Daimonic Reality

Other Books by Patrick Harpur

The Serpents Circle
The Rapture
Mercurius, or the Marriage of Heaven and Earth
The Philosopher's Secret Fire: A History of the Imagination

Daimonic Reality
A Field Guide to the Otherworld

PATRICK HARPUR

Pine Winds Press

Pine Winds Press

PO Box 720. Ravensdale. WA 98051

An imprint of Idyll Arbor, Inc.

Pine Winds Press Editor: Thomas M. Blaschko

ISBN 0-937663-09-3

Library of Congress Cataloging-in-Publication Data

Harpur, Patrick.
  Daimonic reality : a field guide to the otherworld / Patrick Harpur.
      p. cm.
Originally published: Viking, 1994.
Includes bibliographical references and index.
  ISBN 0-937663-09-3 (hardcover : alk. paper)
  1. Supernatural. 2. Apparitions. 3. Visions. I. Title.
  BF1411 .H365 2005
  133--dc21
                                    2002155152

To Merrily

"Every thing possible to be believ'd is an image of truth."

(William Blake)

"It is not possible to speak rightly about the Gods without the Gods."

(Iamblichus)

"... with the ancient philosopher, the deity is an immense and perpetually exuberant fountain whose streams originally filled and continually replenish the world with life. Hence the universe contains in its ample bosom all general natures, divinities visible and invisible, the illustrious race of daemons, the noble army of exalted souls, and man rendered happy by wisdom and virtue."

(Thomas Taylor)

Contents

Part Three Otherworld Journeys

Acknowledgments

Thanks are due to the copyright holders for permission to use extracts from work by the following:

W. Y. Evans-Wentz: to Colin Smythe Ltd for extracts from *The Fairy-Faith in Celtic Countries*, copyright © 1911 W. Y. Evans-Wentz;

Lady Gregory: to Colin Smythe Ltd for extracts from *Visions and Beliefs in the West of Ireland*, copyright © 1920 Lady Augusta Gregory, renewed 1947 by Richard Graham Gregory, Anne Gregory, and Catherine Frances Kennedy;

Aniela Jaffé: to Daimon Verlag for extracts from *Death, Dreams, and Ghosts* (first published in English as *Apparitions and Precognition: A Study from the Viewpoint of C. G. Jung's Analytical Psychology*, 1978);

C. G. Jung: to Routledge Kegan Paul and Pantheon Books, a division of Random House, Inc. for extracts from *Memories, Dreams, Reflections* copyright © 1961, 1962, 1963 by Random House Inc.;

John A. Keel: to the author for extracts from *UFOs: Operation Trojan Horse*;

D. A. MacManus: to Colin Smythe Ltd for extracts from *The Middle Kingdom*, copyright © 1959 by D. A. MacManus.

Every effort has been made to contact all copyright holders. The publishers will be glad to make good any errors or inaccuracies in future editions.

Introduction

An air of embarrassment hangs about a book on apparitions and visions. They are not respectable subjects. They are scarcely mentioned by what we may call the official agents of our culture, such as the academics, the Churches, the reputable press. If the scientists mention them at all, it is usually to denounce them. Apparitions and the like are held to be impossible — if people claim to have seen funny things, then those people are deluded. The trouble is, if it is a delusion, it is one which has persisted throughout history and seems to be as prevalent now as it has ever been, to judge from the number of reported sightings of all kinds of anomalous entities, from ghosts to "flying saucers" and mysterious big black cats, from lake monsters to Virgin Marys and weird "extraterrestrials." There is perhaps nothing especially important about such sightings, except for the questions they raise about the nature of reality or of the mind, or both. It may be, to paraphrase C. S. Lewis, that "their very unimportance is their importance."[1]

For every person who is certain that they have seen something out of this world, there are more who believe that it is possible to see such things or know someone who has. There are no unequivocal statistics for this assertion — I simply base it on conversations I have had over the years with all kinds of people. But my guess that there are at least as many "believers" as there are people who do not believe in the reality of any kind of apparition is partially confirmed by the enormous number of books and small magazines devoted to the subject. These receive little or no notice from the agents of official culture — to read the book reviews, for instance, you would not know they existed. And so it seems that there is not only a deep gulf between believers and non-believers, but also between respectable, official culture and a large section of popular culture.

Such gulfs have always made me uneasy — made me, in fact, look for a book that might bridge them. It would be the sort of book which, rather than denouncing visionary experiences in a high-handed manner, would take them seriously. It would tend to believe that, on the whole, people know what they are seeing. At the same time it would not seek to explain *away* the things they see nor explain them in terms of extravagant, sensational theories. It would nevertheless not be afraid to offend common sense if it became unavoidable to do so. It would certainly not employ long-winded quasi-scientific jargon to give the enterprise an air of respectability. Failing to find a book which satisfied these criteria, I decided to write my own. What, I reasoned, was needed was a kind of framework in which it was possible to entertain the impossible, to think about the unthinkable.

Fortunately I did not have to invent such a framework — one already existed in the form of an intellectual tradition to which this book hopes to draw attention. It is not a system of thought, nor is it a discipline — not a philosophy, religion, psychology, science, etc., although it touches upon all of these. It is more like a way of seeing, a perspective on the world. (It is not necessary to know the body of this tradition to grasp this book — besides, it will become clear as we go along — but I have outlined the bare bones of it in the Epilogue.) In our culture — by which I mean modern Western culture — this perspective has been under siege but has reasserted itself from time to time. One example is the idea of Imagination which, expressed in the work of such Romantic poets as Coleridge, Keats, Shelley, and Blake, reverses our common notion of the imaginative as something unreal, something imagin*ary*, and allows it an autonomous life that includes spontaneous apparitions.

It is by means of ideas such as this that we will begin to understand the kind of experience which overtook Police Constable Alan Godfrey on the night of 28 November 1980, while he was driving around Todmorden, West Yorkshire. His attention was caught by a bright light on the road ahead. He thought at first it was a bus but, approaching to within 100 feet of it, he saw that it was a dome-shaped object, like a child's spinning-top, about fourteen feet high and twenty feet across. It was hovering about five feet above the ground. There was a line of five windows about two thirds of the way up — dark gaps in the body of the shining object which, in the way it reflected the car's headlights, seemed metallic. PC Godfrey tried to call his base on the radio, but it didn't work. Although he was very frightened, he had the presence of mind to make a quick drawing of the object. He was just estimating the size of the windows (about three feet by one foot) when there was a hiccup in the continuity of his perception: he found himself, still in his car, 100 yards farther down the road. The object had disappeared.[2]

It would be convenient to believe that PC Godfrey was prey to delusions or hallucinations. But rigorous psychological tests, and more than one psychiatrist, subsequently concluded that he wasn't. Besides, what he saw was by no means remarkable compared to the thousands of similar objects reported from around the world. People, it seems, see some very funny things — things which leave them profoundly affected, stunned, awestruck, baffled, ecstatic, but, above all, convinced of the reality of a sighting which is outside anything they have previously encountered. Many of them long to know the origin and purpose of such objects, to understand the nature of something that can change their lives in a flash. But to whom can they turn?

You might think that scientists would be curious about so many reports of such anomalous phenomena. Few are. They tend either to ignore or to ridicule experiences like PC Godfrey's; at best they crassly claim that he has misidentified a planet, aircraft, weather balloon, or some such. You might think that psychologists would be interested; but, curiously, few of them are. They might concede — as PC Godfrey's did — that ordinary, sane people see funny things; but they are at a loss as to how to account for them. They are no good to PC Godfrey, who wants to know what the hell *happened.* You might think that the Church, whose central doctrines are founded on supernatural facts, might show a passing interest in an encounter which has a more than passing resemblance to the supernatural and which, moreover, often induces religious awe. No such luck. It often looks as though the Church (almost any Church) is quicker than anyone to dissociate itself from visions of any kind. Even alleged sightings of the Blessed Virgin Mary are received by the Roman Catholic establishment with hostility.

In the end PC Godfrey was drawn to a group of people whom the different orthodoxies could happily unite in reviling as much as his sighting itself: the ufologists. They *were* interested in him. Better still, they took him seriously. In a sense, things got worse: he agreed to undergo hypnosis and was regressed to the incident in order to uncover what had occurred between the time when he had finished his sketch and the time he found himself parked farther up the road. It was revealed that he had met what ufologists call alien entities.

Sightings of such entities are reasonably common. They often fall into one of two categories — benevolent or malevolent, super- or subhuman, beautiful or ugly. For example:

"I awoke to see the loveliest people I have ever seen. A young man and a young girl dressed in olive-green raiment were standing at my bedside. I looked at the girl and noticed that her dress was gathered about her neck into a kind of chain, or perhaps some stiff embroidery... But what filled me with wonder was the miraculous mildness of her face. There are no such faces now... It was peaceful like the faces of animals, or like mountain pools at evening, so peaceful that it was a little sad..."[3]

Or:

"He looked earnestly into a corner of the room, and said, 'There he is — reach me my things — I shall keep an eye on him. There he comes! His eager tongue whisking out of his mouth, a cup in his hand to hold blood and covered with a scaly skin of gold and green;' — as he described him so he drew him...a naked figure with a strong body and a short neck — with burning eyes...and a face worthy of a murderer..."[4]

The young couple appeared to the poet W. B. Yeats; the scaly creature to the Romantic poet and artist William Blake, who called it the "ghost of a flea." PC Godfrey's entities were a mixture of nice and nasty. Under hypnosis he relived an encounter with a shining light, followed by blackness and a sensation of floating. He finds himself in a room in the presence of someone "like a man," about six feet tall, dressed in a white sheet with a skullcap on his head, bearded and with a long thin nose. The "man" smiles at him and Alan Godfrey is reassured. But the man is not alone. There are about eight "horrible" entities, as small as five-year-old boys, whom PC Godfrey thinks of as "robots" since they wear no distinctive clothing, seem to be metallic and have heads "like a lamp" with eyes like vertical lines. They seem to plug themselves into a bracelet which the tall man has placed on PC Godfrey's wrist, causing him acute distress.[5]

Clearly, visions are not the prerogative of poets, just as mystical experiences are not confined to saints. Nor are the appearances of "aliens" the preserve of lunatics. If PC Godfrey had been a Yeats or a Blake he might have used his experience to make poetry or art; but, like most of us, he wasn't. He was a police officer and he wanted to investigate the matter. But to enlist the help of ufologists is a mixed blessing.

They divide loosely into two camps. The first maintains that Alan

Godfrey saw an extraterrestrial spacecraft inhabited by aliens from another planet. This is such a popular hypothesis, especially in the USA, that the acronym UFO (Unidentified Flying Object) has come, quite erroneously, to mean "a flying saucer from outer space." The more extreme proponents of the hypothesis create a certain uneasiness. They would doubtless attribute Henry Vaughan's mystical poem — "I saw Eternity the other night/Like a great Ring of pure and endless light" — to a UFO encounter. However, in many ways their theory does more justice than many another to what I shall boldly call the facts. This camp is analogous, oddly enough, to those believers within the Roman Catholic Church who claim that visions of a graceful, supernatural lady can be identified with the Virgin Mary — despite the fact that the ladies themselves are rarely unambiguous.

PC Godfrey was perhaps fortunate to have fallen in with the second camp of ufologists — those who entertain a wide variety of theories about the nature of UFOs. An open-minded, often ingenious group, their chief aim, it seems, is to persuade scientists to take them and their subject seriously. In this they are like the psychical researchers of a century or so ago who sought, and failed, to convince Science of the truths of Spiritualism. One or two scientists — a Conan Doyle or an Oliver Lodge — might be *converted* (and ufologists, too, net the odd one whom they display like a prize catch); but they will never be convinced. The reasons for this differ according to which scientists are addressed. Like ufologists they fall roughly into two camps.

The first comprises the devotees of scient*ism* who cling, like old Stalinists, to an outmoded cult of dreary mechanistic materialism. Theory has long since hardened into dogma, as rigidly upheld as that of any entrenched extraterrestrialist. (There is a telling film of such customers at work on a rival cult — a bunch of heretical children in Medjugorje, Yugoslavia, who claim visions of the Virgin Mary. At the first sign of ecstasy, they are wired up to inquisitorial machines, poked with sharp instruments, assaulted by loud noises in their ears and flash bulbs in their faces.) Why anyone at the end of the twentieth century still wishes to woo this kind of "scientist" is itself something of a puzzle.

The reason why the second group of scientists — honest, open-minded, reasonable — dismisses the evidence in favor of the paranormal is more of a mystery. Ufologists are inclined to see their silence as a conspiracy or as a fear of the unknown. But I think there is a simpler answer. No one who reviews the evidence for, say, UFOs for an hour is likely to deny that *something* strange is being seen. The trouble is, few people who have been brought up with strict rationalistic principles *can* concentrate on anomalous phenomena for an hour. They are like classically trained musicians who cannot listen to pop songs. A terrible ennui sets in immediately. Messages from the Otherworld, whether delivered by spirits, UFO entities, or Virgin Marys, are so often trivial or banal. In addition, any respectable scientist will be repelled by the sheer absurdity of so many visions. He may be happy to concede that a saint's mystical union with the Godhead is serious and important (though outside his own terms of reference); but what will he make of the testimony of the teenage girls who saw a giant feathered creature at Mawnan, Cornwall, in July 1976?

"It was like a big owl with pointed ears, as big as a man. The eyes were red and glowing. At first, I thought it was someone dressed up…trying to scare us. I laughed at it, we both did, then it went up in the air and we both screamed. When it went up, you could see its feet were like pincers."[6]

I shall be arguing that the very triviality and absurdity of so many visions and apparitions are an essential part of them, pointing to a radical re-alignment of what we commonly regard as reality. In doing this, I want to suggest that the irrational is not necessarily unreasonable nor the incommensurable incomprehensible. I do not want to convince or convert, but merely to persuade people to recall odd experiences of their own which, lacking official sanction, have been forgotten, as dreams are. I would like to stick up for people who, having seen funny things, have set them apart from their otherwise ordinary lives because such things have been outlawed by the orthodox, respectable world of science or literature, of the Churches or even of their own families. Mindful of PC Godfrey's confusion — "*nobody* will convince me that I didn't see what I saw"[7] — I would like to remind people that there have been in the past ways of making sense of weird apparitions and sudden bizarre visions — ways which our age no longer understands. In fact, I shall be suggesting that, if these strange visitations have any purpose at all, it is to subvert the same modern worldview which discredits them.

Now, in order to establish a rough criterion for the kinds of anomalous sightings I will be tackling, I would ask you to consider the three followings stories, each pretty much representative of their genre.

A twenty-five-year-old woman who had just broken off her engagement was walking with her mother across a bridge over the Rhine at Basle: "Suddenly I saw a broad beam of light falling from the sky, across the Rhine; my fiancé was coming towards me on it, and his eyes were fixed on me. I gazed at him in wonder, and heard the words: *that is your way*. The vision vanished and I heard my mother saying: 'Whatever's the matter with you?' " Two years later she married the fiancé and never regretted it.[8]

On 1 July 1965, forty-one-year-old Maurice Masse was about to begin work on his lavender fields near Vallensole, Southern France, when he heard a strange whistling sound. On investigation he found a "machine" shaped like a rugby football with a cupola on top and about the size of a small car. It stood on six thin "legs." Beside the object were two small figures dressed in gray-green one-piece suits. Their bald bare heads were pumpkin-shaped, three times the regular human size, with high fleshy cheeks, big oblique eyes, a lipless mouth, and a pronounced chin. They seemed to be examining M. Masse's lavender plants but, alarmed by his presence, one of them took a cylinder from his belt and aimed a beam at M. Masse who was immediately rooted to the spot, unable to move. He was not especially frightened by this, and observed them apparently conversing in guttural sounds before returning to their "craft," which took off, hovered while the six legs began rotating, and shot off at incredible speed. After only a short flight it disappeared into the blue. "One moment I could see it clearly," said M. Masse, "the next it was gone."[9]

"...I saw five blood-red rays coming down upon me, which were directed towards the hands and feet and heart of my body. Wherefore, perceiving the mystery, I straightaway exclaimed, 'Ah! Lord, my God, I beseech thee, let not the marks appear outwardly on the body.' Then, while I was speaking, before the rays reached me, they changed their blood-red color to splendor, and in the semblance of pure light they came to the five places of my body..."[10]

While there are some similarities between these three supernatural encounters, the first is manifestly *personal* and the last — although it is St. Catherine of Siena's description of how she received stigmata from a personal Christ — is also *impersonal* in that it conforms to the Christian mystic's archetypal experience of the universal Christ. The first is really a ghost story (although the phantom is still living) and I shall not be including such stories because they concern private, individual encounters where the apparition is known to the percipient. There are, however, unknown — as it were *public* — ghosts which seem to attach to places rather than people ("White Ladies" are a standard type) and I might touch on these from time to time.

I am not concerned either with St. Catherine's mystical experience, which is, as it were, the religious equivalent of "high art." This is not to say that my chosen area of visions does not, as we shall see, have religious implications. But in spite — or because — of the fact that it is absurd, almost comical, I shall be concentrating on encounters like my second example — visitations such as M. Masse's which are a curious admixture of the personal and the impersonal, which lie between the private apparition and the transcendent spiritual vision. I will also, incidentally, concentrate on *modern* visitations, roughly within the last century, referring to the past only where the comparison seems illuminating. The next three stories are examples of those I shall be dealing with. Whereas the first three were similar in *kind* but different in *degree,* the following I take to be of the same degree and apparently of the same kind:

"Within the field, just thirty yards away was...a huge silver cigar... Walking from behind the cigar came the figure of a man... [His] height was only about five feet six inches. Yet he was so thin and angular that he looked taller. His joints were peculiar, with pointed elbows and a knee that was three quarters of the way up the leg... He was dressed in a suit of silver, which was thin and hugged him almost like a skin... His head was covered by a sort of balaclava helmet that hid the ears and all but a few sandy wisps of hair. [His] face was long and thin with a flat chin, and extremely pale — almost ghost-like. The most prominent features were the eyes, large and round, with just a tiny dot pupil, pink and no larger than a match head. There was almost no mouth — just a thin line — and the nose was broad and flat."[11]

As she passed the church, she noticed several strange figures in the adjoining field, together with something shaped like an altar, with a white light. She continued on her way — it was raining heavily — but returned with Mrs. Margaret Beirne. They saw three persons, clothed in dazzling white, silverlike garments, standing on top of the grass in the uncut meadow.

They were surrounded by an extraordinarily bright light — "a sight such as you never saw in your life." Within a few minutes eighteen onlookers had assembled in front of the apparitions.[12]

"Suddenly I saw him standing under the drooping branches of a big tree. He was standing there erect. His club was braced against the ground beside him, his hand…on the hilt. He was tall and light-skinned, and his hair nearly descended to the ground behind him. His whole body was painted, and on the outer side of his legs were broad red stripes. His eyes were exactly like two stars…then I lost all courage. My hair stood on end, and…I could not utter a sound because he was looking at me unwaveringly… I kept standing there for a long time after he had vanished."[13]

These three encounters with similar kinds of alien entities are not untypical. In fact, only the first of these was attributed to UFO activity — the alien man was seen by nine-year-old Gaynor Sunderland in North Wales, in July 1976. The second passage describes the experience of a certain Mary McLoughlin who, together with others, identified the shining central figure as the Virgin Mary, standing in front of an altar, with St. Joseph on her right and, possibly, St. John the Evangelist on her left. The vision occurred in 1879 at Knock, County Mayo, in Ireland, which has been a holy place of pilgrimage ever since. The third account belongs to a chief of the Apinayé tribe of eastern Brazil. He identified his visionary figure as the sun god or "father of men."

Thus, while visionary figures conform to cultural expectations and while, within a culture, none of them is ever identical with any other, yet there is a family resemblance between them, as the three examples suggest. By and large I shall be focusing on visions and apparitions in our own Western culture because it is here that they are least regarded. We tend to locate them elsewhere, in our own "unenlightened" past or among credulous peasants or oriental mystics — tend still to disparage as "primitive" those cultures in which the visionary is taken for granted.

I ought to mention parenthetically that, towards the end of the shall be considering a type of apparition which, unlike the other elusive — except as regards its origin and meaning: "they they had been made in one fell swoop. I mean there human doing that, it was far too geometrically ex

Mary Killen of Huish, Wiltshire, w

interlinked circles, 80 meters long, which had appeared overnight in a cornfield in June 1990. My analysis of the mysterious crop circle phenomenon will also provide an opportunity to examine the phenomenology of apparitions in general — the yarns, stories, theories, and hypotheses which surround anomalous sightings and their structural interrelationships.

Lastly, in investigating these visions and apparitions, I ought to mention some of the methods I will *not* be employing. Firstly, I will not be presenting a mass of original research and new material. Rather, I will be using cases that lie to hand, already quite well known and adequately researched. Secondly, I will not be attempting any elaborate classification of the material, which would only impose demarcations that do not strictly exist. It *may* be convenient to distinguish a vision from a hallucination, for instance, but I will be more interested in the common ground underlying both. Thirdly, I will not be pursuing any scientistic fantasy of clarity and rationalism at all costs — a method which is neither possible in this field nor, I would suggest, desirable. If anything, I will be confusing the problem at first in order to get clearer later, at another level. Fourthly, I will not be aiming to *explain* everything because, as the great philosopher of anomalies, Charles Fort, remarked: "There never was an explanation which didn't itself have to be explained." The passion for explanation — *explanationism* — is a peculiarly modern folly. We have come to expect explanations whenever anything mysterious occurs, and there is always an "expert" willing to oblige. No matter ¹ expert's explanation, we are usually
satisf assured that the mystery has been
(I, too, once believed that "will-o'-
neously igniting "marsh gas.")
erceiving the world which, while it
e images, renders them intelligible.
not that we believe, but that we
theatrical production; a way
negative capability — that is
, mysteries, doubts, without
this frame of mind, we can
own twilight, rather than
e can follow where they

lead, providing we are as elusive and allusive, as tricky and contradictory, as they are — as long as we are willing to be led out of our depth where, with luck, we'll be found to be not drowning but waving.

The truth behind apparitions is, I fear, less like a problem to be solved than an initiation into a mystery; less like an investigation than a quest on which we must not be above taking tips from helpful old crones or talking animals in order to wrest the world-transforming treasure from the dragon's cave. We may even have to abandon our idea of truth altogether if we are to find it.

Part One

Apparitions

"There are no conclusive arguments against the hypothesis that these archetypal figures are endowed with personality at the outset and are not just secondary personalizations. In so far as the archetypes do not represent mere functional relationships, they manifest themselves as *daimones*, as personal agencies. In this form they are felt as actual experiences and are not 'figments of the imagination,' as rationalism would have us believe."

(C. G. Jung, *CW* 5, §388)

1

Lights

UFOs and fairy lights

With the exception of ghosts, the most common apparition is an anomalous light in the sky. Ivan Sanderson, the distinguished biologist, who was also an authority on anomalous phenomena, was driving with a colleague in New Jersey on 25 September 1965. It was just after sunset and the sky was clear. Their attention was caught by a red light to the right of Venus. It was much brighter than the planet, lower in the sky, and it was flashing on and off. As they watched, it divided into two parts which continued to flash repeatedly, about twice every second. One light disappeared behind some trees; the other performed a series of tricky maneuvers, including abrupt angular turns, at a speed they estimated at thousands of miles per hour.[1]

If we call this light a UFO — Unidentified Flying Object — it is on the understanding that it is not necessarily an object. Such lights are often, because of their movement, compared to insects or, because of their amorphousness, to organisms. The little lights — called "foo fighters" — which plagued Second World War pilots were often too small to be considered seriously as objects. At the same time their intelligence, apparent from the way they "buzzed" aircraft and followed them, led Allied pilots to think they were some kind of "smart" enemy weapon — until it was discovered that the enemy was thinking exactly the same thing. On 17 July 1957, a larger version of such lights — it was described as "huge" — accompanied a U.S. RB-47 bomber on a training flight for more than 750 miles. All six members of the crew saw it at various times as it flipped from one side of the aircraft to the other in a series of aerodynamically impossible moves. Although it had appeared from nowhere and vanished just as abruptly, the Commander had the impression that the light did in fact emanate from the top of an unseen object — an impression perhaps strengthened by the detection of an object on both ground radar and the aircraft's electronic monitoring equipment.[2] Reports like these have led the acronym UFO, quite erroneously, to imply "extraterrestrial spacecraft."

Dermot MacManus tells us of a sighting which is common not only in his native Ireland but across the world. The witness was a friend of his whom he calls Miss Patricia. When she was eighteen, some time in the nineteenth century, she saw one night at about 9 p.m. a blaze of light across the lough on which her farmhouse was situated. She stared in amazement as the small fort on the far side of the water was lit up by hundreds of little white lights. She saw them "all rise up as one and, keeping their formation, sail steadily through the air across the little lough towards the other fort, not far from the farmhouse. She did not see them settle there, but…hastily retreated to the safety of the house."[3]

The two "forts" on opposite sides of the lough were "fairy forts," also called raths, lisses, or forths. They can be ancient tumuli or barrows but they are more often natural outcrops of land, usually artificially shaped or surrounded by a bank and ditch, whose provenance and purpose has disap-peared beyond history into myth. The forts are said to be where the people of Fairy live. Sudden bursts of light or music have been seen and heard there; sometimes a cavalcade of horsemen is seen passing into them through a hitherto invisible entrance. The lights are fairies. They follow straight paths between their preferred places, like Miss Patricia's two forts, and woe betide anyone who builds on the paths or obstructs their traffic. Thus we see that odd lights have a predilection for certain places and landmarks. They are seen over stone circles or legendary hills or even certain trees. Their appearances favor certain times of day, or certain days. Miss Patricia saw hers on Halloween, when both pagan fairies and Christian souls of the dead are particularly active. Her lough may also have played a part: lights, whether we call them UFOs or fairies, like bodies of water.

In June 1973, a young man woke abruptly at three in the morning and felt compelled to go out onto the landing. Through the large picture window which overlooked Loch Ryan (in Scotland) he saw three yellow-orange spheres hovering above the water. They suddenly shot upwards "at a fantastic speed," and he came round "as if waking from a trance." He found that his parents were standing beside him. They too had woken for no obvious reason and had felt compelled to look out of the same window at the lights.[4]

Witches

It is widely assumed that because anomalous lights in the sky are interpreted as UFOs, whatever that implies, in all Westernized areas of the world, this is the most widespread interpretation. But the natural interpretation of such lights in most tribal societies would be witchcraft. It would be hard to find a society which does not hold, or has not at one time held, a belief in witches. The eminent anthropologist Rodney Needham has taken the trouble to put together a composite picture of witches. Two of the features which can be universally attributed to them are, first, the ability to fly (especially at night), and, second, the emission of a glow or fiery trail as they travel through the air. Needham also points out that anthropologists display in relation to witchcraft the kind of prejudice they studiously avoid in relation to other mystical institutions. They concede, as they must, that the idea of witchcraft must be related to something real in human experience, but they think that "the reality in question consists in social and psychological strains to which the postulation of witchcraft is a social response."[5]

Now, I am not against psycho-social readings of strange beliefs — far from it, as we shall see. But I am against the kind of prejudice which prevents an anthropologist from giving credence to his informants — especially when the anthropologist prides himself on being thoroughly open-minded and scientific. In fact he is neither of these things — they may actually contradict each other — because when he listens to a tale of witches searing their way across the night sky, he simply cannot believe it. It is impossible. And it is impossible because his scientistic ideology tells him that it is. But that does not stop his chosen tribe from seeing funny lights in the sky and calling them witches. Worse still, it does not stop other anthropologists from seeing them: in his classic book *Witchcraft, Oracles and Magic among the Azande* (Oxford, 1937), the father of witchcraft studies himself, E. E. Evans-Pritchard, admitted that he had seen, and been unable to account for, the kind of mysterious lights reported by his informants. Nor is he the only one. Philip Mayer owns up:

"Like Evans-Pritchard...I have seen among the Gusii [of Western Kenya] at night lights moving near my camp, lights that died down and flared up again exactly as the witchcraft myth alleges. Gusii say that witches produce this effect by raising and lowering the lids of covered fire-pots which they carry with them."[6]

The anthropologists v. the Gusii

The problem of the reality or otherwise of witches is one that dogs the interpretation of all apparitions (or alleged apparitions). Ufologists, for instance, can be broadly divided into two camps: those who, like the anthropologists, take a scientific stance towards UFOs, and those who, like the Gusii, don't. The first camp tries to explain away UFOs as natural phenomena (mirages, ball lightning, unexplained atmospheric effects, etc.), as man-made objects (weather balloons, aircraft, etc.), or as psychological aberrations (delusions, hallucinations, etc.). They have even been known to invoke "psycho-social strains." The second camp opt overwhelmingly for the view that UFOs are alien spacecraft from other planets (I shall call these people "extraterrestrialists"). This is the equivalent of the Gusii belief that odd lights do actually appear and are caused by actual beings. Other members of the second camp vary the extraterrestrial view by asserting that UFOs come from secret bases on Earth or from inside the Earth which is hollow; or they suggest that UFOs come from the future (when time travel has been invented), or from other dimensions. The extraordinary behavior of UFOs, defying known physical laws, is explained either by the advanced technological expertise of their authors or by recourse to the idea that they are not physical but spiritual. There have even been attempts to reconcile the two camps with quasi-scientific theories such as the "earthlights" hypothesis which, roughly, asserts that geological faults in the Earth naturally produce aerial lights. These in turn affect the percipients psychologically so that they see the lights as structured craft. Curiously, few (if any) ufologists cite witches as the culprits. But they do occasionally draw attention to the similarity between fairy lore and UFOs. But fairies, of course, are subject to the same controversy as above. On the one hand folklorists, who now replace anthropologists, attribute belief in fairies to a kind if dim "race memory" of (a) the druids, (b) the Celtic gods, or (c) a secret society of witches. Their equivalent of the extraterrestrial theory is that fairies were a race of pigmy people, the Picts, who were forced to live underground after their territory was invaded. However this idea has long been discredited and folklorists have fallen back on, yes, "psycho-social strains."

On the other hand, supernaturalist theories, so to speak, have taken their cue from the original witnesses of, and believers in, fairies, who are largely divided between the views that they are nature spirits, spirits of the dead, fallen angels, or simply a separate, more or less spiritual race of beings who happen to share the planet with us.

I shall not, incidentally, be siding with either camp. That is, I shall not, like the anthropologists, be ruling out any theory on the grounds that it is impossible. Nor, like the Gusii, will I be attributing strange lights to any single agency such as witches.

Ancestral spirits

So far we have seen that, at the very moment of their appearance, anomalous lights are subject to different interpretations. They are never viewed as it were neutrally — some cause or agency is always inferred, regardless of whether it is actually seen. The people of one culture might say that they are alternative manifestations of spirits or fairies; the people of another might say that they emanate from witches or UFOs. Either way we can say that the lights are often accompanied by (for want of a better word) personifications. Let us, for example, return for a moment to Africa. In 1981, at a large estate called La Rochelle outside Mutare, Zimbabwe, several natives saw a large ball of orange light and, shortly afterwards, three or four tall personages dressed in shiny metallic overalls. There was too much light shining from them for their faces to be seen. The incident was not investigated by an anthropologist, who might have seen in the apparitions evidence of witches, but by a ufologist, Cynthia Hind. She naturally asked the chief witness, Clifford Muchena, whether he had heard of people and craft coming from outer space. He was doubtful. Did she mean astronauts? Along with the other witnesses, he was inclined to identify the visitors as ghosts or the spirits of the ancestors. Ms. Hind asked whether silvery overalls were appropriate clothing for the ancestors — didn't they wear fur and necklaces of crocodile teeth? "Times change," said Mr. Muchena.[8]

If his identification was correct, then ancestral spirits would be a more appropriate description of the apparitions than ghosts. They are as widely believed in as witches and they are regarded as both malign and benign, depending on whether one has offended them in any way or not. They are remote from personal life, long-dead, belonging more to the tribe than to the individual. Ghosts on the other hand can be personal, recently dead and intimately connected to the individual. One of the commonest forms of apparition is that of a relative who appears by one's bed in the middle of the night. They are always accompanied by a light and, sometimes, only the light appears while the presence of the relative is intuited. A blacksmith from Tarbes, France, reported:

"In the middle of the night I was awakened by a blinding light. I looked up and saw to the left of my bed a shining disc with a light in it that looked like the steady flame of a nightlamp. I saw no figure and heard no sound..." Thus far, there is nothing to distinguish this experience from countless similar ones which ufologists call "bedroom visitors." UFOs and/or unknown, often alien-looking entities are always turning up under exactly these circumstances. But the blacksmith continued:

"...I had the feeling that a cousin of mine, who lived at Langon and was very ill, was in the room with me. The vision vanished in a few seconds and I lay down again, calling myself an idiot. The next morning ... at 8:30 a.m. I received a telegram with the news that my cousin had died at one o'clock in the night."[9] So the story is a ghost story, not a tale of UFOs; and, to be consistent, we must include the souls of the dead among the possible agents behind anomalous lights.

The cultural context

Furthermore, how do we categorize the following three stories of personified lights?

In 1910 an Oxford student and his friend were riding their horses home from Limerick, through County Kerry, in Ireland. It was midnight and very dark. Nearing Listowel they saw a light about half a mile ahead. They thought at first that it was a house light but, drawing nearer, they noticed it was moving up and down, to and fro, diminishing to a spark, and then expanding into a yellow luminous flame. A further two lights appeared about 100 yards to their right. In the midst of each "we saw a radiant being having a human form. Presently the lights moved toward one another and made contact, whereupon the two beings in them were seen to be walking side by side... So dazzling was the radiance, like a halo, around their heads that we could not distinguish the countenance of the beings..."[10]

In 1846 two children were herding cattle one afternoon in a remote area of France, near La Salette, when one of them, fourteen-year-old Melanie Mathieu, looked down into a ravine and saw "a large circle of brilliant light, vibrant and outshining the sun." She summoned her companion, eleven-year-old Maximin Giraud, who also saw the circle of light. It began to open so that they could make out "the figure of a woman, seated in an attitude of sorrow, weeping."[11]

In 1969 four people were in the kitchen of a café in Pontejos, Spain, when they saw an orange rectangle hovering over the ground against the night sky about thirty meters away. It was about five meters long. The figures of five men were silhouetted within it. They seemed to enter the lighted area from the sides and moved towards the center where they vanished.[12]

It is often said that visions and apparitions are experienced according to the culture in which they appear. To draw a religious parallel, it is a truism to say that no Buddhist ever had a vision of Christ, and no Christian ever had a vision of the Buddha. But I wonder if the witnesses in my three examples were immediately certain of what they were seeing. The radiant beings in the first could reasonably be called angels; but they appear in a book of fairy lore. The children in the second suggested at first that the weeping woman was a great saint. With further sightings she was promoted to the Blessed Virgin Mary. The four Spaniards in the third might have been simply baffled, had their story ended there. In fact, when the orange light went out, they saw a large gray object, like a bowl upturned on a plate, which departed in a blaze of light. They probably called it a UFO. At any rate, regardless of how they are originally experienced, apparitions and visions are inevitably interpreted, on reflection, according to their cultural contexts. These may even co-exist within the same society, as when, for instance, a Christian labels a demon what a ufologist calls an alien.

Pre-literate, tribal, non-Westernized cultures — I'll call them traditional cultures — may be struck by fear or joy at the sight of anomalous lights, with or without accompanying personifications, but they are untroubled by them. Their worldview has a choice of supernatural beings on hand to explain them — gods, witches, ghosts, fairies (or their equivalent), and spirits. And these are not incidental to the culture, but are an essential part of it. You live your life mindful of the proximity of powerful beings, sometimes glimpsed. Our culture simply denies them — officially, that is. Popularly there are a large number of people who believe in all manner of supernatural beings — and not a few who claim to have seen them. (It is not necessary to believe in them in order to see them.) However, we are not satisfied with traditional explanations for anomalous lights. We want, in turn, to explain the explanations — we want to know what witches and spirits are. Above all, we want to know if they are real.

Our own culture has produced a genuine body of what in other cultures we call folklore. I mean UFOs. They are slightly unusual because they do not also manifest directly as personifications. They manifest primarily as structured craft, and any entities associated with them are seen as occupants. A series of opinion polls in the U.S.A. suggests that more than 50 percent of the population believes in UFOs and a high proportion of these people claim to have seen one.[13] "Belief in UFOs" usually implies the belief that they are spaceships visiting us from another planet. Fewer Europeans than Americans seem to hold such beliefs. If they do believe in UFOs, they are more inclined to believe that some pretty funny things are being seen but not necessarily alien spacecraft.

The only thing I can say about anomalous lights in the sky at this stage is that they are the most culturally undifferentiated apparition. They are more like a universal curtain which rises to initiate a drama in which the players can be a wide variety of strange beings. Some witnesses see fairies, others spaceships. Some find that the light has conferred a sudden burst of knowledge on them; others develop psychic powers. Others still return home simply to find their house infested with a poltergeist. These lights are like omens or signs which herald a bizarre experience, a different world, a new way of life. Take the Avis family, for instance, who were driving home one night, minding their own business, when they saw an odd light "pacing" their car. They thought it must be an airplane at first, but it was oval in shape and pale blue in color. It disappeared behind some trees. They assumed that the incident was over; in fact it had only begun. They could no longer hear their car's engine, they drove into a bank of green mist, the car radio crackled and smoked, the engine went dead and then — but I'll save their extraordinary story for later on.

2

UFOs

A Modern Myth

At 2:30 a.m. on 19 May 1979, Mike Sacks was out on the hills near Bacup watching for UFOs with his brother, Ray, and another friend. They all heard a sort of "muted whining howl" and saw a whitish light plunging downwards out of the sky "like a lift out of control." The light "quickly resolved itself into a structured shape, and...the howl became a soft humming." The thing stopped, practically on top of them, spanning a small stream with steep-sided banks. It had a dome on top which sparked with a kind of electric blue light. On the bottom was an aluminum-like rim which seemed translucent, with an internal glow. It tilted away from the witnesses, revealing details of its concave underside, including a row of lights around the edge and both triangular and rectangular inserts. Then the object suddenly raced up the stream and disappeared over a hill.[1]

In describing this encounter, Mike Sacks voiced the frustration common to so many UFO witnesses:

"If only I could make you believe what I saw. It was there. I know it. There is not the slightest bit of doubt whatever. UFOs are real. UFOs are solid, physical craft. Nobody could possibly convince me otherwise after what I saw that night. It is just terrible *knowing* this, and yet being unable to prove it."[2] Indeed, to add to his frustration, the photographs of the UFO taken that night did not come out, although the rest of the film was fine.

Despite Mike Sacks's certainty, the reality of UFOs — and of all apparitions — remains a vexed question. They compel us to ask ourselves what we mean by reality, a very old and knotty philosophical problem. In particular, they ask us to decide whether our encounters with apparitions are subjective or objective — that is, whether a UFO, for example, is somehow a product of our minds or whether it actually exists out there in the world. If it is objectively real, then we have to decide further whether it is physically real or only apparently so; whether, that is, it is material or immaterial (though visible).

Mike Sacks has no doubt that his UFO was both objective and physical. The same might be said of the seven objects, one large and six small, which accompanied a BOAC Stratocruiser on a New York to London flight on 29 June 1954. The objects, seen by both crew and passengers, were described as gray, opaque, hard-edged, and without lights. However, the physical nature of the large object at least was not as clear-cut as it might have been. It seemed to change shape in a mercurial fashion, appearing now as a clearly defined aircraft, now as quite shapeless.[3] In addition, UFOs have an unnerving propensity simply to vanish into thin air.

I will be pegging away at the problem of the physicality or otherwise of apparitions throughout this book. But, for now, I will begin to address the question of their subjectivity or objectivity. And the best place to start is with the great Swiss analytical psychologist C. G. Jung who, in 1956, wrote a long essay called *Flying Saucers: A Modern Myth of Things Seen in the Skies.*[4] It remains one of the most acute analyses of aerial apparitions — but it did no good for Jung's scientific reputation. Respectable scientists have for the most part always steered clear of anomalies, and "flying saucers" are no exception. However, Jung, as always, sided with real life over respectability, arguing that no true scientist could ignore the thousands of reports which flooded in from all over the world concerning these strange lights and stranger objects.

Although the latter have always been seen — Jung reproduces, for instance, two sixteenth-century broadsheets showing aerial apparitions at Nuremberg (1561) and Basel (1566) — ufologists agree that the modern UFO myth was launched on 24 June 1947 by one Kenneth Arnold, who saw nine silvery objects from his light aircraft while flying in the vicinity of Washington State's Mount Rainier. Alerted to their presence by two tremendously bright flashes of light, Arnold described them as flying "like a saucer would if you skipped it across the water."[5] Hence the term "flying saucer." I use the word "myth," incidentally, as Jung uses it in the title of his essay. He did not mean, as is so often casually meant nowadays, a fabrication or a story that is untrue. He meant, on the contrary, a story that is true. The precise nature of this truth, like the nature of reality, will unfold as we go along. For the moment, what Jung said of flying saucers is as true today as it was then. *"Something is seen,"* he says, *"but one doesn't know what*…one thing is certain: they have become a *living myth.*"[6]

The collective unconscious

Before we can decide whether or not UFOs are "all in the mind," we have to decide what we mean by "mind." Jung's model of the psyche provides the best — perhaps the only — framework for understanding visionary experiences. As a follower of Freud he understood that apart from our conscious lives, which we quite mistakenly think of as our selves, there is a subconscious life of which we are normally unaware. The subconscious is the repository of our past experience, some of which can be recalled at will to consciousness (memory) but other parts of which cannot be, because they have been repressed. A repressed content, however, does not merely go away — it continues to exert a hidden influence on our lives, reappearing indirectly as a neurosis. The task of psychoanalysis, roughly, is to encourage the patient to bring this forgotten or repressed experience to light — it often lies in childhood — and so dissolve the psychological knot which is producing the neurosis and its undesirable symptoms.

But, unlike Freud, Jung dealt with patients who were more seriously disturbed, psychotic rather than neurotic, and he noticed in their delusions and fantasies a number of images and motifs which could not possibly be explained by recourse to their personal lives. For example, a patient might hold fantastic ideas and beliefs which had no counterpart anywhere except in some esoteric Gnostic myth. So Jung was forced to recognize a deeper level of the psyche which contained the past experience not just of our personal lives but of the entire race. He called this level of the psyche the collective unconscious, to distinguish it from Freud's subconscious (which, in turn, he re-named the personal unconscious).

If Jung described the unconscious in terms of strata or levels, this was only a manner of speaking. The unconscious cannot be described in itself; it can only be represented by metaphors. It does not divide neatly into levels, for instance. Rather, it is oceanic, shifting, seething, constantly in flux. Indeed, the ocean was a favorite metaphor of Jung's, according to which consciousness is, of course, only a small island rising out of, and surrounded by, the vast ~~idity.~~

The content ~~scious~~ is a sea of images. These are usually, but not exclusively, visu~~they~~ can be abstractions, patterns, ideas, inspirations and even moods. The images of the collective unconscious are representations of what Jung called archetypes. This was not a new idea — it goes back to Plato, who postulated an ideal world of forms, of which everything in this world was merely a copy — but it was a new idea in psychology. The archetypes are paradoxical. They cannot be known in themselves, but they can be known indirectly through their images. They are, by definition, impersonal but they can manifest personally. For example, the archetype which lies, so to speak, nearest the surface is called the *shadow*. At a personal level, it embodies our inferior side, all our repressed traits. It might appear in dreams and fantasies, therefore, as a dark twin or a despised acquaintance or an idiot half-brother. At the same time, our personal shadows are rooted in an impersonal collective shadow, the archetype of evil, such as the Christian Devil represents.

It is more common to encounter an archetypal image indirectly than directly — that is, in *projection*. Here, the aptness of the word "shadow" is evident. For the archetype bypasses consciousness altogether and throws a shadow over the external world. Then we encounter what is within us as if it were outside. Any object or person in the world can receive a projection and suddenly be charged with archetypal significance. Whenever we fall madly in love with someone about whom we know very little, we are more often than not falling prey to an "anima projection" which overlays the actual person and imbues them with almost sacred significance. The *anima* (or, in a woman, animus) is the second major archetype uncovered by Jung. She is the female principle in a man, the personification of the unconscious itself. As such there is no end to the images by which she represents herself — virgin, crone, wife, girl-next-door, goddess, nymph, lamia, and so on.

The archetype which most concerns us is the one Jung called the *self*. It is the goal of all psychic life, all personal development, which he called *individuation*. This process forms the major task of our lives, in the course of which we are supposed to make conscious, as far as possible, the contents of our unconscious — for instance, by withdrawing our projections onto the world. The result is an expansion of personality and, finally, a state of wholeness which embraces even the dark and contradictory sides of ourselves. The self archetype is foreshadowed in the image of the Wise Old Man and consummated in his mystic marriage with the anima. But such personifications are not the only images of the self. They also occur in abstract form, most notably in circular patterns, often divided into four, which oriental religions have long understood and called mandalas. Such images can occur spontaneously near the beginning of the individuation process, or at a crisis in our psychic lives, as a guide to and token of the final goal. Jung believed that "flying saucers" were like mandalas; that UFOs, in other words, are projections of the collective unconscious. (However, I shall have more, and more critical, things to say about "projection" later on.)

The soul

Jung's assertion was in many ways traditional. After all, in early and medieval times, the totality of the psyche — or soul, as it used to be called — was pictured in a number of ways: as an airy or ethereal body, as a homunculus (a little person or child), as a bird (in Celtic and Islamic lore), and as a bright or fiery sphere. According to Caesarius of Heisterbach[7] (*c.* 1170–1240), the Abbot of Morimond saw in a vision that his own soul was shaped like "a glassy spherical vessel, with eyes before and behind, all-knowing and seeing everything at once." This aura of omniscience is a hallmark of many UFO encounters. Another visionary cited by Caesarius found that his soul was "a spiritual substance, spherical in nature, like the globe of the moon." (The moon is itself a traditional symbol of the soul.) Caesarius sums up with an interesting distinction: to mortal eyes the soul appears to have a bodily form, but to those freed from the flesh the soul appears as the two visionaries describe it, as a luminous sphere.[8]

In his treatise *The Immortality of the Soul,* the great seventeenth-century Cambridge Platonist, Henry More, drawing perhaps on the same Neoplatonic tradition as Caesarius, describes how the soul after death takes on an "airy body" in the same shape as our earthly body. However, this is exchanged for a "shining" or "ethereal" body which, immortal, "lives while in its true condition an unimaginable life and is sometimes described as of 'a round or oval figure' and as always circling among gods and among stars, and sometimes as having more dimensions than our penury can comprehend."[9] It is interesting to note that both Caesarius and More consider the abstract image of the soul a higher form than the personified image.

One way, then, of regarding luminous apparitions is as images of the soul projected by the soul itself. Jung also remarked on the frequency with which many such apparitions appeared, representing a disintegration and fragmentation of the psyche. These can be seen as "partial souls" which may appear in quite ordinary circumstances. One of his patients dreamt that many shining spheres were hanging in the curtains of her room. Jung interpreted these as split-off fragments of psyche which were seeking to be reintegrated into the personality in order to attain or restore psychic wholeness. Furthermore, he knew that as long as these fragments remain in a state of projection or "exteriorized," they can produce all kinds of parapsychological phenomena. Sure enough, just as his patient woke up, she heard a loud report: the upper part of the glass she kept by her bedside had broken off in the shape of a perfect circle whose edge was completely smooth.[10]

Experiences like these are not uncommon among so-called UFO contactees. Many of them, including Mike Sacks whom we met at the beginning of this chapter, remember playing as children with balls of light which were numinous and quasi-intelligent, just as Jung's projected psychic fragments or partial souls are said to be. Gaynor Sunderland who, in my introduction, was described as seeing two "aliens" next to a "spacecraft" in a field, remembers that, as a baby, lights of only a few inches in diameter used to fly through the walls and windows, and play with her — only to vanish just before someone entered the room.[11] Moreover, such people seem marked out for parapsychological experiences, as Jung predicts. Mike Sacks had already seen two UFOs when he had the close encounter I quoted; and the fact that he actually saw a UFO on a night when he had specifically gone out to see one makes him an unusual chap, to say the least. Gaynor's long history of paranormal happenings took a whole book to document.

Jung argues that the appearance of large balls of light on a grand scale reflects a tension which is no longer confined to the individual psyche but to the collective. There is a split in the psychological world, between consciousness and the unconscious, and also in the political world, between East and West. At a time when humanity was contemplating space travel and worried about overpopulation and the Bomb, it was natural that "signs in the heavens" should appear as UFOs in shapes that reflect our own technological fantasy.

UFOs are ambiguous. On the one hand they symbolize the disintegration of psychic unity by arriving in numbers and in a multitude of shapes — not merely disc-like or circular, but huge or tiny, lenticular or conical, winged or wingless, with or without fins, etc. (Hardly any two sightings are identical, which argues against the spacecraft hypothesis.) On the other hand, they symbolize the potential for reintegration — wholeness, the self — by also appearing singly and in mandala-like forms. They do not have a purpose, Jung would argue, any more than a myth has a purpose. They are natural phenomena produced by the need for psychic equilibrium; and we are left to reflect on them, as they reflect us, in the hope of healing whatever psychic breach besets us.

As a psychologist, Jung did not address the question of the physical nature of UFOs. He noted that many sightings seemed to be of solid objects — which, moreover, registered on radar screens. But he insisted that, even if UFOs did have some sort of physical reality, this in no way altered his thesis. For "…either psychic projections throw back a radar echo, or else the appearance of real objects affords an opportunity for mythological projections."[12] In other words, he thought it possible that projections from the collective unconscious might have a physical aspect; or else, although UFOs might be physical, they were not necessarily extraterrestrial space-craft. We project this interpretation on them by an unconscious need for a myth that embodies, say, the notion of heavenly intervention by superhuman powers.

Jung's real contribution to the debate, however, lay in his discovery of a part of the psyche — the collective unconscious — which is objective. Thus he dissolves the question as to whether UFOs are subjective ("all in the mind") or objective ("really out there"), and asserts that they are always objective, but they derive from the inner realm of the psyche. We know that they can appear outwardly, as projections, but to be consistent we would also expect them to appear inwardly, as fantasies and, above all, as dreams. And so they do.

Dreams

It must be emphasized that although dreams are inner experiences they are not subjective. That is, our conscious minds do not create them. They do not belong to us; they happen to us. The ancient Greeks were correct when they never spoke of *having* a dream, but always of *seeing* a dream. They also made a fundamental distinction between significant dreams and non-significant.[13] Jung, who analyzed thousands of dreams in the course of a long life, agreed with them. Ordinary dreams, whose contents could be traced back to events in our lives, were products of the personal unconscious. But there are also archetypal dreams, deriving from the collective unconscious, which the Greeks called "significant" and which tribal societies call "big dreams." These have a quite different atmosphere from ordinary dreams. They are distinguished by their vividness, clarity, and, above all, their sense of *reality*. They are felt to be sacred and, sometimes, prophetic. A typical example, cited by Jung, is that of a woman who dreamed she was traveling down the Champs-Élysées in a bus. The air-raid warning sounded. The passengers in the bus jumped out and disappeared into the surrounding houses. Last to leave the bus, the woman tried to get into a house but all the doors were shut. The whole street was empty. She pressed against a wall and looked up at the sky. Instead of the expected bombers she saw "a sort of Flying Saucer, a metallic sphere shaped like a drop. It was flying along quite slowly from north to east, and [she] had the impression that [she] was being observed." In the silence she heard the high heels of a woman walking down the empty street. "The atmosphere was most uncanny."[14]

Here, we can see the transition from the personal unconscious, as it were, to the collective: the woman is traveling along quite normally when the "air-raid" warning sounds. She is left alone to face a dramatic, but quite usual, scene of enemy aircraft. Instead, something altogether out of this world appears, an epiphany, accompanied by the aura of uncanniness which surrounds UFO sightings.

About a month later, she had another dream:

"I was walking, at night, in the streets of a city. Interplanetary 'machines' appeared in the sky, and everyone fled. The 'machines' looked like large steel cigars. I did not flee. One of the 'machines' spotted me and came straight towards me at an oblique angle. I think: Professor Jung says that one should not run away, so I stand still and look at the machine. From the front, seen close to, it looked like a circular eye, half blue, half white."[15]

Here the sense of epiphany — of a god or God manifesting himself — intensifies. The single eye is like the many-eyed all-seeing soul cited by Caesarius. But although Jung's advice to his patient may have been sound, it must be borne in mind that direct contact with spiritual powers is equivocal — dangerous as well as beneficent — as the second part of the same dream makes clear. The woman finds herself in a room in a hospital. "My two chiefs come in, very worried, and ask my sister how it was going. My sister replied that the mere sight of the machine had burnt my whole face. Only then did I realize that they were talking about me, and that my whole head was bandaged, although I could not see it."[16]

This is an effect often reported by UFO witnesses. Their faces are burnt, they develop rashes, skin irritations, conjunctivitis. Extraterrestrialists attribute these symptoms to "radiation." But we see that not all radiation need be literal. The searing archetypal images leave their mark in a psychic, symbolic sense, as well as a physical, literal sense. Moses had to cover his face after seeing the burning bush, not because it was burnt by radiation but because, irradiated by the glory of the Lord, it could not be looked upon.

And so, UFOs can appear in dreams with a lifelike — even more than lifelike — lucidity. But, conversely, waking visions of UFOs are often hedged about by a strange dream-like atmosphere, the same stillness and uncanniness reported in dreams. At about 5 p.m. on 26 May 1981, for example, a couple had just left their home in Pitsea, Essex, when an enormous oval object appeared from near an oil refinery. It had a red light at the back and four white "headlights." It flew very low and so slowly that it "took ages" to pass over. "Time virtually stood still, they felt, and later the witnesses realized that unless the object had taken about half an hour to pass over this busy rush-hour street such a large chunk of time was totally unaccounted for. There were no other witnesses."[17]

Again and again in UFO reports we hear of time "standing still," of an uncanny hush despite the presence of heavy traffic, say. Witnesses describe a feeling of isolation and absorption as if (as in the dream example) everybody else had suddenly vanished; a feeling of oneness with the perceived object in which initial apprehension or fear can be replaced by a sensation of subdued calm.

Another oddity of UFO sightings is demonstrated by the case of Nigel Mortimer of West Yorkshire, who woke one night "for no apparent reason" and felt an urge to look out of his bedroom window. He saw a bright "star" moving across the sky to the west. He thought it was a meteor until it slowed down and hovered over a nearby field. It now resembled a metallic, bluish-gray, oval object. Nigel said later that he felt very alert and rather elated by the sight. When the object flew off at an enormous speed, he felt sad. Returning to bed, he found himself suddenly overcome by tiredness and unwilling to believe what he had seen, almost as if something were trying to make him forget. As a precaution, he wrote down a full description of the sighting. It was just as well he did, for he had forgotten everything the next day until he was reminded by his written account.[18]

Just as we sometimes, amazingly, forget "big dreams" until some slight reminder recalls them, so it seems that people who have seen UFOs while wide awake, driving along a motorway perhaps, can also forget the whole incident until they read a report about it from another witness. But I am not drawing attention to the similarity between dream and waking encounters with UFOs in order to reduce the latter to the former — to say, as people will, "It was only a dream." On the contrary, I want to emphasize the importance of dreams and to insist on their reality, albeit a different order of reality from that which we are pleased to call normal. It is an eccentricity of our culture to undervalue dreams when we consider what a major role they play, and have always played, not only in traditional cultures, but also, for instance, in the great religions of the world.

Jung considered dreams the *via regia* — the royal path — to the unconscious and hence to self-knowledge. He never ceased paying attention to his dreams, many of which were decisive in shaping the course of both his inner and outer life. He understood the paradox of the unconscious: that it is unconscious only from the standpoint of ordinary waking consciousness. When the latter sleeps or is placed in abeyance, the "unconscious" reveals a striking consciousness of its own which often sees and knows more than we do. Sleeping and waking need not be treated as opposites. The one can invade the other. Dreams can be seen as sleeping visions, and visions as waking dreams. The first takes place inwardly, the second outwardly. But they are the same in kind, as the Apinayé chief I quoted in my introduction understood. You will recall that, while out hunting, he met his sun god who stood with his club beside a tree, his body painted, his legs red-striped, and his eyes like two stars. That same night he reappeared to our chief while he slept:

"I addressed him, but he said he had been waiting for me in the Steppe to talk to me, but since I had not approached he had gone away. He led me some distance behind the house and there showed me a spot on the ground where, he said, something was lying in storage for me. Then he vanished.

"The next morning I immediately went there and touched the ground with the tip of my foot, perceiving something hard buried there. But others came to call me to go hunting… When we returned, I at once went back to the site he had shown me, but did not find anything any more. Today I know that I was very stupid then…"[19]

Ah yes, the tale of the lost treasure is familiar across the world, like the crocks of gold pointed out to the Irish by the people of Fairy. The visionary condition is a fragile thing. Once the enchantment is broken by the summons of expediency and common sense, the treasure evaporates and the great Secret is forgotten, like the remainder of Coleridge's poem, "Kubla Khan," from which he was called away by the unfortunate person from Porlock.

3

Aliens and Fairies

Prefatory sightings

Having looked at anomalous lights and putative UFOs, it is time to look more closely at the entities associated with them. The two following sightings can be called classic or archetypal. They are chosen at random from dozens of similar cases.

As a young man, Mr. T. C. Kermode, a member of parliament on the Isle of Man, was walking with a friend to a party at Cronk-a-Voddy one October night when the friend happened to look across a small river and say: "Oh look, there are the fairies. Did you ever see them?" Mr. Kermode duly looked and "saw a circle of supernatural light which I have now come to regard as the 'astral light' or the Light of Nature, as it is called by the mystics and in which spirits become visible." The spot where the light appeared was a flat space surrounded by low hills. Into this space and the circle of light "I saw come in twos and threes a great crowd of little beings...who appeared like soldiers...dressed in red. They moved back and forth amid the circle of light, as they formed into order like troops drilling." They all vanished when his friend struck a wall with his stick and shouted.[1]

A forty-year-old businessman, Señor Angelu, was riding his motorcycle near Figueras, Spain, one October evening in 1958 when he saw something fall from the sky as if crashing into a nearby wood. He went to offer help, but found not a crashed, but a landed object. It had a classic UFO shape — like one plate inverted on another, about eight meters in diameter, and standing on legs. A figure was visible in the transparent "cockpit" on top, and two more were on the ground outside, moving about and gathering something. They were human in appearance, except for over-large heads, and were only about one meter tall. They rejoined their "ship," which rose

23

into the air and accelerated quickly out of sight.[2]

For the moment I will call the kind of entity in this second example an alien, to distinguish it from the fairies of the first. That this is largely a matter of convenience is made clear by these next examples, which I invite you to classify.

On the night of 9 June 1960, a woman driving to California caught a small figure in the headlights. It turned to face her and then ran off. It was three feet tall, broad-shouldered, long-armed, dark in color, with a head shaped like a pumpkin and two yellowish-orange glowing eyes. She had the impression that its body was hairy or furry.[3]

Driving through Stockton, Georgia, on 3 July 1955, Mrs. Wesley Symonds saw four "bug-eyed" creatures near the road. The one facing her had large, bulging eyes, a cup-like affair on its head, no visible mouth, a long pointed nose, and a chin that came to a sharp point. Long, thin arms ended in claw-like appendages.[4]

On 20 October 1954, near Como, Italy, a man had just parked his car in his garage when he saw a strange being about 1.30 meters tall. It was wearing a luminous suit and was standing near a tree. It aimed a beam at him from a sort of flashlight and the witness was paralyzed until he clenched his fist around his garage keys — a movement that seemed to free him. He went for the being who promptly rose into the air and disappeared with a whirring noise.[5]

The President of the Wellington Women's Institute was on holiday in Cornwall with her daughter when, walking down a winding lane, they came across a small man by a gate. He was all in green with a pointed hood and pointed ears, and he was watching them. They both saw him, the little girl screamed, they were both "cold with terror." They ran as fast as they could towards the ferry below them.[6]

Despite the absence of any UFOs, the first three sightings appeared in the UFO literature — perhaps because this is now the main, or even the only, repository for non-human apparitions. However, there is little to distinguish them from the fourth example, which is quoted in a book about fairies. The third encounter even has a classic touch — the fairies are famous for dreading anything made of iron, and it was the man's iron keys which broke the spell of the alien's beam.

I ought to say here that I am only using examples of fairy sightings to compare with those of more modern and fashionable aliens because fairies are nearer to me historically and geographically (and personally — members of my family have seen them) than any other species of anomalous being. But they are in no way exceptional. They are simply the name given in Celtic cultures — notably Ireland — to those beings which have their counterparts in every culture, whether the elves of Anglo-Saxon culture, for instance, or the trolls of Scandinavian. Modern culture, which we call Western, has done away with all these. They are relegated to the "superstitious past." But modern tribal societies still see, and believe in, their own equivalents. And perhaps, after all, we do too, if the above examples are anything to go by. Some ufologists argue that apparitions of aliens are only the old fairies, or whatever, reappearing in a new guise.

I'm not at all sure that the guise is actually all that new. The extreme diversity of aliens is more plausibly compared to the plethora of folklore entities than to thousands of different extraterrestrial species. The two features which, I suppose, are most commonly seized upon to set aliens apart are their clothing and their "spaceships." But even these have historical or anthropological parallels, if one cares to dig for them. When we hear of the shiny metallic skins or suits of the aliens, we naturally think of our own astronauts. But we might also remember the shiny little metal-men — earth-spirits and kobolds — who haunted the mines and mountains;[7] the hooded manikins called Cabiri who figure famously in Goethe's *Faust;* and the small but mighty Dactyls, gods of invention, who were known to the ancient Greeks.[8] We have already seen that fairies and their like can travel the skies as lights resembling UFOs. But the *ihk'al* of the Tzeltal Indians in Mexico fly about with a kind of rocket attached to their backs. They are described as three-foot-tall, hairy humanoids who occasionally use their means of propulsion to carry people off.[9] Flying vehicles of a technology appropriate to the culture in which they appear are not uncommon. A native American myth tells of Algon, a Chippewa hunter who stumbled across a circular pathway worn by many feet in the grass. To find out who made it, he hid and waited, eventually hearing music. As it grew louder, he saw in the air an osier (willow) car carrying four pretty women who landed and danced beautifully in a circle. When Algon approached, they fled to their car and soared away.[10] The story is particularly interesting, combining fairy elements (music and dancing) with UFO lore and even crop circle mythology.

It is curious that even those UFO investigators who are *not* committed to some extraterrestrial hypothesis seem never to inquire about the local folklore in the area where an "alien" sighting has taken place. Might it not turn out that similar critters had been seen before, maybe for hundreds of years? This would be especially useful in South American countries where the reports of aliens are so outlandish in many cases, and so unlike anything we might think of as "spacemen," that one suspects a transition is taking place from traditional entities to modern Western "ufonauts."

Alien classification

In 1987 Walt Andrus, director of America's Mutual UFO Network, announced that, after studying "thousands of cases," the organization had concluded that there were just four types of alien visiting Earth: the human-like entity, the small humanoids, the experimental animal, and the robot.[11] This classification reflects a commitment to extraterrestrialism — there are in effect two species of alien who are responsible for artificially creating two more. It is broadly true that amid the chaos of aliens in the 1950s a species of human-like, handsome, flowing-haired, benevolent entity showed a certain preponderance. It is also true that these were largely supplanted from the mid-1960s on by consistent contact with a kind of small, big-headed, gray-colored alien (I will especially be looking at these later on). But neither assertions are quite true enough. Exceptions still abounded.

Another survey claimed that about a fifth of the aliens spotted were more or less human-like; just over a third were small bipeds with huge heads; just under a third were not seen because of some clothing or helmet. Five percent were hairy bipeds. The remaining 11 or so percent were a miscellaneous bunch of complete weirdos.[12]

A valiant attempt by Peter Hough to classify them by their features reveals that they are as varied as the craft they appear to travel in. Reports describe the aliens as tall or small, human-like or headless, solid-looking or able to pass through walls or to levitate; friendly or hostile or just plain indifferent.[13] On the one hand such a catalogue of contradictions makes one despair of ever satisfactorily classifying the aliens; on the other hand, it provides a real clue as to their nature — which is to be essentially contra-dictory. It is almost as if their variety is specifically designed to refute any theory we might hold about them.

To show further the difficulty of classification (and as an excuse to indicate more of the flavor of alien encounters), I will briefly consider a favorite (though somewhat desperate) way of labeling them — that is, by size. The examples I have already cited may lead us to believe that both aliens and fairies tend to be *small,* between about three feet and four and a half feet tall. This is not the case:

On 12 September 1952, in Flatwoods, West Virginia, a group of youngsters saw a "meteor" land on the top of a nearby hill. On their way to investigate they collected Mrs. Kathleen Hill, her two sons, and seventeen-year-old National Guardsman Gae Lemon (*sic*). At the top of the hill they all saw a large globe "as big as a house," according to one of the boys. At that point another member of the group saw what he thought was a pair of animal eyes in the branches of a tree. He shone a flashlight towards them, whereupon everyone saw "a huge figure just under the lower branch of the tree. It seemed to be about ten or fifteen feet tall, had a blood-red 'face' and glowing greenish-orange 'eyes'... The apparition floated slowly towards the observers, who fled hysterically down the hillside..." The next day, investigators found parallel skid marks, a large circular area of flattened grass and a strange, unpleasant odor close to the ground.[14]

In November 1958, two Territorial Army soldiers were guarding a small hilltop near Braemar in the region of Aberdeen, Scotland, when, at dawn, they heard a "gurgling" noise behind some trees. As they went to investigate, two huge figures — more than seven feet tall — came towards them from among the trees. The soldiers turned and ran. As they fled they heard a swishing sound and, glancing back, saw a shining disc-shaped object swoop over their heads, pulsating as it went and trailing a shower of sparks. The two young men were in a state of shock when they were given shelter soon afterwards by Post Office engineers in an isolated hut near the scene of the incident.[15]

While aliens are often of sub- or superhuman stature, they are also, as it were, life-size.

At six o'clock on a May morning in 1957, Miss Frances Stichler was doing her chores in the barn at her farm in Milford, Pennsylvania, when she was alerted by a whining sound to a rimmed, bowl-shaped object about twenty feet in diameter which hove into view, stopped, and hovered about fifteen feet from the ground. A man in a loose shiny gray suit and tight-fitting helmet sat perched on the object's rim. He seemed to be of average size. His face, lightly tanned, had deep-set eyes and bore a "quizzical" expression. No sooner had Miss Stichler overcome her initial shock than the object streaked out of sight with a "spinning" sound.[16]

In November 1976, Joyce Bowles and Ted Pratt were driving near Winchester (England) when, noticing an orange glow in the sky, they lost control of the car, which swerved on to a grass verge along the narrow country lane. Ahead of them, hovering just off the ground, was an orange cigar-shaped object, fifteen feet "in size." A "man" passed through the side of the "cigar" and approached their car. He was about six feet tall, slim, and wearing a one-piece foil-like suit which zipped up to his chin. His hair was long and blond, but his beard was dark. His complexion was pale. Reaching the car, he put one hand on the roof and peered inside, enabling Joyce and Ted to see that his nose was long and pointed, and his eyes were entirely pink, without irises or pupils. They may even have been luminescent because, when Joyce turned her head away, an after-image remained on her retina — similar to the effect of staring at a naked electric lamp.[17]

The fearless and tireless UFO investigator John Keel pointed out that ufologists — like the astronomers who deliberately ignore anomalous aerial objects — are not above ignoring certain data themselves, if it does not suit them. "Among the great heaps of neglected and ignored UFO data," he said, "we find hundreds of minipeople accounts. These are very rarely published anywhere because they are so unbelievable. Most of them are identical to the fairy and gnome stories of yesteryear. The minipeople are only a few inches in height. Some dress like spacemen, complete with transparent helmets, while others are described in much the same way as Irish leprechauns."[18]

He goes on to relate the example given to him by a woman from Seattle, Washington, who woke up at 2 a.m. one morning in August 1965 to find that she could not move a muscle. Her window was open, and suddenly a football-sized, dull object floated through and hovered near her bed. Three tripod legs were lowered and it settled on the floor. A small ramp descended from this mini-UFO and five or six tiny people climbed out and began to work on their craft, as if repairing it. They wore tight-fitting clothes. When they had finished, they retreated up the ramp, and the object took off and sailed out of the window. The witness was then able to move. She was quite certain that she had been wide awake.

Keel is right about their similarity to fairies. There is a school of thought among folklorists that the belief in a race of tiny English fairies derives from the literary fancies of Shakespeare and his contemporaries. This is not the case — some of the very earliest fairies to be mentioned, the Portunes, were described by Gervase of Tilbury (*c.* 1211) as being only half an inch high.[19] At the same time, the popular conception of fairies — formed by late Victorian illustrations — as little winged creatures buzzing around flowers, etc. is mistaken. Fairies, like aliens, come in all sizes. They are not much mentioned in medieval manuscripts but, where they are, all the later types to be described are present, from Gervase's half-inchers, to child-size, to human-size, and even to giants.[20]

Fairy classification

I may be prejudiced, but of all the Celtic fairies, I like the Irish best. They are less dark than their Scottish counterparts, more beautiful even than the Welsh Tylwyth Teg (Fair Family), more noble than the Cornish piskies (pisgies, pixies), less associated with the dead than the Breton korrigans. I am not referring to the child-size or tiny fairies already mentioned but to that race of fairy variously called Tuatha de Danann, Sidhe, Good People or, by one "peasant-seer" of Sligo, the Gentry:

"The folk are the grandest I have ever seen. They are far superior to us, and that is why they are called the Gentry. They are…a military-aristocratic class, tall and noble appearing. They are a distinct race between our race and that of spirits, as they have told me. Their qualifications are tremendous. 'We could cut off half the human race, but would not,' they said, 'for we are expecting salvation.' And I knew a man three or four years ago whom they struck down with paralysis. Their sight is so penetrating that I think they would see through the earth. They have a silvery voice, quick and sweet. The music they play is most beautiful. They take the whole body and soul of young and intellectual people who are interesting, transmuting the body to a body like their own…"[21]

At one time such beings were frequently seen and perhaps would be still, were it not that belief in them is now considered risible. Perhaps they *are* still seen but are no longer reported for the same reason. Certainly both Lady Gregory and Dermot MacManus, who collected eyewitness accounts, did not have to look far. They had only, in fact, to ask around their estates and the surrounding area to find witnesses in abundance. For example, Mrs. Sheridan told Lady Gregory:

"I never saw fire go up in the air [presumably 'fairy lights'], but in the wood beyond the tree at Raheen I used often to see like a door open at night, and the light shining through it, just as it might shine through the house door, with the candle and the fire inside... Many of *them* I have seen — they are like ourselves only wearing bracket [i.e. speckled] clothes, and their bodies are not so strong or so thick as ours, and their eyes are more shining than our eyes..."[22]

When MacManus was a boy, around the turn of the century, I guess, the head gardener told him of a sighting at Lis Ard, the famous "fairy fort" on MacManus land. He had been working in the field below when "...he had looked up and seen the bank lined with a score or more of the fairy folk, all life-sized, the women mostly young and good-looking and with shawls over their heads. The men wore red or brown coats and some were bareheaded...while others wore conical hats...all of them had penetrating, staring eyes which...seemed to pierce right through him."[23]

Of course, there is a whole range of fairies which folklorists have had as little success in classifying as ufologists have had with aliens. I shall quote only one brave attempt, by an informant of Evans-Wentz's, because she at least claimed to have seen all her categories of fairy and, besides, it's as good as any. She is described as "a cultured Irishwoman now [i.e. 1910] living in County Dublin."

The fairies we have just been discussing she calls the Good People, who are "tall beautiful beings, as tall as ourselves." They are distinct from, on the one hand, the gods "who are really the Tuatha de Danann and taller than ourselves" and, on the other, from the Little People who are "quite good-looking" and, naturally, "very small." These in turn are separate from gnomes and leprechauns. The gnomes she saw on the side of Ben Bulben (a well-known Sligo mountain) had "rather round heads, dark thick-set bodies" and stood about two and a half feet tall. She called them "earth-spirits." Leprechauns are also small and "full of mischief." She followed one from the town of Wicklow out to the Carraig Sidhe (Rock of the Fairies), where he disappeared. "He had a very merry face, and beckoned to me with his finger."[24]

If these are just some of the fairies in one culture, the problem of classification is compounded when we consider that every culture has, or used to have, their equivalent, whose characteristics sometimes overlap, sometimes differ, from culture to culture, from tribe to tribe, and even perhaps from individual to individual. English fairies are named differently from county to county. There are Danes (Somerset), Derricks (Devon/Hants), Farisees (Suffolk), Feeorin (Lancashire), Piskies (Cornwall), and so on — to say nothing of assorted boggarts, brownies, gnomes, goblins, hobs, imps, and a host of fairy animals from "water-horses" to fairy cats.[25]

However, the great variety of fairies may be only apparent. Evans-Wentz's "peasant-seer" stressed that the Gentry were "able to appear in different forms. One once appeared to me, and seemed only four feet high, and stoutly built. He said, 'I am bigger than I appear to you now. We can make the old young, the big small, the small big.' "[26] This is a respectable and ancient view. Proclus (412–85) says much the same thing in his commentary on Plato's *Republic:* "In all initiations and mysteries" — elsewhere he adds "dreams and true visions"[27] — "the gods exhibit many forms of themselves, and appear in a variety of shapes, and sometimes, indeed, an unfigured light of themselves is held forth to view; sometimes this light is figured according to a human form, and sometimes it proceeds into a different shape."[28]

The Christian-scientific view

It is amusing and interesting to make distinctions between types of fairy and between, say, fairies and aliens. But formal classification is not possible nor, I think, desirable. Classification presupposes a kind of thinking which cannot apply to the apparitional or visionary world. And, besides, the apparitions themselves resist it. As soon as one characteristic is predicated of them it is contradicted by another. So, instead of compelling the apparitions into one category or another, it is more sensible to let them take the lead in the way they should be looked at. This means changing our point of view, which, overtly or implicitly, has been formed by Christianity and, more recently, by science.

Christianity holds no brief for fairies, aliens, and the like. Its officials can scarcely tolerate reputable visions of the Virgin Mary. On the whole, it wishes apparitions would go away. If they don't, it is tempted to call them the work of the devil. Science very properly ignores them. Apparitions and visions, contrary to the belief of most ufologists for instance, have little to do with science. Despite the best efforts of quasi-scientists, such as parapsychologists, to prove their existence, they will remain (like most things in life) rumors, hearsay, anecdotes, stories, and private experiences. There will always be abundant stories of proof — claims that fairies and aliens have been caught, shot, photographed, or whatever — but never unequivocal proof itself. However, proof itself doesn't prove anything. No one who has seen or felt the full force of an apparition demands proof. If they feel compelled to try and prove it to others, it is only because they feel obliged to, by the scientific tenor of the times.

If science were content merely to ignore apparitions, all would be well. Unhappily, it has bred an ideology, scientism (roughly, a mixture of logical positivism and philosophical materialism) which sees fit to pronounce on matters, including visionary experience, which do not concern it. Since these matters do not conform to its scheme of things, scientism condemns them with all the zeal of a Christian convert. At best, it adopts a superior stance, as if it had the right to some higher moral ground, and invokes psychology (by which it means "all in the mind") or, yes, "psycho-social strains." It would not dream of crediting the evidence of ordinary people's eyes. It is an intrinsic part of both "official" Christianity and scientism, incidentally, to project themselves as superior (real Christians and scientists suffer from doubt and humility).

To understand apparitions, we have to cultivate a view of the world which is different from that based on Christianity, science, and their ideological legacies. As we have seen from Jung, who held such a view, a large part of it involves turning assumptions upside down, reassessing "reality," and reinstating the importance of dreams, unconscious contents, soul-images. Fortunately this is not as difficult as Jung's difficult, often turgid psychology suggests. For the same worldview existed everywhere in pre-Christian times and still exists in non-monotheistic cultures. It even exists, against the odds, unofficially — instinctively — among groups and individuals in our culture. What such people often lack is a sense of precedent for their view, an historical context for the evidence of their own eyes; and this is partly what this book hopes to provide.

Psychic reality

More than anyone else in the twentieth century, Jung held a worldview which made apparitions intelligible. He discovered it empirically by examining his patients' dreams and fantasies, which led him to uncover a deep collective level of the unconscious containing archetypal images that lived an independent objective life. Naturally, he cast about for some historical counterpart to his idea, and he found it in, of all things, alchemy. Far from being merely a primitive form of chemistry, this turned out to be a complex ritual system of self-initiation — a whole "science of the soul," in fact.

We can imagine his excitement when, for instance, he read in an alchemical text the casual remark that "the soul is only partly confined to the body, just as God is only partly enclosed in the body of the world."[29] It confirmed his own conclusion that "the psyche is only partly identical with our empirical conscious being; for the rest it is projected and in this state it imagines or represents those things which the body cannot grasp..."[30] Here, the objective nature of the psyche is firmly established. But Jung still clings to the fundamental inwardness of the psyche, whose outward manifestations are only projections. By the time of his magnum opus — *Mysterium Coniunctionis* (1955–6) — even this conviction has been shaken. "It may well be a prejudice," Jung muses, "to restrict the psyche to being 'inside the body.' In so far as the psyche has a non-spatial aspect, there may be a psyche 'outside-the-body,' a region so utterly different from 'my' psychic sphere that one has to get out of oneself...to get there."[31]

Jung imagined this region as an "alien country outside the ego" such as tribal peoples believed in — a whole world, invisible but present in this one, which was inhabited both by the spirits of the ancestors and by spirits whose world it was (and who had never been incarnate). It could also, of course, be felt as a "psychic" world "inside," as a world in miniature. In other words, Jung now thinks less in terms of two worlds, one inside and one outside, and more in terms of two aspects of the same world: a microcosm and a macrocosm. He called this world *psychic reality*.

It is difficult for us to grasp psychic reality because our worldview has been doggedly dualistic for so long. Dualism caught on in the early seventeenth century with the new empiricism of Francis Bacon and the philosophy of René Descartes, who divided the world firmly between Mind (subject) and Extension (object). But the groundwork for such a division had been laid centuries before, at the Church Council of 869, which established dogmatically that man was composed of two parts, body and spirit. The third component — soul — was subsumed under spirit, and so an essential distinction was lost. For it is precisely to soul (Greek *psyche;* Latin *anima*) that psychic reality refers: an intermediate world between the physical and spiritual, partaking of both.

Jung understood psychic reality because he encountered it directly — in a dream. There appeared to him "a winged being sailing across the sky. I saw that it was an old man with the horns of a bull. He held a bunch of four keys, one of which he clutched as if he were about to open a lock." This mysterious figure introduced himself as Philemon; and it was the start of a beautiful relationship. He visited Jung often, not only in dreams but while he was awake as well: "At times he seemed to me quite real, as if he were a living personality. I went walking up and down the garden with him, and to me he was what the Indians call a guru... Philemon brought home to me the crucial insight that there are things in the psyche which I do not produce, but which have their own life... I held conversations with him and he said things which I had not consciously thought... He said I treated thoughts as if I generate them myself but in his view thoughts were like animals in the forest, or people in a room... It was he who taught me psychic objectivity, the reality of the psyche."[32]

One of the details that Jung tells us about Philemon is that he "brought with him an Egypto-Hellenistic atmosphere with a Gnostic coloration." In other words he came from the Greek-speaking culture which extended around the eastern Mediterranean in the early centuries after the birth of Christ. At this time Christianity was simply another set of beliefs competing for sovereignty with several others, such as Gnosticism, Hermeticism and, especially, Neoplatonism. These were eventually either declared heretical or partially absorbed into Christianity, which became the official religion of the Holy Roman Empire. Cast out with them was a belief they took for granted — a belief in what Jung called psychic reality. And so Philemon, who had done so much to initiate Jung into this world, was truly his spiritual ancestor.

Plato's daimons

The great authorities on the intermediate world of psychic reality were the Neoplatonists who flourished from about the middle of the third century A.D. to the middle of the sixth. Following Plato's most mystical dialogue, the *Timaeus,* they called the intermediate region the Soul of the World, widely known in Latin as *Anima Mundi.* Just as the human soul mediated between spirit and body, so the world-soul mediated between the One (which, like God, was the transcendent source of all things) and the material, sensory world. The agents of this mediation were called daimons (sometimes spelled daemons) — who, as it were, populated the Soul of the World and provided the connection between gods and men.

Christianity later, and unjustly, pronounced the daimons *demons.* But originally they were simply the beings who thronged myth and folklore, from the Greek nymphs, satyrs, fauns, dryads, etc. to elves, gnomes, trolls, jinn, and so on. I am therefore proposing, for the sake of convenience, to call all apparitional figures, including our fairies and aliens, by the general name of daimons.

Daimons were essential to the Gnostic–Hermetic–Neoplatonic tradition of philosophy — which was more like psychology (in the Jungian sense) or a mystical discipline than the logical exercises philosophy became. But the daimons of myth evolved into a sort more suited to these philosophies, whether angels, souls, archons, thrones, or powers — many of which later infiltrated Christianity. Ever-flexible, the daimons changed their shape to suit the times, even becoming abstractions when necessary (the Neoplatonic henads, for example) but preferring if possible to remain personified. Jung's cast of archetypal personages — shadow, anima/animus, Great Mother, Wise Old Man — placed him firmly in this tradition.

Never quite divine nor quite human, the daimons erupted out of the Soul of the World. They were neither spiritual nor physical, but both. Neither were they, as Jung discovered, wholly inner nor wholly outer, but both. They were paradoxical beings, both good and bad, benign and frightening, guiding and warning, protecting and maddening. Plato has Diotima describe them in the *Symposium,* a dialogue devoted to the most neglected of topics in modern philosophy — love.

"Everything that is daimonic is intermediate between god and mortal.

Interpreting and conveying the wishes of men to Gods and the will of Gods to men, it stands between the two and fills the gap... God has no contact with men; only through the daimonic is there intercourse and conversation between men and Gods, whether in the waking state or during sleep. And the man who is an expert in such intercourse is a daimonic man..."[33]

Jung was clearly just such a man. In his terms, the daimons are archetypal images which, in the process of individuation, conduct us towards the archetypes (gods) themselves. They did not have to convey messages; they were themselves the message. The Greeks understood from early times that daimons could be psychological, in Jung's sense. They attributed to daimons "those irrational impulses which arise in a man against his will to tempt him — hope, for instance, or fear."[34] Daimons of passion or jealousy and hatred still possess us, as they always have, causing us to cry forlornly: "I don't know what got into me. I was beside myself." But while daimonic activity is most noticeable in irrational, obsessive behavior, it is always quietly at work behind the scenes. Our task is to identify the daimon behind our deepest needs and desires, our projects and ideologies for, as we have seen, they always have a religious concern, coming from and returning to the divine, archetypal ground of being. The one thing we must not do is ignore them because, as Plutarch (46?–120?) warned, he who denies the daimons breaks the chain that unites the world to God.[35]

4

Daimons

Guardian angels

Mrs. Hope MacDonald, a devout Christian and wife of a missionary, compiled a rather sweet book called *When Angels Appear* (Grand Rapids, Michigan, 1982) in which she recounts anecdotes of angelic visitations gathered from among friends and acquaintances, presumably also Christian. The stories are not especially memorable. Many of what she calls angel stories could be called something else. Some of them are dubious (for example, she cites a classic piece of modern folklore, known as the "Vanishing Hitchhiker," as an angelic encounter). But they do draw attention to the large number of people who have experienced something they think of as miraculous. Mrs. MacDonald found that most of her informants had three things in common: they had never told their story before; the experience had made a great difference to their lives; and they were grateful for the opportunity of describing it. John Keel tells of similar reactions when questioning the large body of "silent contactees" whose UFO experiences have never been publicized. I, too, have heard remarkable stories from the most unlikely people just because I happened to ask and because I seemed likely to take the story seriously. All such stories would of course be derided by conventional wisdom, which takes no account of the importance and frequency of paranormal intervention in our ordinary lives.

One of the more sensational stories Mrs. MacDonald has to tell concerns a young mother who saw that her three-year-old daughter, Lisa, had escaped from the garden and was sitting on the railway tracks beyond. At that moment a train came around the bend, its whistle blowing persistently. "As she raced from the house screaming her daughter's name, she suddenly saw a striking figure, clothed in pure white, lifting Lisa off the tracks. While the train roared past, this glorious being stood by the track with an arm around the child… When the mother reached the daughter's side, Lisa was standing alone."[1]

However, it is more usual for one's angel to remain unseen and merely to warn or arrest one in a course of action with a single word or sentence, or silently, with a touch on the shoulder. Even less tangible are the sudden hunches and intuitions, also the work of "guardian angels," which appear out of the blue to make us miss the plane that is doomed to crash or simply to search an unlikely place for a lost object. As Mrs. MacDonald remarks, people by and large have little desire to speak about their daimonic experiences, let alone prove them to others. They know instinctively that they belong to a separate fragile reality which must be cherished in silence rather than blabbed about. And this is one reason we hear so little about them.

Personal daimons

Guardian angels derived from Neoplatonism and, along with other classes of angels, became part of the Christian dogma at the Council of Nicaea (AD 325). But, long before this, the ancient Greeks believed that individuals were attached at birth to a daimon who determined, wholly or in part, their destiny.[2] Philemon was clearly such a daimon for Jung, who emphasized the crucial part this strange Gnostic figure played in his life and work.[3] Plato's mentor, Socrates, had a daimon who was famous for always saying "No." It did not enter into rational discourse with Socrates; it merely warned him when he was about to do something wrong (especially something displeasing to the gods),[4] like the prompting of conscience or, indeed, like the cryptic guardian angels cited by Mrs. MacDonald.

However, Plato in the *Timaeus* identified the individual daimon with the element of pure reason in man and so it became "a sort of lofty spirit-guide, or Freudian super-ego."[5] This may be true of certain, perhaps exceptional individuals, but it is also true — as we shall see — that daimons are as likely to represent unreason or at least to be equivocal. But meanwhile it is instructive to consider the case of Napoleon. He had a familiar spirit "which protected him, which guided him, as a daemon, and which at particular moments took on the shape of a shining sphere, which he called his star, or which visited him in the figure of a dwarf clothed in red that warned him."[6]

This reminds us that personal daimons favor two forms by which to manifest: the abstract light, globe, oval, and (as here) shining sphere, or the personification — angelic, manikin-like, or whatever. It confirms, in other words, my speculation in Chapter 1 that the two forms are different manifestations of each other, with (in Napoleon's case) different functions: the star guides, the dwarf warns. Both are images of the soul, which is another way of understanding the daimon.

Indeed, it seems that, next to personification, daimons prefer luminous appearances or "phasmata," as the Syrian Neoplatonist Iamblichus (d. 326) called them. He was a real expert on daimons, and ufologists could do worse than study the distinctions he makes between phasmata. For instance, while phasmata of archangels are both "terrible and mild," their images "full of supernatural light," the phasmata of daimons are "various" and "dreadful." They appear "at different times…in a different form, and appear at one time great, but at another small, yet are still recognized to be the phasmata of daemons." As we have seen, this could equally well describe their personifications. Their "operations," interestingly, "appear to be more rapid than they are in reality" (an observation which might be borne in mind by ufologists). Their images are "obscure," presenting themselves within a "turbid fire" which is "unstable."[7]

The first of the great Neoplatonists, Plotinus (AD 204–70), maintained that the individual daimon was "not an anthropomorphic daemon, but an inner psychological principle, viz: the level above that on which we consciously live, and so is *both within us and yet transcendent*"[8] (my italics). Like Jung, he takes it as read that daimons are objective phenomena and thinks to emphasize only that, paradoxically, they manifest both inwardly (dreams, inspirations, thoughts, fantasies) and outwardly or transcendently (visions and apparitions). Plotinus does not, we notice — like the early Jung — speak of daimons as primarily "inner" and as seen outwardly only in "projection." He seems to agree with the later Jung — that there is a psyche "outside the body." However, his use of the word "transcendent" also suggests that the real distinction to be made is not between inner and outer, but between personal and impersonal. There is a sense, he seems to be saying, in which daimons can be both at once.

This is illustrated by a story told of Plotinus himself.[9] He was invited by some colleagues to attend an invocation of his personal daimon. Although he was not in favor of this sort of theurgical practice, he agreed. The invokers were abashed, however, when his daimon appeared — and turned out to be a god. This is more than an amusing story, for a god (unlike God the Father) is by definition inhuman and impersonal — and yet it can be a personal daimon. Moreover, the story intimates that personal daimons are not fixed but can develop or unfold according to our own spiritual development. Jung might say: in the course of individuation, we move beyond the personal unconscious to the impersonal, collective unconscious, through the daimonic to the divine. According to Iamblichus, we are assigned a daimon at birth to govern and direct our lives but our task is to obtain a god in its place.[10]

As a poet, W. B. Yeats experienced his daimon differently: "…I think it was Heraclitus who said: the Daimon is our destiny. When I think of life as a struggle with the Daimon who would ever set us to the hardest work among those not impossible, I understand why there is a deep enmity between a man and his destiny, and why a man loves nothing but his destiny… I am persuaded that the Daimon delivers and deceives us, and that he wove the netting from the stars and threw the net from his shoulder…"[11]

Here is a picture of the personal daimon both daunting and beautiful. It is a hard taskmaster, instilling in us the desire to perform the most difficult deeds possible for us, stretching us to the limit. The relationship is thus ambivalent: we feel both enmity and love for our daimon who, we notice, both "delivers and deceives us." Deceit is one of the daimonic attributes it is hardest for us to accept — we hear little or nothing of it in relation to guardian angels, for example — but we will be hearing more.

Towards the end of his life, Jung speaks wistfully of having been all his days in the grip of a daimon which, while it drove him towards the completion of his work and of his self, also drove him apart from the companionship of others. "The daimon of creativity has ruthlessly had its way with me," he remarked;[12] and ruthlessness, too, is another unpalatable characteristic of daimons we will have to swallow. Nor was this simply a manner of speaking — for Jung as for Plotinus, the daimon was a living, powerful personality.

Helping spirits

Not all daimons are as lofty and singular as philosophical and poetic ones. It's part of the vocation of all tribal medicine men or shamans to gain the help of their daimons. Often hostile to begin with, the daimons have to be won over. They can never be controlled as fully as they can control the individual to whom they are attached, but, after rigorous initiation rites, their aid can be enlisted at will. Knud Rasmussen quotes an Eskimo shaman:

"My first helping spirit became my name, a little *aua*. When it came to me, it was as if the door and roof rose and I received such power of vision that I could see right through the house, into the earth and up into the sky. It was the little *aua* that brought me all this inner light, by soaring over me so long as I sang. Then it stood in a corner of the doorway, invisible to everyone, but always ready when I called it."[13]

Here we see the enhanced vision that a consciousness of one's daimon can bring. Surely such a powerful and illuminating being must be equally striking in appearance — and so it is, but not perhaps in the way we might imagine:

"An *aua* is a little spirit, a woman, who lives down on the shore. There are many of these shore spirits. They run about with pointed skin caps on their heads, their trousers are quaintly short and of bearskin. They have high boots with black patterns and furs of sealskin. Their feet are turned upwards and they seem to walk only on their heels. They hold their hands with the thumbs always pressed against their palms... They are gay and jolly when you call them and look like small, charming, living dolls, for when standing up straight they are no taller than an arm's length."[14]

The comical and highly idiosyncratic appearance of the little *aua* is worthy of any fairy or alien. Clearly, it is not an individual daimon in the earlier sense of one's "destiny" or, as Philemon was to Jung, in the sense of being a guru. And yet its transforming effect on the shaman is not far removed in importance from these functions. One striking feature of the shaman's account is the matter-of-factness with which he describes the independent existence of the shore spirits and, at the same time, their willingness to attach themselves to individuals like himself. The same might be said of the following entities who appeared to people unversed in shamanic lore:

"I've never seen a ghost, but I did see a fairy. It was on the Berkshire Downs, and we'd lost our way and didn't know what track to take. When I looked round, there was a small man in green standing at my elbow. He had a round smiling face, and he said, 'You take that one; you'll be all right.' Then he didn't disappear, but he just wasn't there any more. Did I see him?

Or didn't I?"

This story was told to R. L. Tongue in 1962 by a farmer's wife near Timberscombe, Somerset.[15] The fairy was as benign as the fairy who appeared to the mother and daughter in Cornwall was frightening. A similar but even more striking instance was given to the well-known folklorist Katharine Briggs by a friend of hers, a clergyman's widow. She suffered from an injured foot and was sitting one day on a seat in London's Regent's Park, wondering how she would find the strength to limp home, when suddenly she saw a tiny man in green who looked at her very kindly and said, " 'Go home. We promise that your foot shan't pain you tonight.' Then he disappeared. But the intense pain in her foot had gone. She walked home easily and slept painlessly all night."[16]

These traditional "little green men" surely deserve to be called individual daimons, fulfilling a function of guiding, comforting and healing, as do the more familiar Christian "guardian angels." Like the little *aua,* too, their diminutive size and quaint appearance is misleading. They may be compared to the dwarfish Cabiri of Greek mythology who were also known as *megaloi theoi* — great gods; or to the homunculi that appeared in the vessels of the alchemists (like aliens in UFOs) and whom Jung reckoned manifestations of the Wise Old Man, one of the more powerful and profound archetypes. Particularly appealing is their lack of drama and fuss and their practical help — quite the opposite of so many encounters with "ufonauts," of which this is a typical example:

Law professor João de Freitas Guimares was sitting near the seashore at São Sebastião, Brazil, one July evening in 1957 when he saw a luminous hat-shaped craft approach from the sea and land on the edge of the water. The "pot-bellied" craft opened and two men, over five feet ten inches tall, with long fair hair to their shoulders, descended a metal stairway. They were youthful, fair-complexioned and with "wise and understanding eyes." They wore greenish one-piece suits fitting closely at the neck, wrists, and ankles. They invited the professor — telepathically — aboard their craft. He accepted. Taking his place on a circular seat in an illuminated compartment with three or four other crew members, he was taken for a flight lasting about half an hour (he could not be sure, since his watch had stopped working on his return). He told newspapers that he thought his hosts were advanced beings who wished to warn Earthlings about the dangers threatening them.[17]

The tradition of the visionary journey is something I will be looking at in detail later on. For the moment it is enough to remark that, on the one hand, aliens conform in part to the notion of individual daimons — they are definitely to do with the professor (it was he, after all, and not someone else who saw them). They have significance for him; they are even like Jung's Philemon with their apparent wisdom and understanding, even if they are rather more banal. Many contactees of this kind report revolutionary changes in their lives as a result of such encounters, which haunt them and present an obstacle to their former smooth perception of the world, opening up extraordinary possibilities.

On the other hand, his experience was not to do with him — was, in fact, truly alien. The witness feels that the same events would have occurred regardless of his presence, would have happened to anyone who chanced to be sitting on the same seashore. Compared to the previous fairy encounters, the experience errs on the side of the impersonal.

In the end, all apparitions are ambiguous, both personal and impersonal. As we saw earlier, even the most obviously personal — the ghosts of relatives known to us — often contain impersonal elements, as when they seem to represent the more general "ancestors," or when they appear as an abstract "shiny disc," a globe of light, an amorphous soul. Conversely, no encounter is so impersonal as to be free of personal significance, even in the absence of some intimate message. And so, like any reality worth the name, daimons are paradoxical; and it is as well to grapple with this idea now if any understanding is to be gained later.

Two horrors

We would like to believe that all daimons are, at least potentially, helpful and protective. This is not the case. There are daimons to which, frankly, it is difficult to attach rhyme or reason. Far from being articulate, wise, or superhuman, they appear to be brutal and subhuman. We would like to think that they have nothing to do with us, but of this we cannot be sure. Nevertheless they do seem to be as impersonal as, if not more so than, those daimons at the top end of the spiritual spectrum (so to speak) which shade into gods. They may only seem especially alien and frightening because we cannot, by definition, make any personal connection with them. At any rate, no description of psychic reality is complete without them, and so I offer two random examples. The first would be hilarious were it not so grotesque; the second is a daimon which does not merely appear nasty at first, only to reveal positive attributes later on — it seems to be a personification of malignity, a veritable demon.

On 16 November 1963, four young people were walking along a country road near Sandling Park, Hythe, Kent. Seventeen-year-old John Flaxton was the first to draw attention to a bright "star" which seemed to be moving over the woods at Slaybrook corner. The group grew alarmed when the "star" started to drop towards them. As they ran for safety they became aware of an oval-shaped golden light floating about ten feet above an adjoining field. They stopped running — and the light stopped moving. They felt they were being watched...

Up until now, the encounter is typical: the anomalous light heralds the advent of some visitation — a ring of fairies perhaps or a blond "spaceman" with a stirring message for mankind. Instead, "the glowing disappeared behind the trees, and the next thing the young people knew was that a dark figure was shambling across the field towards them. It seemed to be completely black, human-sized but with no head [and]...to have wings of the kind associated with bats... The youngsters are convinced they saw a ghost. Mervyn Hutchinson, eighteen, said it was like a bat, with webbed feet and no head."[18]

Dermot MacManus tells us that his father, when aged about fourteen, was playing hide-and-seek with his brother one late afternoon when it was not yet dark. He was tiptoeing along the granary when he heard the horses in the stable below snorting and trampling. He opened a trap door in the floor and looked down into the stable where two horses "in a mad panic of terror" were trying to get as far away as possible from something in the manger.

"He looked across and saw, not twelve feet from his head...a sight that he never forgot all the days of his life. There crouched a figure of evil with baleful eyes, blazing red like glowing coals of fire. It was huddling in a compact ball, as a boy of his own age might look when squatting on his haunches. My father remembered only those awful eyes, the squatness of the body hunched in a dark corner of the manger, and one awful hand, a human hand, but how different! The fingers were bone and sinew and ended not in human nails but in curved, pointed claws."[19]

Complexes, archetypes, myths

In his earlier work Jung would have called the personal daimons *complexes* — those parts of his patients' unconscious psyches which, having been denied or repressed, tend to split off and take on a quasi-autonomy, much as we find in cases of "multiple personality disorder." These psychic fragments are like personalities in their own right, with their own voices. The aim of psychotherapy was (broadly) to trace the cause of the splitting off in the patient's history and bring it to consciousness so that the fragment or complex might be reintegrated and so cease to make itself heard through undesirable symptoms. Strictly speaking, we do not have complexes — *they* have us. We are powerless in the grip of obsessions, compulsions, fixations, aversions, and so on.

But even as the complexes are unraveled they reveal contents which do not belong to personal history — contents which point downwards, as it were, to the impersonal world of the *archetypes*. Here we find daimons in whose grip we are equally powerless, no longer in the neurotic sense, but in the sense of being impelled by destiny, called by a god.

Jung's great triumph was not to follow the usual Western philosophical tradition in always translating images and personifications into concepts and thought-abstractions. Instead he remained faithful to the images themselves, retaining their personified nature as, for instance, Shadow, Hero, Anima, Great Mother, etc. (And here I must stress that I am not using the word personification in the usual anthropomorphic sense, implying that we make the gods and daimons in our own image, or that they are our projections. On the contrary, the appearance of gods and daimons *precedes* the concept of personification. *We do not personify;* rather, *the daimons come as persons.*)[20]

In addition, Jung recognized that it is the nature of the ego — the sense of "I-ness" — to deceive us into believing that we are single unified personalities. But in reality the psyche is composed of many different personalities, each with claims of its own, which the ego is driven to ignore, subordinate, or annihilate. Jung therefore wanted to shift the center of the personality away from the ego and towards the self, which he conceived as a *complexio oppositorum,* a complex of opposites where our different and opposing personalities could be harmoniously accommodated, allowed to co-inhere as a kind of paradoxical multiplicity-in-unity.

Jung granted the relative autonomy of the complexes by calling them the "little people." He saw that they related to the archetypes as the daimons related to, and flowed into, the gods. This relationship is not static but dynamic; it forms archetypal *patterns* — narrative actions which we call *myths*.

Freud recognized that our ideas and actions conform to certain archetypal and mythological motifs, but he tended to reduce these to just a few, e.g. the myth of Oedipus. Jung on the other hand saw that, deep in the collective unconscious, all myths were alive and well, living their own lives. The covert influence they exert on us sometimes surfaces spontaneously, as in the psychotic patients who were found to be acting out some arcane myth of which they could have no conscious knowledge. Alternatively, men and women of exceptional vision and self-knowledge can become aware of the myth they are living out, just as Jung was conscious of recapitulating in his work the ancient processes of alchemy, not chemically but psychologically.

In other words, "mythology is ancient psychology and psychology is recent mythology."[21] And for Western culture since the Renaissance, mythology has meant Greek, or Greco-Roman, mythology. Not that Jung neglected other mythologies — indeed, the recurrence of disturbing motifs from Germanic myths, which he detected in the unconscious psyches of his German patients, enabled him to foresee as early as the 1920s the outbreak of the Second World War. But, for the most part, it is the incomparably subtle, detailed, and elaborate mythology of the ancient Greeks which provides the most reliable guide to the deep life of the collective psyche.

And so we have to revise, even reverse, our view of myths as we had to revise our view of dreams. Instead of seeing them as archaic tales and primitive fabrications, we must see them as the embodiment of psychological truths, archetypal stories which tell us in symbolic, poetic form how it really is with us. There are even myths, as we shall see, which foreshadow the denial of myth itself. They are true stories, describing events which never occurred in history but which took place, as they are still taking place, in the timeless realm of the collective unconscious. If their protagonists, the gods and daimons, change shape — appearing now as aliens from other planets, say — they are only cutting their cloth to fit the times.

The Soul of the World

As I noted at the end of the last chapter, the Neoplatonists described the intermediate world of gods and daimons as *Anima Mundi,* the Soul of the World. They derived it from Plato who imagined a world-soul, diffused by the Demiurge (his creator-god) throughout the body of the world, making of it a living creature.[22] As such it remains the mythical model or root metaphor behind modern ecological concerns which picture the world as an organism, or personify it as a goddess such as Gaia.

It is also directly analogous to Jung's collective unconscious, itself part of the philosophical tradition for which it seeks to account. Jung dressed the Soul of the World in a new, more scientific garb. Since neither the Soul of the World nor the collective unconscious can be known in themselves, it might be better to say that they are metaphors for each other. They are like a mirror, empty in itself, but reflecting everything. They are like vast storehouses of images but they do not exist separately from the images they contain.

In fact the images are not *in* them at all — they *are* them. "Image *is* psyche," said Jung;[23] and this is why we cannot say what *Anima Mundi* is, only what it is *like,* for among its images are images of itself, including concepts such as *Anima Mundi* and collective unconscious! In many ways these abstract concepts do less justice to the reality than concrete images such as a mirror or a storehouse. W. B. Yeats thought of *Anima Mundi* "as a great pool or garden where it moves through its allotted growth like a great water-plant or frequently branches in the air..."[24] But this is perhaps too tame an image for *Anima Mundi.* Jung frequently compared it to the sea, an image which appears alike in individual dreams and primitive myth, where the ocean is often portrayed as a mirror-universe containing replicas or reflections of everything on Earth. He certainly acknowledged, at the end of his autobiography, that "unconscious" was perhaps too neutral and rational a term, better replaced by *mana,* daimon, or God.[25]

In alchemy he found perhaps the most sophisticated representation of the world-soul — Mercurius (Mercury), who personified both a dynamic spirit immanent in matter and the collective unconscious itself. The mythical figure of Proteus, a favorite image of the Renaissance, represented a combination of the sea image and the personification: as daimonic offspring

of the sea-god Poseidon, Proteus is the shape-changer *par excellence* —
always himself, yet always appearing as something else.

When Jung spoke of images, he referred especially of course to those
archetypal images we encounter as daimons and gods. We must not be
misled by the word "images" into thinking of them as somehow unreal. We
should, on the contrary, approach them as Jung approached daimons like his
Philemon — "as if they were real people" to whom he "listened
attentively."[26] He did not, we notice, treat them as literally real, as we
(mistakenly) treat hallucinations or (correctly) treat people in the street. He
did not treat them as "extraterrestrials." Nor did he treat them as parts of
himself, illusions or *mere* projections. He treated them as metaphorical
beings, *as if* they were real people. And it is this metaphorical reality, as real
as (if not more so than) literal reality — as real as Philemon — that he called
psychic reality. In order to remove the taint of subjectivity which popularly
attaches to the word "psychic," I shall call it *daimonic reality.*

The advantage of *Anima Mundi* over the collective unconscious as a root
metaphor for daimonic reality is that it returns us to the idea of *soul,* with all
its religious connotations, instead of *psyche* which has lost these
connotations in the hands of almost everyone except Jung. Also, it does not
suggest, as the "unconscious" does, a world *within* us easily reduced to
"mere psychology." Instead it re-introduces the idea of an objective ensouled
world "out there."

"If all our mental images no less than apparitions (and I see no reason to
distinguish)," wrote Yeats, "are forms existing in the general vehicle of
Anima Mundi, and mirrored in our particular vehicle, many crooked things
are made straight."[27] From our point of view, the soul is a microcosm, a
"little world" in itself, which includes a profound collective level or world-
soul where all individual souls meet. From the world-soul's point of view, it
is a macrocosm, a whole impersonal world, which can paradoxically manifest itself in a personal way — as individual human souls. Jung understood
that if we penetrate deeply enough into ourselves, so to speak, the unconscious turns inside out: " 'At bottom' the psyche is simply 'the world'."[28]

Animism

All traditional societies recognize *Anima Mundi.* They may not have a
concept for it (Jung's mention of mana is the exception rather than the rule)

but they know it, directly, through every big dream, daimonic encounter, and epiphany. This sense of *anima* in Nature, shivering with vibrant life, is pejoratively called animism by Western culture, which has long since emptied Nature of soul and reduced it to dead matter obeying mechanical laws. The word "animism" effectively writes off what it claims to describe. But to cultures we describe as animistic, there is no such thing as animism — there is only Nature presenting itself in all its immediacy as daimon-ridden. There are genii of forest and mountain, *numina* of trees and streams, demons in caves, spirits on the seashore. These haunters of the wilderness have their counterparts, too, within the boundaries of habitat, from the spirits of the ancestors to the cozier household gods. No part of everyday life is without some presiding daimon who has to be accorded its portion and due if trouble is to be avoided. "All things," as Proclus remarked, "are full of gods."

Outside the sacred precinct — the temenos — of the village, sacred sites housed daimons who, naturally, prefer one place over another, a certain tree here, a rock there. Inside, man-made shrines — hearths, graves, temples — accommodated domestic gods and ancestral spirits. For the daimons need to be heeded. The lights which hang over tumuli or stone circles, rise up from sacred graves or holy wells, are signs of a daimonic place. UFOs hover over military bases, power stations, reservoirs because these are the shrines of our modern secular culture whose technological preoccupations are mirrored in the shadow display of high-tech alien "spacecraft."

Places where there is a high incidence of UFOs are called "windows." Not a bad name for a sacred site, suggesting a greater transparency between daimonic and ordinary reality. Daimons notoriously favor boundaries what the anthropologist Victor Turn These may be within us (between sl the unconscious) or outside us — cr at certain times, between day and ni the year. Caravan sites or trailer par UFOs or by strange creatures, perha between town and country, habitat knows a place of enchantment, privately. Here, the laws of time a attenuated; and we glimpse for an ins

5

A Little History of Daimons

In polytheistic religions, many gods are mediated by a multitude of daimons, who are often perceived as being virtually gods or, at least, godlings themselves (the seamless continuity between gods and daimons is a source of endless confusion to the classifying mind). Monotheistic religions are impatient of daimons. In the case of Christianity, they have to be expunged for the simple reason that only one mediator between mankind and the One God can be permitted: Jesus Christ.

Demons

Christianity's chief method for getting rid of the daimons was to *demonize* them. This process began with the earliest of the New Testament writings, the epistles of St. Paul; "...the things which the gentiles sacrifice," said Paul reproachfully, "they sacrifice to the devils, and not to God."[1] The Greek word he used for devils was *daimonia*: daimons. At a stroke, the host of intermediate beings recognized by all pagan peoples everywhere were stigmatized as demons in the service of Satan (*diabolos*). At best, the complex daimonic realm such as the one revered by Greco-Roman polytheism was subsumed under the Christian angelic realm; and all the old daimons were, of course, classed with the demonic angels who had been cast out of heaven along with Satan.

The Christian idea of angels derived from the daimons of neighboring, competing doctrines, such as Gnosticism and Neoplatonism, which were condemned as heretical. At first, since Christianity imagined its angels as having bodies of air and light, its demons were supposed to have similarly ethereal bodies which, according to St. Augustine, gave them extraordinary powers of perception and enabled them to move through the air at extraordinary speeds.[2] However, over the centuries, they shed their bodies and became purely spiritual. How else, it was asked in the twelfth century, could a legion of demons — 6,666 in number — be contained within a man?

The man most responsible for this spiritualizing process was the anonymous fifth-century mystic known as Dionysius the Areopagite. He was thoroughly Neoplatonic — his works reflect, and even quote, Proclus who was teaching in Athens around AD 430 — but he was also a Christian. Thus, when in the sixth century the Neoplatonic school at Athens closed down and the one at Alexandria passed into Christian hands, Dionysius's influence ensured that the daimons were assimilated to Christianity — not in their original form, as partly physical and partly spiritual, but as purely spiritual.

Hand in hand with the progressive spiritualization of the daimons went an opposite trend. As early as the fifth century, St. Jerome intimated that demons could take on grotesque forms, and be seen, heard, or felt by human beings. Christendom's early confidence in its power to overcome the demons gave way to doubt. They began to be seen as more forceful and threatening to Christian souls than anyone had bargained for. By the time of the Middle Ages demons were thought to be capable of appearing physically on earth. In the thirteenth century, Caesarius of Heisterbach was telling stories of demons in the guise of "big, ugly men dressed in black or, when set on seducing a woman, as a fine smartly dressed fellow"[3] — or even as horses, dogs, cats, bears, and other animals. Around 1270 it was thought advisable to compose the discourses of Richelmus, Abbot of Schönthal, into a book for the purpose of warning novice monks about the dangerous, highly organized hierarchy of demons. "The first and most cunning demons," he averred, "dwell in the air, and…issue instructions to demons of a cruder sort, who patrol the earth itself."[4]

In all this we see the polarizing tendency of Christianity which removes the category of intermediacy from daimons and makes them *either* purely spiritual *or* physical, compelling them the while to be in both cases *literal* beings. This literalizing drive is the same as that found among modern students of apparitions, especially ufologists. For them, there is no alternative to the proposition that aliens and the like are either literally real or else spirits and phantoms — except that nowadays, of course, even the category spirit has been all but abolished, leaving a choice between literally real and purely illusory, "all in the mind." Thus, whereas aliens have often been seen as updated versions of fairy-like entities, their true ancestors may well be instead the Christian angels and demons who also inhabit the "lower air" and divide sharply into good and evil, just as the aliens seem to. Fairies do not divide neatly in this way. True to their daimonic nature, they represent a third reality, remaining both spiritual and physical. They may inhabit the air, but are more likely to be terrestrial, adopting an aerial form on occasions. They are ambiguous at all times, benevolent and malign, but never simply demonic, purely angelic.

However, in medieval times, fairies were given short shrift by the authorities. Chaucer's Wife of Bath gives an ironical but unwittingly chilling description of how fairies were scoured from the landscape. In the old days, she says, the land was full of fairies, but now no one sees elves any more. The reason for this is the activity of holy friars and "limitours" — friars who were granted a license to beg within certain prescribed limits. "As thick as motes in the sunbeam," these holy men went about blessing everything, from halls, kitchens, and bowers; to cities, burghs, and castles; to woods, streams, and dairies "that maketh that ther ben no fayries."

> For wherever there used to walk an elf
> There now walks none but the limitour himself.[5]

The lines evoke images of the cowled, incense-bearing armies of Christendom as they marched across Europe, driving the native daimons into ever remoter places. This casting out of daimons was tantamount to demonizing them. It was not at all the same as the second principal method of dealing with them, namely to *Christianize* them. For, just as gentle Christian missionaries have tried to adapt tribal beliefs to Christianity, so in the early days of Christendom some cultures were converted relatively smoothly. The Celts in general, and the Irish in particular, seem to have found Christianity congenial to their existing beliefs. At any rate they appear to have converted without bitterness and bloodshed. (Legend relates that St. Patrick converted the Irish by engaging their druids in a spiritual contest which he won by superior theurgy.)

The daimons of such cultures were, so to speak, either converted alongside the humans, becoming adapted to Christianity; or else they lived on in their original form, frowned on, but more or less tolerated by the priests. The Puritan spirit which principally denied the daimons was common to Catholics and Protestants alike; but it was less evident among the Catholics and so it was in Catholic countries for the most part that the daimons were accommodated as vague "fallen angels," or were re-baptized with the name of a local saint who continued to mediate between human and God. Above all, they lived on in cults of the Virgin Mary who was — and still is — especially worshipped at holy wells and springs where she was adopted in place of the nymphs and genii of old. She performs the daimonic function *par excellence*: as the mother of Christ she is ideally placed to mediate between us and God, mitigating the severity of God's judgment.

The Longaevi

In his book *The Discarded Image,* C. S. Lewis tries to depict the universe as it was seen through the eyes of a medieval person. He describes their view of the heavens, with its precise system of crystalline spheres towering like a great cathedral, vast but finite, into space. And he is just about to describe their view of Earth and its inhabitants who occupy the lower end of the Great Chain of Being, which stretches down from God and the angels, to man, animals, vegetables, and even stones, when he finds himself obliged to pause and consider an anomalous class of beings. They are not only strange to him, as a literary historian and Christian apologist, but they are also at odds with the cosmology he is outlining — a world even more precise and orderly than our own worldview. Following the Roman writer Martianus Capella, he calls these beings *longaevi* (presumably "long-lived ones") — "dancing companies" of which "haunt woods, glades, and groves, and lakes, and springs and brooks; whose names are Pans, Fauns,…Satyrs, Silvans, Nymphs." They are, of course, our daimons.

"In a sense," says Lewis, "their unimportance is their importance. They are marginal fugitive creatures. They are perhaps the only creatures to whom the Model [i.e. the medieval cosmos] does not assign, as it were, an official status."[6] And this is as true of our own model of the cosmos as it was then. It is the nature of the daimons to be always unofficial, constituting a stumbling block to the orderly structures by which we envisage Creation. To his credit, Lewis does not disapprove of them. "Herein lies their imaginative value," he says. "They introduce a welcome hint of wildness and uncertainty into the universe that is in danger of being a little too self-explanatory, too luminous."[7] Lewis's private attempt to reconcile the daimons with a

Christian cosmos took the form of his famous Narnia books for children of all ages.

In the Middle Ages, too, the daimons of myth begin to infiltrate art. That is, they emerge from collective oral culture into medieval romances, written by individuals. In *Sir Orfeo* (*c.* 1330), for example, the story derives from the perennial motif of a human abducted by the fairies. The latter are no shadowy figures, but appear in a blaze of wealth, luxury, and hard material splendor. The Fairy King, who has threatened to take Orfeo's wife, arrives with over a hundred knights and a hundred ladies on white horses. In his own country he has a hundred towns and a crystal castle with a moat and buttresses of gold. But, for all this, he remains as elusive as ever: despite Orfeo's precautions, surrounding his wife with a thousand knights, she is taken all the same. The impression made by the fairies is one of violent passionate life. They are both beautiful and dangerous like the damsels of the later Grail romances, whose Christian veneer barely conceals their ancient pagan roots.

Sir Orfeo also rehearses the current view of fairies, which turns out to be as mixed as traditional views. For instance, the author cannot decide whether the place to which Orfeo's wife is abducted is the land of the dead or not. It is certainly full of people who were presumed dead but aren't (lines 389–90), but it is also full of people who really have died (391–400). It contains as well those who have been taken there in their sleep (401–4). Running concurrently with such debates were the usual views: that fairies were a separate rational species, distinct from angels and men; or that they were angels who had not quite fallen (they did not join Satan's rebellion but were, so to speak, fellow-travelers). Lastly, of course, they were thought of as fallen angels proper and, as such, demons.

Unfortunately, it was this last view which came to prevail in England. The process of demonization took on new impetus with the Reformation. The Protestants were in no mood to accommodate the daimons; nor were their Catholic counterparts, the new breed of narrow counter-reformationists. Both sides quoted the early Christian Fathers, who had identified the pagan gods with devils, to support their own identification of fairies with demons. By 1584, Reginald Scot could complain loudly in his *Discoverie of Witchcraft* (vii, xv) that "our mothers' maids have so terrified us with…spirits, witches, urchins, elves, hags, fairies, satyrs, pans, faunes,…dwarfs, giants, nymphs, Incubus, Robin Good Fellow,…and other such bugs." Here we see the fear and exasperation of a mind which has ceased to discriminate between daimons and is merely oppressed, lumping them all together in a demonic body. With the accession of James I to the throne in 1603, together with the rise of Puritanism, the demonization of fairies was all but complete in educated circles. James was opposed to daimons of any kind, as he had previously made clear in his own book *Daemonologie*. From the outset he calls them devils — "That kinde of Devils conversing in the earth may be divided in foure different kinds…the fourth is these kinde of spirites that are called vulgarlie the Fayrie" (III, i).[8]

What really did for the fairies, however, was their association with witches. Even as the poet Edmund Spenser could compliment Elizabeth I by identifying her with the Fairie Queene, a woman could be burned at Edinburgh in 1576 for "repairing with" the fairies and the "Queen of Elfame."[9] As late as 1662, the lovely red-haired Scottish witch Isobel Gowdie — a well-educated young woman of good family — was saying, in the first of her four famous confessions, "I was in the Downie Hills and got meat there, more than I could eat. The Queen of Fairie is bravely clothed in white linen…and the King of Fairie is a brave man, well-favored and broad faced…"[10]

The history of witchcraft in Europe is extremely complex. (I will touch on the subject later on.) It's enough to say here that, as the sixteenth century drew to a close, it became increasingly hag-ridden. Daimons, and fairies in particular, were implicated in the hysteria, phobia, and paranoia which surrounded witchcraft and the persecution of its alleged practitioners. This was also a period, of course, which saw the rise of empiricism which led eventually to the modern, essentially scientific, view of the world. On the face of it, this view could be seen as responsible for the ensuing decay of daimonic beliefs. But I am inclined to agree with C. S. Lewis when he says: "One might have expected the High Fairies to have been expelled by science; I think they were actually expelled by a darkening of superstition."[11]

Reason and the decline of daimons

"I often entangle myself in arguments…as to what is the true nature of apparitions. But at other times I say as Socrates said when they told him a learned opinion about a nymph of the Ilissus, 'the common opinion is enough for me,' and believe that all nature is full of invisible people, and that some of them are ugly and grotesque, some wicked or foolish, many beautiful beyond any one we have ever seen...they are surely there, the divine people, for only we who have neither simplicity nor wisdom have denied them, and the simple of all times and the wise men of ancient times have seen them and even spoken to them..." (W. B. Yeats)[12]

In the seventeenth century there were a few wise men left — the Hermetic philosopher Robert Fludd, for instance, one or two Cambridge Platonists, even Isaac Newton who spent twenty years on the study of alchemy. But for the most part the educated elite were, then as now, less than wise. They embraced the new emerging worldview — scientific, secular, skeptical — which even after three centuries is still more or less intact. This worldview did not so much demonize the daimons, let alone Christianize them, as simply refuse to recognize them. They were impossible — and so they did not exist.

Central to this development was the dualistic philosophy of Descartes who, as I have mentioned, effectively divided the world into Mind and Extension, that is, a subjective consciousness and an objective, external world. Nature was no longer a living entity in which we participated; it was a separate realm full of soulless objects. So, forced out of Nature, the daimons were compelled, as it were, to take refuge in the other half of the permitted world — in the subjective realm of Mind.

But Mind was more or less identified with consciousness and, shortly, Reason. It, too, had no room for the daimonic realm, which was forced "underground," into the unconscious region of Mind. In fact, it might be argued that the "unconscious" was formed during this period; that the Soul of the World was withdrawn from "outside" and re-located "within," as the collective unconscious, eventually to be rediscovered by depth psychology.

Meanwhile the eighteenth-century humanists, who had no concept of an unconscious, ascribed the daimonic to the faculty of imagination. The first volume of *The Gentleman's Magazine,* the epitome of mannerly eighteenth-century culture, sounded a distinctly modern note when it announced that "Apparitions, Genii, Demons, Hobgoblins, Sorcerers, and Magicians, are now reckon'd idle stories."[13] That is, they were reckoned to be imaginary and harmless. But, at the same time, imagination was feared as a threat to

Reason, as a source of irrational "enthusiasm." It was demonized, just as Nature had been demonized by the Puritans — just as the unconscious was later to be demonized by psychologists who branded it a dangerous jungle, a cesspit, a seething cauldron of unbridled desires. Imagination was characterized in much the same way in the eighteenth century. It was approved only so long as it remained moderate, voluntary, and controlled. However, at the turn of the nineteenth century a grander view of imagination came into its own — as we shall see — through the Romantic poets, and the imprisoned daimons erupted once more into life.

But this summary of the daimons' fate in relation to the educated classes takes no account of their fate among the uneducated. What happened to them among Yeats's "simple of all ages?" First of all, it should be noted that whereas intellectuals had always disdained popular "superstition," the appearance in the mid-seventeenth century of "well-born collectors of popular folk lore, like Sir Thomas Browne in his *Vulgar Errors* or John Aubrey in his *Remaines of Gentilisme and Judaisme*,"[14] opened an unprecedented gulf between educated and popular belief, a gulf that remains with us today. It was not that Browne and Aubrey were unsympathetic to traditional beliefs; it was more that they "were acutely conscious of belonging to a different mental world."[15] From the standpoint of "high" culture, "low" culture was barely culture at all; it was pejoratively called "superstition" and "folk lore."

From this lofty standpoint the popular belief in daimons was seen as increasingly besieged by inimical changes. Their wildernesses were being cultivated and the great forests — where apparitions were always around a corner, where Grail knights went astray only to encounter enchantment — were being cut down. Like the Celts before them the daimons were marginalized, driven back into the mountain fastnesses. The forlorn remark of John Dunbar, a Scottish highlander, at the turn of the last century echoed that of preceding generations: "I believe people saw fairies," he told Evans-Wentz, "but I think one reason no one sees them now is because every place in this parish where they used to appear has been put into sheep, and deer, and grouse, and shooting…"[16]

The decline of oral culture, too, was seen as contributing to the decline in daimonic belief. The prosaic printed word was more forceful, more focused than the stories which fed on the expressions and gestures of the teller. It dispelled the shadows cast by firelight on which daimonic tales depend for their power. In recent times, a man who saw a daimonic monster in Canada's Lake Aylmer actually chose to contradict the evidence of his own eyes, and to believe it had been a giant sturgeon, as a result of reading a Government book on the subject — a book, however, which had been inspired by his own sighting in the first place![17] Books insist on being fact or fiction. But daimons, like the stories about them, are not so easily classified. They straddle the border between fact and fiction, as they do so many borders. (Oral culture was further undermined from the eighteenth century onwards by the increasing cleavage between the classes, by the uprooting of the poor from the land and their move to a life of labor in the cities where, with no time for leisure, their own "folk" culture starved — but that's another story.)

While there is a case to be made for the decline of daimonic belief, I doubt that there has been a decline in daimonic manifestations themselves. Daimons have continued to appear, and never more so than today with the plethora of UFO sightings, "phantom" beasts, visions of the Virgin Mary, angelic visitations, spirit communications, and so on. I even doubt that traditional daimons, such as — in our culture — fairies, have been super-seded or are extinct. For it is part of fairy belief itself to claim that fairies are no longer being seen, just as John Dunbar claimed. But his contention that fairies were dying out has many precedents (Aubrey, for instance, thought that fairy beliefs had ceased during the English Civil War) and many subsequent echoes: fairies are always ascribed to an earlier time, yet they go on turning up (I will expand on this point later on). Accordingly, I myself was ready to assert that they really had disappeared nowadays — until I came across, quite by chance, two people who told me of their recent sightings, not even in the old Celtic strongholds, but in Dorset and Wiltshire. In the former case, Dominic French saw a troop of fairies dancing in a wood — known locally as the "fairy wood" — near Winterbourne Stickland.[18] He did not believe in them until then. (They were described, incidentally, as about four feet tall, colorful, and semi-transparent.)

I also beg leave to doubt whether the received wisdom is right in maintaining that the decline of oral culture has led to the decline of popular belief in daimons. Has there not merely been a change in its dissemination?

The printed word, which was formerly so inimical to such a belief, now spreads it through a mass of popular books and tabloid newspaper stories, aided by television and movies. Besides, people still tell apparitional stories, and folklorists have even discerned a new species of modern "urban" folklore.

Furthermore, I am not convinced that the cultivation and subsequent "disenchantment" of the landscape has done away with the daimons whose natural habitat it was. They may well be returning in new and unexpected forms, like the mystery big cats which lurk in the suburbs or the bizarre circular patterns impressed on the cornfields. If there ever was a time when the cultivation of wild Nature and the decline of oral culture led to a loss of daimonic belief, it was probably in the nineteenth century when daimonic activity principally moved from the countryside to the séance room.

Spiritualism

While Christianity had polarized daimonic reality into its two halves of spirit and matter, the rise of philosophical materialism in the nineteenth century abolished the spiritual altogether. Reality became matter. The Church tried to fight this off, but tended to do so by invoking Biblical authority — which suffered a frightful blow from Darwin and his notion that mankind was not divinely created but had naturally evolved. During the Victorian period, scientism reached a peak of confidence. It was robustly asserted that the mysteries of the universe would all be unraveled within a few short years. The confidence turned out, of course, to be misplaced; but a similar faith in the capacity of science still exists today. The tenor of reverence with which science is still treated was set 150 years ago.

It would be wrong to think that scientism had it all its own way. Scientific materialism has never quite been able to shake off vitalism — the idea, broadly, that there is a soul in matter. "Vitalist theories of the nature of life attributed its purposive organization to non-material souls, or vital factors, under a variety of other names. Mechanistic theories have always denied the existence of such 'mystical entities,' but have then had to reinvent them in new guises."[19] Daimonic reality always subverts the very disciplines which are designed to exclude it.

However, the daimons I wish to mention here are not those which plagued scientism from within, but those which it constellated as its opposite, like a half-witted brother. For the Victorian era was, paradoxically, prey to a vast daimonic phenomenon which shadowed the bright new daylight world of optimistic progress with the old penumbral world of "superstition," in which hollow-voiced ancestors spoke from beyond the grave.

There was something at once impressive and gruesome about the golden age of Spiritualism. Its mediums were attractively robust compared to their modern-day counterparts, the "channelers," who relay vapid messages from a myriad entities ranging from obscure African deities to far-out "space brothers." In a Victorian séance, trumpets sounded, bells rang, tables turned; objects materialized and apports flew through the walls; ghostly hands imprinted themselves on hot wax and pale spirits molded bodies for themselves from the sickly ectoplasm that gushed from the medium. Yet, ironically, these spectacular manifestations now seem merely to reflect the materialism they set out to confound. There was something crude about them, something distinctly unspiritual. Nevertheless, they were perhaps what was needed to shake the faith of a materialistic age.

Like the theatrical world with which it has a traditional affinity, Spiritualism had its stars and its hams, its comics and its tragedians. But not even its greatest star, D. D. Home, could shake off the shadiness which, of its nature, attaches to all daimonic phenomena. He moved pianos at will while he was tied to chairs in front of dozens of eminent people in brightly lit rooms. He levitated himself; he floated out of a window — and back through another. He performed endless feats of this kind, to order.[20] A top scientist, Sir William Crookes, was sent to debunk him and was converted instead. His colleagues were outraged — what Home was doing, they said, was impossible. "I never said it was possible," replied the despairing Crookes. "I said it was true."[21] But, for as many as believed in the reality of psychic powers, there were more who believed it was all trickery, even to the extent of disbelieving their own eyes.

There is a fine line between trickery and the genuine article. Daimons are themselves tricky. Sincere mediums were more likely to be the victims of their own spirits than out-and-out charlatans. If occasionally they conjured up an appropriate message when the spirits failed to communicate, it was usually — simple souls that they often were — a desire to please. The daimons on which psychic powers depend are easily bored and cease to function under enforced repetition, as ESP researchers discover in their laboratories: their subjects will show startling precognitive or psychokinetic abilities and then, as the dreary card-guessing tests progress, the results will tail off. Daimons do not take kindly to rigor, insistence, orders. They are capricious and whimsical. When we are asked to judge whether a medium is authentic or a fake, we have to say that the issue is less clear-cut than this.

Take the case of the "psychic surgeons" of the Philippines. Instead of healing people at a distance like Western Spiritualist healers, or healing by a simple laying on of hands, these "surgeons" appeared to slice their patients open with their fingers, spilling blood and hauling out pieces of intestine and sealing them up again without a stitch. Debunkers saw nothing but prestidigitation, even claiming that the blood and guts were fake or came from animals. Yet incurables continued to insist that they had been cured by these unpromising procedures.

I do not believe it is possible to know exactly what is going on. Psychic healers of all kinds do not themselves know quite how they do it. (They claim, in any case, that God or a god or spirits do it.) But we are entitled to consider the possibilities which the psychic surgeons raise. We have to bear in mind that traditional native shamanism or witch doctoring, though related to Western Spiritualism, is also quite different. Perhaps the psychic surgeons were not performing conjuring tricks but magic. Perhaps the blood and guts were materialized as part of the operation rather than being hidden up their sleeves (actually they had no sleeves). Daimonic events are nothing if not theatrical. They like to leave enigmatic pieces of evidence which turn out to confuse the issue further, to deepen rather than prove the mystery. And what if the "evidence" *were* "faked" by the surgeons? Might it not be a necessary aid to a magical procedure which requires dramatic props in order to work? Nothing is straightforward in the Twilight Zone, least of all Spiritualism.

For example, who are the mediums talking to? What produces their paranormal effects? The mediums, of course, say that they are talking to their "guides" or "controls." These are very like personal daimons (or "guardian angels") except that they claim to have once been alive on earth, as humans, which is not always the case with personal daimons. These spirits are typically Red Indians or Chinese doctors who speak with funny voices. They tend to be exalted souls who have advanced to the higher echelons of the afterlife and so are well placed to put us in touch with dead relatives and friends whom they keep in order. Occasionally, the spirit who takes possession of the medium is very high up indeed, almost a god, and, as such, not connected personally to the medium. Nor do they help deliver personal messages but tend to philosophize. Silver Birch and White Eagle are examples, both of whom have maintained substantial followings for fifty years or more. Their messages are best described as a kind of theosophy, preaching peace and love, recognizing Jesus as a great teacher, endorsing reincarnation and so on — unarguable but general and unexceptional (though less banal than the creeds channeled by most New Agers). Philosophy, it seems, is best left to the living.

However, there are exceptions, one of which is the book dictated to W. B. Yeats by his entranced wife. The spirit communicators told him that their purpose was to provide him with symbols for his poetry. The result was *A Vision*, a complex, almost Hermetic, system of philosophy and cosmology. But even here the dictation was disrupted by other spirits whom Yeats called the "Frustrators." They mimicked the genuine communicators so successfully that Yeats often wrote down messages for months before he either recognized that they were gibberish or was informed of their bogusness by the return of the "real" spirits.

A psychologist might argue, as Jung did to begin with, that a medium is really talking to other parts of himself — those autonomous, split-off fragments of the total psyche which lead a relatively independent life. In one sense they would know more than us — being unencumbered by space and time, they might have intimations of the future, for instance. In another sense they would be inferior as well as superior — not well-differentiated, half in darkness. On the whole, as we have seen, and as Jung came to realize, this view won't wash. Comforting though it is to think of the spirits as somehow belonging to us, safely contained within the psyche and therefore "subjective," we have been compelled to recognize that just as the psyche is, finally, objective and impersonal, so are its daimonic manifestations or personifications.

In fact there has been too much emphasis in Spiritualism on the afterlife, the realm of the dead. We have seen the tendency of daimons to conflate in the daimonic realm, and the realm of Spiritualism is no exception. If the dead — spirits, ancestors — are found among the fairies, might not the reverse be true? One man who thought so was the French astronomer and pioneer psychical researcher, Camille Flammarion, who noticed the striking similarity between so-called spirit manifestations and those of fairies:

"The greater part of the phenomena observed — noises, movement of tables, confusions, disturbances, raps, replies to questions asked — are really childish, puerile, vulgar, often ridiculous, and rather resemble the presences of mischievous boys than serious *bona fide* actions. It is impossible not to notice this... Either it is we who produce these phenomena or it is spirits. But mark this well: these spirits are not necessarily the souls of the dead; for other kinds of spiritual beings may exist, and space may be full of them without our ever knowing anything about it... Do we not find in the ancient literatures, demons, angels, gnomes, goblins, sprites, specters, elementals, etc.? Perhaps these legends are not without some foundation in fact."[22]

In modern times, the daimons appear much as they have always done. They appear externally as a host of apparitions; and internally, as muses who inspire and as devils who possess us and drive us mad. As ever they appear above all in dreams. Modern depth psychology came about because the daimons would no longer be ignored. They made themselves felt in neurotic symptoms, in obsessions and psychoses. Freud and his followers documented the complexes which cried out from within us with alien voices; Jung followed their call into the depths, beyond the personal, beyond even the human, to the world of archetypal psychological principles in which he saw the gods returning in a new guise. Freud could not follow him down. He feared the daimons of the unconscious, demonized them, warning Jung that he must set up a bulwark "against the black tide of mud" of "occultism."[23] But Jung dared to make his own journey into the collective unconscious and found there something altogether different, something — as we will see — unimaginable. Other schools of psychology became increasingly materialistic and reductive, treating the daimons as if they were purely physiological. Soul was reduced to mind, and mind to brain. The daimons were not so much demonized as *medicalized*. "The gods have become diseases," Jung was fond of lamenting.[24]

Dreams are probably less valued or heeded now than at any other time in our history. Since they hold a mirror up to us, reflecting our conscious stances, their neglect is itself reflected in images of weakness or vulnerability. Nightmares of crippled children, the baby we fail to rescue from fire or flood, the animal killed on the road — these are images of the debilitated soul wherein the daimons dwell. Or else the daimons turn on us, compelling recognition in dreams of menace and destruction: the hag who appears by our bedside, the friend who betrays, the husband who mocks, the wife who wields a scalpel.

Just as it is a psychological law — a law of the soul — that whatever is repressed returns in a different form, so the daimons plague the creeds and disciplines which refuse to admit them. They begin by making mischief, then they turn ugly and, finally, demonic. Over-masculine authoritarian Christianity is vexed by subversive visions of the Blessed Virgin Mary (BVM); over-ascetic monks are tormented by the arch-daimon Eros who insinuates himself into their lonely cells. The over-rational are haunted by a demonic hatred and fear of daimons; the over-materialistic are beset, like the Victorians, by spirits. The daimons are against extremes; they are the middle way. Like Freudian slips, they are the banana skins on which the over-proud come a cropper.

It would be wrong to imagine that the daimons have altogether abandoned Nature. Apparitions still abound there, while Nature lovers — even if they do not see it (as visionaries like William Blake saw it) as peopled with daimons — still have intimations of its autonomous life, its soul. But scientism has taken its toll: officially we no longer seek to see into, and participate in, the heart of Dame Kind (as Nature used to be called), but to examine, interrogate, and operate on her. Obediently she reflects our attitude towards her, appearing as essentially impersonal, objective, inhuman, and soulless. But at the poles of our investigations into the world — in subatomic- and astrophysics — the daimons return as minute, impish, but powerful particles and as white dwarfs, red giants, or ogreish black holes. The language of fairytales is telling. At the very edge of the "known universe" inconceivably huge Somethings recede from us at inconceivable speeds. They are called quasi-stellar objects — quasars — but we cannot agree about what we are looking at. They may as well be called unidentified flying objects.

6

Beasts

In Chapter 4 I began by discussing personal daimons and moved towards more impersonal ones, suggesting that all daimons were, finally, both personal and impersonal — that is, they exist on a continuum, some appearing at the personal end, others at the impersonal. Finally I drew attention to the traditional doctrine of a world-soul which was believed to animate the world. Like the collective unconscious, it expresses the idea that there is a psyche or soul which may manifest through us but which does not exclusively belong to us. If anything, we belong to, and participate in, it. Unlike the collective unconscious, perhaps, the idea of a world-soul emphasizes the outer and impersonal aspects of what I have called daimonic reality; and, to illustrate these, I want to look at the kind of apparitions which attach themselves to Nature and to a particular topography rather than, say, to particular individuals.

The most striking of these apparitions come in animal form, notably bird-like creatures, black dogs and cats, lake monsters, and "big hairy monsters" (I shall be touching on all of these except the first). Already these suggest an affinity with a certain element or type of landscape, as the Neoplatonists noticed. Olympiodorus, for example, remarked that daimons can be celestial, ethereal, aerial, aquatic, or subterranean. (He adds, for the benefit of ufologists, that "irrational daimons originate from the aerial governors"...[1]) Iamblichus notes that each daimonic nature is allotted its place on Earth, such as certain "sacred" regions or groves.[2] And it is true that black dogs, for instance, haunt particular stretches of road, certain lakesides, specific woods in a manner analogous to UFO and fairy preference for certain sacred sites. (The predilection of these to be linked by straight lines — "fairy paths," *lung-mei* or Chinese "dragon paths," and "leys" — has been documented by students of so-called earth mysteries.)³

Mysterious beasts have always been taken for granted by traditional cultures, who call them ghosts, spirits, phantoms, devils — or, at least, these are the words *we* use to translate *their* words for them. In fact, such cultures recognize them as daimons — that is, partly material as well as spiritual — instead of merely spirit-like, ghostly, and immaterial. It is our culture which is divided over whether these animals are spirits and ghosts or whether — absurd as it must seem to a tribal society — they are actual, literal animals. We even have a quasi-science — crypto-zoology — whose adherents go out hunting for black cats or Bigfoot. They are to mystery animals what extraterrestrialists are to UFOs. However, they are not to be despised — everyone who has had an encounter with one of these beasts, no less than with a UFO, cannot doubt its reality. The only question is: what sort of reality are we talking about? Their case for literal reality is apparently strengthened by the many pieces of what they call physical evidence, from footprints to recorded sounds, which I shall be calling something else in Chapter 10. Meanwhile, let us hear from some witnesses.

Black dogs

East Anglia is haunted by a black dog. In Norfolk it is called Shuck (Black Shuck, Old Shuck, Old Shock). Its name is imitative, some say, of the sound of chains which it drags. In Suffolk it tends to be called Scarfe, Galley Trot, or Moddy Dhoe. There are probably several of them. A Norfolk man heard it in May 1945 — the baying, as of a hound, which grew louder until it was "ear-splitting." At the same time he heard a sound like a chain being dragged along the road. He ran for his life.⁴

Seven years earlier Ernest Whitehead saw a black object approaching him as he was walking home along the Bungay to Ditchingham road on the Suffolk/Norfolk border. It turned out to be a large dog with a long black shaggy coat, about two and a half feet tall. When Ernest drew level with it, it vanished.⁵ Coastguard Graham Grant got a good look at it on 19 April 1972. It was on the beach at Gorleston, Norfolk, and "it was running then stopping, as if looking for someone." He watched it for a minute or two and then "it vanished before [his] eyes." He went on looking for a while but it did not reappear.⁶

The black dogs of Lancashire and Yorkshire are known as Barguest,

Trash, and Skriker. Trash makes a sound like heavy shoes splashing through mud; Skriker screams. In Staffordshire it is called Padfoot; in Warwickshire, Hooter. But it is not only British. Reports of black dogs are also found in France, Italy, Croatia, Germany, and Austria. In the USA they are seen mostly in Pennsylvania, Mississippi, and Missouri — where, in Peniscot county, for instance, some hunters threw an axe at an eight-foot-long black dog. The axe passed through it and stuck in a tree.[7] In Nova Scotia, Canada's prime black dog country, the one often seen at Rous' Brook sometimes appears only as a bright light, but can seem rather more substantial: a man who was emboldened by strong drink to face the thing that was following him was pounced on and nearly choked to death. "It looked like a black dog," he said, "but when it got [me] by the throat it seemed more like a person."[8]

However, black dogs are as likely to be friendly as hostile, even acting on occasion as "guardian angels." Early this century, a woman walking home from Scunthorpe to Crosby in Lincolnshire "found herself accompanied by a strange dog as she passed a group of [so-called] Irish laborers who were saying what they would have done to her if the dog weren't with her."[9] In the same county, in the thirties, a schoolmistress who often cycled at night along a lonely lane near Manton was frequently accompanied by a very large dog trotting along the grass verge. Its presence reassured her.[10]

Popular beliefs about what black dogs are are divided. They are ghosts of dogs, some say, or ghosts of the dead taking animal form. In earlier times — sightings of them have been continuous down through the centuries — they were thought of as a manifestation of the Devil or, at least, as witches' familiars. They certainly possess all the usual daimonic ambiguity, as well as an archetypal resonance which echoes the black dogs that guard treasure in fairy tales, and extends all the way back to such mythical dogs as triple-headed Cerberus who guards the Underworld. In Celtic cultures they fit naturally into the usual fairy framework, whether as the Isle of Man's Buggane or Moddy Dhoe, or as the Scottish Highlands' *cu sith*. In Ireland, black dogs are only one of many fairy creatures. Dermot MacManus gives us a dramatic sighting by a friend of his, a Mr. Martin, who was trout-fishing near his home in County Derry in 1928 when "…he saw a huge black animal come into sight, padding along in the shallow water. He could not at first make out what it was, whether dog, panther, or what, but he felt it to be intensely menacing, so…he dropped his rod and jumped for the nearest tree on the bank."[11]

Meanwhile, the animal advanced steadily and "as it passed it looked up at him with almost human intelligence and bared its teeth with a mixture of snarl and jeering grin. His flesh crept as he stared back into its fearsome, blazing red eyes, which seemed like live coals inside the monstrous head." Thinking that it was an escaped circus animal, Mr. Martin went home for his shotgun and hunted it. But no one he met had seen it and he was forced to give up. A few months later he happened to see a cigarette card, one of a series illustrating Irish place names. It depicted Poulaphuca (Pool of the Pooka) with its famous waterfall in the background. In the foreground was a very life-like portrait of the animal he had seen, the Pooka itself, a great black fairy dog. He began to inquire of the people local to his home and soon gathered plenty of stories of sightings. A creature like his had often been seen over the years, "usually standing in or by the river near the local bridge, but always in the gloaming…it was fifty or more years since anyone had claimed to have seen it in broad daylight."[12]

There are several classic features to this apparition. Firstly, we see how the Pooka, like all black dogs, is associated with a particular place, such as a pool or a stretch of road, and especially with a *liminal* place — a bridge, a river bank, a crossroads. Secondly it is most often seen at a liminal time, such as twilight ("the gloaming"). Thirdly, it shares with anomalous cats, lake monsters, Bigfoot, and so on, blazing red eyes. A friend of Walter Gill, the Manx author, met a black dog near Ramsay on the Isle of Man in 1927: it had long shaggy hair and eyes like coals of fire and would not let him pass. (His father died shortly afterwards, supporting the common view that black dogs are death portents.)[13] Fourthly, there is the matter of the animal's transfixing look. A young woman whom MacManus met described it in the same terms as Mr. Martin: she saw a Pooka in broad daylight — a black dog as high as her shoulder (Martin's was "as tall as a mantelpiece") only four yards away. It looked at her "with interest rather than hostility, but to her its eyes *seemed almost human in their intelligence*," (my italics). It walked past her and clean through a solid iron gate.[14]

Mystery cats

Mr. Martin's initial doubt about what he was seeing — "whether dog, panther, or what" — is echoed in more recent sightings of animals which are generally identified as big black *cats*. "At first I thought it was a dog and spoke to it," said Alan Pestell of Thorganby, Yorkshire, who encountered a large animal while walking along a main road on the night of 9 August 1976, "...but then I realized it had a cat's face and a long tail! I was scared stiff. I froze for a few seconds and then decided to keep on walking to the pub. I thought if I turned and ran it might jump on my back." He described the creature as three to four feet long and nearly three feet high, and said that it sat up and looked at him with its right paw lifted until he passed.[15]

In 1983 an animal which the press called the "Exmoor Beast" was assumed to have killed a large number of sheep in southern Exmoor around the Devon/Somerset border. The sheep were certainly slaughtered in the rather meticulous way characteristic of big cats. It is almost impossible to believe that a "phantom" animal — an apparition — can kill sheep. And yet the usual inquiries about escaped circus animals drew a blank, and no cats were missing from zoos or private menageries. In addition, people who saw the Exmoor Beast said that it looked more like a dog than a cat and its tracks, three and a half inches across, were dog-like — claw marks were visible (cats, of course, retract their claws). An enormous effort was made to kill or capture this creature. The Royal Marines were even called in to lie in wait for it with night-sights on their powerful rifles; but, although it was seen, it evaded everyone.[16]

Something similar to the Exmoor Beast is well known in the USA. It is generally referred to, or reported as, "a black panther." This makes no literal sense because a black panther is only a melanistic — i.e. all-black — leopard which is extremely rare at the best of times. Nevertheless, many such creatures have been, and continue to be, seen. In September 1975, something was heard screaming at night in Stockbridge, near Atlanta, Georgia. A "black panther" was seen. It had huge glowing eyes. It began to appear on highways in broad daylight. It was held responsible for killing a goat and, later, two cows. In neither case did the owners, sleeping nearby, hear anything. Search parties were launched, but no trace of the animal came to light. Like the Exmoor Beast, its reign of terror ceased as abruptly as it had begun. The only people perhaps unsurprised by the animal were the local Seminole Indians who were familiar from their legends with "ghost panthers" that preyed on deer and even people, and could only be killed by spears blessed by their holy man.[17]

It is difficult to know whether the black dogs of folklore are really black cats, or vice versa. Like the Pooka and the ghost panther they show the daimonic trait of amorphousness. Always recognizable, they also appear slightly different in detail to each observer. The animal which terrorized Bay Springs, Mississippi, throughout 1977 was described by Joe McCullough as waist-high, with a large head and short ears. Black and gray in color, it "slightly resembled a dog and had a long shaggy tail." It turned on Joe and others as they were hunting it and he only just managed to escape. Joseph Dixon saw it as "bigger than any German shepherd [Alsatian]…longer than any dog… Jumping further than any dog could jump." He held it responsible for the sinister attack on his pigs whose ears — and *only* their ears — had been eaten off. Nothing was caught or shot.[18]

The "black panther" is only one type of mystery cat reported in the USA. There are thousands more stories involving cats of a puma-, lion-, or tiger-like nature. One begins to wonder whether (granted that some may be real indigenous cats) they are different types of cat apparition or whether they are different manifestations of the same Pooka-like phenomenon which shape-changes. Different kinds of cat may be only a variation on the theme of dog-like cat. A spate of sightings at Wellington College, a boys' school near Crowthorne, Berkshire, in 1981 tends to support this notion.

In June, a teacher saw a fox-like animal run out of some long grass at an amazing speed — he timed it as taking twelve seconds to cover 150 yards. He was fascinated by the animal's sinuous way of moving, in which hind and front legs met each other in a bounding action. It was about the size of his Irish setter, reddish-brown in color, and with a long tail, more like a cat than a dog.[19] On 2 July three boys saw something as big as a Labrador, jet-black, with a smooth, glossy coat. It was about four feet long and moved very fast with long strides. It was agreed to be a "huge feline" animal, and certainly not a domestic cat or dog.[20] On 6 July a shopkeeper corroborated the boys' sighting, having spotted the "cat" in a field on the college grounds. He added that "the tail was as long as the body…the most noticeable feature was its bright red eyes, they almost seemed to flash — as if they were lit by a battery."[21]

However, on the same day as the boys' sighting, a retired couple was walking in nearby Crowthorne woods, about a quarter of a mile from Devil's Highway, when they saw at a distance of forty yards or so a "female lioness." It was "bigger than an Alsatian" with "a smooth brown-gold coat" and it crossed the track "in a slow graceful movement."[22] On 11 July another teacher was strolling through the college grounds with his wife and parents. They all saw a large, dark brown cat-like animal which stopped and looked at them for a few seconds.[23]

We are reminded of the strange feline manifestations, collectively known as the Surrey Puma, which appeared from 1962 onwards around the 300-acre Bushylease Farm between Ewshot and Crondall. (Nearby Godalming police accumulated 362 sightings of puma-like animals between 1962 and 1964.)[24] From the first it presented a number of characteristics both folkloric and anomalous. Screaming and howling noises were heard; it appeared largely at night or on foggy days; it left no footprints in snow but prints were later found in mud. The farm manager, Edward Blanks, had unleashed his dogs to track it but they refused to follow the scent and seemed terrified. Lights shone on the roofs of the farm buildings at night for no apparent reason and every time they appeared, the strange creature was seen in the area shortly afterwards. Blanks and his family saw, variously, a cat the size of a spaniel, ginger with darker spots and stripes; a larger puma-like beast; and a dark leopard-like animal.[25] Mrs. Christabel Arnold of Crondall was walking near the farm when she saw a creature she described as not at all like a puma: "I got the stench of it first a long way up the lane... I froze and we just looked at one another, then it spat all the time. It had marks like a cheetah on its face and was grayish, browny-beige with spots and stripes. Its back was deep red-brown...it had a beautiful striped red-brown and beigy white-tipped tail... It had yellow slanted eyes, wire-like whiskers and tufted ears..." She subsequently saw it again several times.[26]

I would not say exactly that black dogs are an endangered species of apparition (I read about a sighting the other day), but they do seem to have been somewhat usurped in the popular imagination by mystery cats, leading to a diminution of ambiguity and richness. For black dogs have the wider range of symbolic appeal, appearing now as omens of death or misfortune, now as protectors of women, and even as guardians of treasure and sacred places. In Chapter 40 of Thomas Hardy's *Far From the Madding Crowd*, the wretched Fanny is comforted by the apparition of a huge black dog which materializes in typical fashion near Grey's Bridge on the outskirts of Casterbridge

(Dorchester): "…a huge, heavy, quiet creature…of too strange and mysterious a nature to belong to any variety among those of popular nomenclature…the ideal embodiment of canine greatness."

But we discover that this black dog is no actual beast, but a metaphor — Hardy is referring to "Night, in its sad, solemn and benevolent aspect…personified." It is usual to speak of melancholy as a "black dog," and, in dreams, it often features powerfully as a dangerous but not necessarily malignant guardian. The metaphorical range of big cats is perhaps more limited but it exists and, above all, exists in a different way. In dreams, big cats are common images of unresolved affects — bursts of emotional or instinctual life — which spring on us suddenly from out of the unconscious "jungle." It is tempting, by extension, to see the Surrey puma as a return of wild instinctual life to the suburban, commuterized Home Counties; to see it as that fanged unconscious force which menaces the bland surface of stockbroker-belt consciousness. Is it like the wild circular patterns which plague our cultivated fields? Or, worse, is it like that new breed of alien which, since the sixties — the hour of the puma — has been abducting wayfarers and performing unspeakable operations on them? Are the daimons, unwilling to wait longer for recognition, returning to attract our attention by force? These are questions I shall be addressing again.

Kaptars, Yowies, Yetis

In late July 1957, Professor V. K. Leontiev was camping in the Caucasus Mountains at the head of the Jurmut River when he found some unusual footprints in the snow. They were unlike any prints he had ever seen. That night he heard a strange cry. The following day, he saw something crossing a nearby snowfield. The professor knew at once that it was a Kaptar. "He was walking on his feet, not touching the ground with his hands. His shoulders were unusually wide. His body was covered with long dark hair. He was about 2.2 meters [some 7 feet] tall." The Kaptar's general appearance was like a tall, massively built, hairy human. Nonetheless, the Professor fired a shot at its feet but either missed or failed to affect the creature because it ran out of sight among some rocks.[27]

It must be obvious that this Caucasian Kaptar is the same, or the same type, of creature as the more famous Himalayan Yeti, known in Tibetan as Kangmi, or the Californian Bigfoot. It is called Chuchuna in northeastern

Siberia, Sasquatch in British Columbia (Canada), and, in Australia, the Yowie. It doesn't seem to be much in evidence in Europe, perhaps because its preferred habitat appears to be vast, pretty much uninhabited, usually mountainous areas — although I suspect that it has something in common with Scandinavian trolls. Whenever it encounters men it shows curiosity but not fear. It watches what we do but rarely interferes.

On 29 January 1978, a six-foot hairy creature peered through the door of a house at Spinbrook, Queensland. Its eyes were deep-set in an egg-shaped head; its nose was small, flat and screwed up; its ears, flat. Black in color, it smelled like a badly kept public lavatory. The owner threw a chair at it and it "hopped or limped away."[28] This Yowie was rather smaller than the one which, in 1924, watched kangaroo-hunter David Squires skinning one of his victims, to the west of Dubbo, New South Wales. It stood eight feet tall and had thick, coarse, grayish hair about three inches long, large gray-blue eyes, and a face half-human, half-apelike. It reached up and scratched the tree it was standing beside before walking slowly away into the undergrowth. The scratch marks were later measured at thirteen feet above the ground.[29]

Rex Gilroy of New South Wales has collected over 3,000 sightings of Yowies.[30] The Bords have gathered reports of sightings of the American equivalent in forty states and five Canadian provinces, with details of nearly

Figure 1. Tracks in the snow February 17, 2002, near Poopanelly Creek, Oregon. The tracks were six inches by 16 inches and the length of the stride was eight feet from one right foot to the other. From http://www.oregonbigfoot.com

500 separate locations at which there have often been more than one sighting by a number of witnesses. If we consider, too, that — as with all anomalous phenomena — only a small number of sightings are ever reported (or, if reported, do not pass into wider circulation than the locality), the total sum of sightings probably runs into the thousands. The vast majority of these have occurred or, at least, come to light since 1940. But the modern descriptions of, say, Bigfoot, in no way differ from Native American descriptions, which go back centuries, nor from those of early settlers. Mr. Trimble of Crawford County, Kansas, noted in 1869 that "it has so near a resemblance to the human form that the men are unwilling to shoot it... It has a stooping gait, very long arms with immense hands or claws; it has a hairy face...a most ferocious expression...generally walks on its hind legs but sometimes on all fours."[31]

In the nineteenth century the creatures were called "mountain gorillas" or, in recognition of their unearthly behavior, "mountain devils." They were variously thought to be ghosts, or kinds of ape or bear, or else survivals of prehistoric men such as *Gigantopithecus* (rather in the same way that fairies were thought to be remnants of the Picts). In other words, the same mythologizing surrounds these big hairy monsters as surrounds, on the one hand, other mystery animals and, on the other, fairies or fairy creatures. If they only behaved in the manner of my first three examples, we could easily accept some naturalistic explanation for them. But, alas, they are every bit as impossible as our dogs and cats.

In the autumn of 1957, Gary Joanis and Jim Newall were hunting deer at Wanoga Butte, near Bend, Oregon. Gary shot a deer, but before he could reach it a hairy creature all of nine feet tall came into the clearing, picked up the deer and carried it off under his arm. Gary was furious. He fired shots repeatedly into the beast's back, but it gave no sign that it had been injured, unless its "strange whistling scream" was a cry of pain. It simply kept on walking.[32] There are many recorded cases of Bigfoot being shot; but, apart from the occasional trace of blood, the bullets seem to have no effect.

One of several young men who were camping in woods near Davis, West Virginia, during the summer of 1960, had gone to cut firewood when he felt someone poking him in the ribs. Thinking it was one of his friends, he turned around — only to find himself confronted by a "horrible monster." It had "two huge eyes that shone like big balls of fire and...stood every bit of eight feet tall and had shaggy hair all over its body." It just stared for a while and then wandered off, leaving some giant footprints in evidence of the visitation.[33] So far, so (nearly) tangible. But there are more elusive encounters with Bigfoot, like the one which a Mrs. A. had on 6 February 1974, near Uniontown, Pennsylvania. Hearing suspicious noises outside while she was watching TV, she doughtily went out onto her porch with a shotgun. A seven-foot Bigfoot was standing in front of her. It raised both its arms above its head. Terrified, Mrs. A. fired the gun at its midriff. There was a brilliant flash of light and the creature vanished, leaving no trace.[34]

On 5 November 1977, a posse led by Lieutenant Verdell Veo chased a Bigfoot for hours in the vicinity of Little Eagle, South Dakota. They finally surrounded it with cars and blazing lights, but still it managed to escape. One of the ranchers present remarked: "I put my flashlight where I could plainly hear it, only where it should have been there was nothing in sight. Now what I'm wondering is, can this thing make itself invisible when things get too close for comfort?"[35]

An even stranger confrontation, reminiscent of many "UFO entity" cases, occurred to a Mrs. Lister, then eighteen years old, one night in 1964. She was sitting with her husband-to-be in a parked car when they saw in the beam of the headlights a creature hopping and leaping towards them. It passed through a triple-strand barbed wire fence as if it were as insubstantial as mist. Mrs. Lister screamed as the beast tried to grab her companion through a window. She felt hypnotized by its glowing eyes, as if she had "had a time lapse or like [she] was living in another time..." She could see that the creature was six feet tall, wide-shouldered, covered with yellowish fuzz, with a horrible head that was pointed at the top and narrow at the chin. Its brow was wrinkled, its ears and nose like a pig's, its eyes glowing orange. As she watched, it turned into another form: its hands became paws and it went down on all fours. Then it vanished into thin air.[36]

There is a nightmarish atmosphere about this sighting which reminds one of the dream-like distortion of time and form in the presence of daimons such as we saw earlier in certain UFO sightings. Everything is preternaturally vivid and real yet, at the same time, curiously otherworldly. Daimonic events are shrouded in their own enchanted space. The odd aftermath of the following sighting is also something we have come across, stamping it with the hallmark of the daimonic.

In 1952, a man was driving to Orleans, California, on a remote dirt road running through Bear Valley, when he had to stop and get out of his car to remove a sapling that had fallen across the road. It was dark and had been raining heavily. He heard the thud of feet coming down the road behind him and saw a "shaggy human-like monster." It began to circle him, snarling and bellowing very menacingly. Its eyes were round and rather luminous; its head low and rounded with short hair on top; its eye-teeth were longer than a human's; its chest was rather bare of hair and leathery-looking. As the creature became increasingly menacing, he was forced to dash for his car, start it up, and smash through the sapling while the creature clawed at the window. He got away. But it was not until he later read a newspaper report about a Bigfoot sighting in Northern California that he began to remember, bit by bit, his own encounter in all its vividness. He had hitherto *forgotten the whole event,* even failing to remember when a friend had asked him how he had got the big dent in the grille of his car.[37]

Bigfoot and fairies

Even from this smattering of Bigfoot sightings it is clear that we are not dealing with a rare species of animal. We have another daimon on our hands. It has the characteristic huge, glowing or fiery eyes; it is sometimes invisible or vanishes into thin air; it is impervious to gunfire; it leaves suggestive traces of itself like blood or footprints, or, like a UFO, it leaves peripheral damage to cars and buildings and so on — but it is not able to be nailed down. It also leaves no footprints when it should and when it does leave prints they are contradictory: they have different numbers of toes — two, four, six and, above all, three. Not five. Like the fingers of UFO entities, it prefers non-human numbers.

Other features include the noises it makes — it whistles, screams, sounds like a pig grunting or a child crying, whines, or roars. But it prefers to whistle, and this is a sound frequently reported of the fairies. Bigfoot also moves on occasions with supernatural speed. It has been seen racing across open country like a deer, hurdling fences. On the other hand, it is often lumbering and slow. If it has one unique feature it is its stench of rotting meat, garbage, and decay. It smells like the very devil. I need hardly add that it has been seen in connection with UFOs, leading fanciful ufologists to speculate that it may be a kind of alien or even an experimental animal engineered by aliens for their own inscrutable purposes. Its behavior is usually meek and enigmatic but even when it pokes, grabs, snarls at, or menaces people, it does not in the end damage them. In short, it shares so many attributes with the beings I have been pleased to call fairies that it may be regarded for the sake of convenience (and if you'll pardon the expression) as a Big Fairy... As such, it should not really be bracketed with other "alien animals" such as black dogs and anomalous cats which, although they may be usefully called fairy creatures, are not themselves fairies.

A typical example of Bigfoot's "fairy" behavior occurred at Roachdale, Indiana, in August 1972. The first thing that Randy and Lou Rogers heard was a lot of loud banging on their walls and windows several nights in a row. It was very like poltergeist ("noisy ghost") phenomena. But poltergeists are themselves notoriously difficult to fathom. As with all daimonic manifestations, there is some personal connection — notably to pubescent females. There is also an impersonal aspect, usually a ghost or unquiet spirit, but sometimes a traditional class of fairy — the English boggart is an example — whose behavior is indistinguishable from that of poltergeists. Noisy, mischievous, childish, it is a pretty rudimentary kind of fairy, more of a nuisance than anything else. The fairy component, so to speak, in the nexus of beliefs surrounding poltergeists has not been pointed out often enough.

Anyway, after the initial banging, the Rogerses glimpsed a heavily built, six-foot Bigfoot loping away into a nearby cornfield. For the next two or three weeks it returned regularly between ten and ten-thirty at night, announcing itself with an appalling smell of dead animal or rotting garbage. Instinctively Mrs. Rogers treated it as it is traditional to treat mildly troublesome fairy manifestations: she left food out for it — a practice which goes back to antiquity and includes the appeasing of household gods and ancestral spirits with offerings of food. The Bigfoot took the food, sometimes staying to watch Mrs. Rogers through the kitchen window. She recognized that it was not altogether of this world because it left no traces, even when running through mud. In fact it hardly touched the ground when it ran and made no sound as it passed through undergrowth. Sometimes the Rogerses thought that they could see through it, as if it were semi-transparent.[38]

Another, sadly extinct kind of English fairy was the Brownie. Unlike its brilliant and handsome Celtic cousins, it was a poor unintelligent creature, entirely covered with hair, which attached itself to particular households, often tidying the place up at night — a function shared by Celtic "little people." (It was thus the converse of the poltergeist, bringing order instead of chaos. In fact, it might be more accurate to see fairies in terms of their different manifestations, chaotic or orderly, rather than to postulate separate entities.) Brownies were harmless drudges but could grow truculent if left unpropitiated. They remind me of the Bigfoot which plagued the Lee family of the Watova settlement, near Nowata, Oklahoma, in 1974. After several sightings of the six-foot Bigfoot over a number of weeks, the Lees lost their fear of it and even became quite fond of it when it began to play a game with them. Every day it left a feed pail in front of their barn, and every day they took the pail away and hid it — only to find it back in front of the barn the following day. The only time Mrs. Margie Lee heard it make a noise was when it seemed to laugh. Eventually it became a nuisance, thrashing around in the barn and crashing through a chicken-wired window when chased away. It also took a neighbor's chicken. It was seen as well by two deputy sheriffs who had been called in to help deal with the creature. They shot at it, but it escaped into the woods. The next day Mrs. Lee heard a thump on the wall outside while she was taking a shower. She dashed to the window but was too late — she never saw her Bigfoot again.[39]

It is a sad tale, and a cautionary one. I should have thought that the Bigfoot's leaving out the feed pail was as clear an indication as you could get of what was required. No wonder it became a nuisance when it was ignored. Daimons do not literally need feeding; they need *heeding*. We must give them their due, leaving a portion of the harvest for them or something off the table. Otherwise they might take something for themselves. The Lees got off lightly with the loss of only a neighbor's chicken. To be visited by fairies (even Big Fairies!) is good luck, if we treat them right. But, if it is bad enough not to feed or heed them, it is potentially disastrous to try and shoot them. Mrs. Lee was fortunate to receive only that last, curiously poignant, thump of farewell.

Investigators of apparitions are often frustrated by the way that no apparition exists in isolation. One leads to another. We cannot investigate dogs without cats; cats without fairies; fairies without Bigfoot and lake monsters; any of these without UFOs and aliens. The investigation always *broadens* to embrace, in the end, all apparitions, as if there were a single principle at work capable of manifesting itself in a myriad forms. At the same time, the investigation always *deepens,* pointing to the continuity of apparitions in time, leading us into the past, into folklore and myth. Both characteristics of broadening and deepening are made intelligible — though not, of course, explained — by the two models I have so far outlined: the collective unconscious and *Anima Mundi.* If apparitions cannot be understood in isolation from each other, neither can they be understood separately from the witness who sees them. Thus it is time now to shift emphasis away from what is seen to how and why it is seen.

Part Two

Vision

"This world of Imagination is the world of Eternity; it is the divine bosom into which we shall all go after the death of the Vegetated body. This World of Imagination is Infinite and Eternal, whereas the world of Generation, or Vegetation, is Finite and Temporal. There Exist in that Eternal World the Permanent Realities of Every Thing which we see reflected in this Vegetable Glass of Nature. All Things are comprehended in their Eternal Forms in the divine body of the Saviour, the True Vine of Eternity, The Human Imagination…"

(William Blake, *A Vision of the Last Judgment*)

7

Seeing Things

Misidentification

I have always felt uneasy about the complacency with which ufologists repeat the assertion that 90 percent (or 95 percent) of UFO sightings are misidentifications of ordinary aerial objects such as stars, planets, birds, clouds, aircraft, etc. (I don't believe in weather balloons); or else of natural phenomena such as patches of light, optical reflections, etc. I don't like the superior air which creeps into reports of UFOs which turn out to have one of these simple explanations. It reminds me of a school seniority system: the scientists look down on the ufologists for believing in UFOs, and the ufologists, who want to become (of all things) scientists, look down on poor benighted passers-by who mistake simple weather balloons (or whatever) for what they are pleased to call genuine UFOs.

At a UFO conference some years ago, we listened briefly to a radio phone-in on UFOs which happened to coincide with the conference. How we all hooted when Val of Peckham rang in to say that she had been disturbed by a weird light in the sky! It had seemed to be watching her, it was definitely intelligent, she had come over all funny, etc. It was obvious from her description that the light in question was a planet. John Rimmer, our kindly host and editor of *Magonia,* quelled the derision by reminding us that Val's experience was in a sense the very stuff of ufology — indeed, that many of the eminent ufologists present had been seized by the subject through just such an encounter, mistaken or not. We were suitably chastened.

Val had the kind of experience we all have at some time, especially as children: that of seeing a world we had been told was dead as alive, intelligent, watchful (we all remember the sinister dressing-gown up to no good on the back of the bedroom door). In other words, that way of seeing the world, and being seen by it, which has been labeled "animism" is not the prerogative of poor benighted primitives (nor even of children), but is an experience of reality which can strike at any time, just as it struck a couple (one of whom was, of all things, a *scientist*) who were driving from Shropshire to Cheshire one night in October 1983. They were lengthily and systematically hounded by an aerial object which shone menacing beams of light into their car, terrifying them. In a state of shock, and after much thought, they reported it to (of all things) the Jodrell Bank Radio Telescope, who passed the report on to ufologist Jenny Randles. She kindly wrote it down for us. It turned out that the couple had misperceived the moon.

Perhaps ufology should be less concerned with the nature of what is seen than with the nature of seeing. Here, for instance, is another well-known case of misidentification:

"...do you not see a round disk of fire somewhat like a Guinea? O no, no, I see an Innumerable Company of the Heavenly host crying 'Holy, Holy, Holy is the Lord God Almighty.' "[1]

The percipient is of course the visionary poet and artist William Blake; the "disk of fire" is the sun. Blake insisted that his poems were not mere figures of speech but true accounts of the natural world, transformed (invariably personified) by the power of the creative imagination. He could see the sun perfectly well as everyone else does, as a golden Guinea; but he could also see its deeper reality, as a heavenly host. He distinguished between seeing *with* the eye and seeing *through* it.

I am not saying that there are no such things as visual errors. We have all seen lights in the sky which might have been UFOs, but which on closer inspection turned out to be aircraft lights or whatever. But even such simple misidentifications are not wholly neutral or without significance. They are like visual equivalents of Freudian or, more accurately, Jungian slips: they point for a moment to the Unknown which lies both in our depths and in the heights of the sky. Even when we see with and not through the eye, as it were, we are already imagining what we see. Blake's description of the normal sun is already embroidered by a simile, "like a Guinea." The whole world is an imaginative construct. There is no such thing as a simple, unadorned perception, nor a simple misperception — let alone Val of Peckham's sighting, charged as it was with potentially frightful significance.

Was Val satisfied by the explanation that her sighting was "only a planet?" Was she not made to feel a little foolish, even a little cheated? And what of Mrs. A. of Hollington, East Sussex, who was watching TV on 4 October 1981 when she felt "compelled" to go to the window, only to see a large bright yellow object in the sky? She was joined by her daughter-in-law, Janette, and the two women watched astonished for half an hour as the object wobbled, pulsated, and repeatedly changed shape. Several times, as an aircraft passed nearby, the object emitted smoke and hid itself behind a cloud. Janette saw lights on, and structured sides to, the object. Both women suffered severe recurrent headaches over the following weeks — a sure sign of a close encounter — and Mrs. A. experienced a fourteen-hour blackout four days after the sighting. The witnesses were convinced they had seen a spacecraft piloted by aliens. Investigation revealed that the object had been the moon.[2]

Projection

As I noted in Chapter 2, the usual psychological explanation for the two women's experience — and it applies to Val of Peckham's — is "projection." The idea of projection supposes that unconscious images are thrown forward — projected — onto the world, where they are perceived as something external. This has come to mean that the images are "merely subjective" but are wrongly seen as objective. But I have already insisted that unconscious images are outside the ego and therefore, by definition, objective, even when they are perceived "within" us (as in dreams). However, the taint of subjectivity lingers so long as we maintain that images "within" are projected "outside." I would like to dismantle the idea of projection which fosters this misleading dualism.

Lee Worth Bailey, among others, has argued that "projection" is a metaphor drawn from the model of the magic lanterns which caused so much excitement in the nineteenth century.[3] While the common people were astounded and terrified by the slide-shows which tended to project images of ghosts and demons, experts and debunkers delighted in exposing the "fraudulence" of these images. Scientists like David Brewster (d. 1868) published widely read descriptions of how the magic lanterns worked and went on to claim that all so-called visions and apparitions were attributable to it. He asserted that ancient priestcraft employed similar devices to trick people into believing that gods and daimons existed when they were, in fact, only projected illusions. This notion was to influence Freud, who deprecated visions as "nothing but projections." And, naturally, just as we tend to model the psyche on our own machines (it's computers now), so it was not long before the magic lantern became the model for our own heads, out of which subjective images were projected onto a soulless world of objects. The psyche became restricted to the skull, and any of its images encountered outside became delusions which had to be withdrawn back inside. Thus the autonomous, image-forming unconscious was reduced to a kind of cine-projector which mechanically threw out fraudulent visual images — and to hell with the powerful, affecting visions of poor bystanders.

I suggest instead that the idea of projection won't wash. We should rethink our epistemology along the lines of a Blake, understanding that our primary mode of perception is *imaginative*. We simultaneously see and transform the world. As the ancients knew, the moon is not just a barren planet but also a dangerous goddess liable to induce delusions or revelations, madness or mystical experience; and if my two examples are anything to go by, she potentially still is.

Jung became equivocal about projection, as he had initially understood it, largely as a result of his alchemical studies. Nevertheless he could not quite bring himself to discard it, until he had a dream late in life — October 1958 — which caused him to stand the whole idea on its head. In the dream he saw "two lens-shaped metallically gleaming discs, which hurtled in a narrow arc over the house and down to the lake. They were two U.F.O.s... Then another body came flying directly towards me. It was a perfectly circular lens, like the objective of a telescope. At a distance of four or five hundred yards it stood still for a moment, and then flew off. Immediately afterwards, another came speeding through the air: a lens with a metallic extension which led to a box — a magic lantern. At a distance of sixty or seventy yards it stood still in the air, pointing straight at me. I awoke with a feeling of astonishment. Still half in the dream, the thought passed through my head: 'we always think that the U.F.O.s are projections of ours. Now it turns out that we are their projections. I am projected by the magic lantern as C. G. Jung. But who manipulates the apparatus?' "[4]

The aim of this dream, says Jung, is "to effect a reversal of the relationship between ego-consciousness and the unconscious, and to represent the unconscious as the generator of the empirical personality."[5] In other words, from the point of view of the unconscious — that is, of daimonic reality — its existence is the real one and our conscious world is a dream, a pattern of images such as we conceive *it* to be... "Mirror on mirror mirrored is all the show."[6]

Our trouble is that we have been brought up with a literal-minded worldview. We demand that objects have only a single identity or meaning. We are educated to see with the eye only, in single vision. When the preternatural breaks in upon us, transforming the profane into something sacred, amazing, we are unequipped for it. Instead of seizing on the vision, reflecting on it — writing poetry, if necessary — we react with fright and panic. Instead of countering like with like — that is, assimilating through imagination the complexity of the image presented to us — we feebly telephone scientists for reassurance. We are told we are only "seeing things" and so we miss the opportunity to grasp that different, daimonic order of reality which lies behind the merely literal.

The distinction between daimonic and literal will become clearer as we go along, through repetition in different contexts. But because it is an essential part of my argument, I ought to say a few prefatory words about literalism here. In one sense it is extraordinarily difficult for us to understand literalism because the world we inhabit is determined by it — words such as "real," "factual," "true" invariably mean *literally* real, factual, true. But in another sense, it is easy to understand another kind of reality, of truth — for example, whenever we watch a drama on stage or screen. If it is good enough (we might say: if it is art), we feel that we are watching a revelation of some deeper reality, normally concealed in the muddle of our mundane lives. Even if it is not great art, we still — astonishingly — suffer all the emotions of suspense, joy, pity, and terror as if the drama were real. We are seized by it as we are seized by the daimonic. We are seized because the drama is real — not *literally* real but *imaginatively* real. We stumble out of the theater, rubbing our eyes as if we had just seen a "big dream" or a vision; we look about us at the ordinary world which now seems curiously unreal compared to the drama; we can half believe that we really are "such stuff as dreams are made on."

The trouble is that we find it difficult to take such imaginative reality seriously for long. Literal-mindedness reasserts itself. It even persuades us that powerful imagina*tive* experiences are only imagin*ary,* treating imagination with the same disdain as it treats daimonic reality. But for poets and visionaries such as William Blake, imagination is the primary, and most important, mode of apprehending the world. (In Chapter 9 I shall be reevaluating imagination as another model for daimonic reality.)

By way of an initial summary, then, I would assert that literal reality is only one kind of reality, deriving from a superordinate reality — here called daimonic — which is metaphorical rather than literal, imaginative rather than empirical. Literal reality is therefore, if anything, *less* real than daimonic reality. Moreover, in relation to the history of our culture, and also to traditional cultures, a belief in the literalness of reality is the exception rather than the rule. Literal reality is the product of literalism, which is really a way of seeing the world, a perspective on the world, but which insists that it is a property inherent in the world. It insists that it is the only reality and, as such, actively denies other kinds of reality, especially the daimonic, which it calls unreal, fictional, even delusional.

I am not suggesting that we strive only to see the world as visionaries. To perceive all aerial objects as angels — to see only the heavenly-host sun and not the guinea sun — leads to the madhouse. It is just as literal-minded as seeing a light in the sky as *only* a ball of hot gas or a barren planet (or an extraterrestrial spacecraft). This, too, is a kind of madness, albeit established and called normal. The remedy is to cultivate a sense of metaphor which, as its etymology suggests, is the ability to "carry across" — to translate one view of the world in terms of another. Sanity is the possession of what Blake called "double vision," which allowed him, for example, to see "with my inward eye…an old man gray / With my outward a thistle across my way."[7]

If Blake had been running the phone-in when Val of Peckham rang in, he would not have told her that she had misidentified a planet: he would have said she was privileged to have glimpsed the awesome form of foam-born Venus rising in splendor from the sea of night. She might then have been emboldened to prize wider that momentary crack in literal reality and to enter that other, imaginative reality which alone infuses the world with beauty and terror. We don't need to see UFOs in order to enter that reality because, to the poetic imagination, everything in the sky — stars, birds, clouds, the Earth itself — is a UFO whose final reality can never be known.

Paranoia

People have always "seen things." The question has always been: are the apparitions they see, or the visions they have, true or false? Are they, that is, revelations or delusions? This used to be a question which was referred to theologians. They allowed that both were possible but that one had to distinguish carefully between them. Subsequently, scientists became the arbiters; and, since their worldview did not allow supernatural revelations, the latter were stigmatized as delusions. By and large, witnesses to apparitions collude in this view by trying to prove that the apparition was literal, actual, empirically real — and that they were therefore not deluded. Christian visionaries — seers of angels, Jesus, the Virgin Mary — ignore scientific demands and place their visions firmly in a religious context. They are not always supported in this by the Church, whose traditional skepticism about revelations has been stiffened by its fear of being made to look ridiculous in the eyes of scientism.

But popular Christianity is right to regard visions religiously. As revelations they are by definition to do with religion. For religion, by definition, is to do with the revelation of daimon, of deity, or of a hidden order of the world. What was concealed is suddenly made manifest. At the moment of manifestation, revelations are to the witness complete, self-contained, self-explanatory, self-justifying. Only afterwards do the arguments about validity, reality, and so on, begin. Even if the witness can in time be persuaded that the revelation was false — i.e. a delusion — at the time of its occurrence it was simply itself and, by definition, true. But revelation cannot be understood without considering its opposite, delusion; and delusion cannot be considered without touching upon paranoia, whose determinant characteristic is the presence of delusions.

Paranoia is the mental disorder *par excellence.*[8] No other syndrome has so completely escaped being reduced to physiology — that is, it cannot be accounted for by recourse to organic explanations. Literally meaning "besides-thinking" — thinking that is flawed or skewed — paranoia popularly refers to the delusion that one is being watched, followed, spied on, persecuted by unseen enemies. But in fact its delusions can take many other forms, including the delusion of jealousy (my wife gives signs to other men behind my back); delusions of reference (certain things me because of others); and delusions of grandeur (I have a special "vocation," I am high-born, I am divine, I shall survive the coming world disaster, etc.). In every other way paranoiacs are normal; if their delusions were true they would pretty much pass for ordinary citizens.

A false belief can be proved false. It is corrigible. So is a hallucination, which, as a perceptual disorder, can be falsified with reference to the perceived world. But a delusion is incorrigible. No amount of reason, persuasion, and sensory evidence can convince paranoiacs that they are deluded. On the contrary, everything that happens seems to support the delusion. The sufferer is trapped in a single reality which imposes its meaning on all other events. In other words, paranoia is a *meaning* disorder and, as such, it relates in Jungian terms to the archetype of meaning, the self. The paranoiac is someone who has been overwhelmed by the self and its preoccupations with God, oneness, unity, spirit, transcendence, and cosmic grandeur. Everything in the world is charged with preternatural significance for good or for ill. Thus the same archetype whose manifestations are pregnant with revelations can also be responsible for delusions.

This is why delusions are so often of a religious nature. Nothing is as it seems. The paranoiac always sees a hidden (but often menacing) order behind the phenomenal world. Humans become spirits or even gods hiding behind masks which he alone is able to see through. And after all, a similar experience can beset the best of us: under the sway of love or hate, do we not also sometimes glimpse the lineaments of the beloved or the hated in the face or bearing of total strangers?[9] The paranoiac only takes this to extremes — he sees the same friend or enemy in *everyone.* Gradually he "sees through" everyone until they become the same person. The world becomes more and more impoverished until only his enemy remains.

It is their narrowness, I suppose, which enables us to spot a paranoiac.
en he attributes certain persecutions to the
when the neighbor is blamed for everything
e begin to realize we are dealing with a

seeing a hidden meaning behind everything
r causal relations, which finally becomes an
ens to him is chance or coincidence; there is
found if searched for. Everything unknown

can be traced back to something known. Every strange object can be unmasked and revealed as something one already possesses."[10] (Thus it may be that our modern preoccupation with cause and effect is a touch paranoid. We certainly dislike and distrust the spontaneous, the acausal, the synchronistic — whatever, that is, transgresses our "laws" and seems heedless and free, such as all paranormal phenomena.)

Delusion and revelation

What is the difference, then, between delusion and revelation, between the paranoiac and the religious leader? We feel that there must be some difference in the *contents* of a delusion as compared to a revelation. But in fact the same mixture of weird, irrational, cosmogonic, and even blasphemous material appears equally in the writings of the sane and the insane. (Consider only the Revelation of St. John, the last book in the New Testament.) Typical contents urge mission and prophecy. The paranoiac often claims to be privy to some secret plan of God's. He has been chosen to spread the word and especially entrusted with certain secret facts which will be verified in the future — notably, he warns us that the world is going to end.

In 1954 Dr. Charles A. Langhead, an MD on the staff of Michigan University, began communicating with a range of entities from outer space, largely through trance mediums. From this rich mixture of ufology and spiritualism there arose a principal entity named Ashtar, a high-ranking member of the Intergalactic Federation, whose prophecies — admittedly minor and personal — all came true. This is a common daimonic trick: true revelations, such as intimate knowledge of the recipients' private lives or accurate, if trivial, predictions of coming events, are succeeded — just as the recipients are convinced of the truth of the messages — by false revelations or delusions. Ashtar suddenly announced that the world would end on 21 December 1954. A few people, including Dr. Langhead and his friends, would be saved by spaceships. Naturally they gathered together on the appointed day to await rescue, having first alerted the press. (They were told, by the way, to wear no metal. We recall the fairies' aversion to metal.) They waited. And waited...[11]

No doubt the press had a good laugh at their expense. But when we consider that they may not have been very different from the small group of ridiculed Christians who huddled together after Christ's death in expectation of his immediate return and the world's end, we should not perhaps be too quick to laugh. A great many Christians are still expecting the Apocalypse any day now. Millennial expectations recur throughout history — only the causes change, cutting their cloth to suit the concerns of the age. During the outburst of millennialism in mid-seventeenth-century England, a wide range of enthusiastic cults — Ranters, Shakers, Muggletonians and the like — took the view that the world's sin would prompt Christ's world-ending return. Nowadays (or, at least, during the 1950s and 1960s) it is more likely to be nuclear war which rings down the curtain on Creation; and the messengers who warn us of this are more likely to be tall blond UFO entities than, say, angels of the Lord. Currently, the fashionable cause of coming doom is ecological. And, sure enough, the same kind of entity, either "channeled" or appearing directly, warns us against the abuse of Nature.

Prophecy is not the preserve of paranoiacs, then — unless we say that all leaders and members of cults (and, indeed, of major religions) are paranoid. Delusion cannot be distinguished from revelation as far as its contents are concerned. Can it be differentiated by any other criteria? Well, it has been suggested that one can judge paranoiacs because their ideas are harmful and dangerous or because they transcend the limits of social acceptability. But what religious ideas are not potentially harmful and dangerous? And what defines social acceptability? Paranoid notions may not be acceptable according to standard norms, but as soon as a few people share them, as in the kind of cults I have mentioned, they cannot be clinically diagnosed as paranoid.

There are even beliefs which, although they have not been systematized into a formal organization, exhibit paranoid tendencies. Often widely held, they are comparable to folklore beliefs. For example, many people (mostly Americans) believe that benign aliens or "space brothers" are watching over us like angels and guiding our development. They are like the "guides" of spiritualism but instead of being dead humans in the world beyond the grave, they are living aliens in worlds beyond the solar system. Just as many Americans believe an inverted version of this. A malignant species of small gray alien — we shall be meeting these later — has landed on earth and, having established secret bases, is abducting human beings for genetic experiments or for breeding purposes in order to strengthen its own race.

The government knows about them and colludes with them in exchange for their advanced technology.

This belief is a recent variant of the perennial belief that somehow "They" are watching, manipulating, threatening us — whether "They" are the Government, the CIA, aliens, or even our neighbors. "Grays" who appear with malevolent intent in our bedrooms have replaced "Reds under the bed." The paranoia is reciprocal: we fear them and they fear us. Most power structures are a touch paranoid. They suspect and fear whatever lies outside their power. Cult leaders grow more suspicious of their disciples' loyalty the more power-crazed they become. The disciples of scientism and of fundamentalist Christianity alike rabidly denounce the mildest daimonic phenomenon as crazy nonsense or the work of Satan respectively. They feel threatened. At the height of its power, the Catholic Church sensed frightful aliens in its midst — witches, indistinguishable from humans except by hidden "witch-marks," who had to be uncovered and destroyed.

This is what happens when daimons are made literal: they become polarized, either demonic or angelic, responsible for all bad or for all good. Conspiracy theories flourish because, in a sense, there has been a conspiracy against the daimons. Suppressed, covered-up, they return to infiltrate our thinking from below, conferring secret diabolical intentions on actual institutions. The sense of conspiracy everywhere is the reverse side of the religious idea that there is an underlying order, benign and protective, beneath or behind appearances. Paranoid "seeing through" is the negative aspect of artistic or religious insight. There may be a profound truth in the folklore belief that if we see the fairies first, they will be benevolent; but if they see us first they will be malign, and we, cursed.

There is religion in paranoia and paranoia in religion. The suspicion that dark forces lie behind phenomena is an inversion of the intuition that another, possibly divine, reality underwrites the world. The deep attention paid by the artist to the world, and the contemplation of God by the mystic, are shadowed by the fearful hypervigilance of the paranoiac. But which of us has not been (as the textbooks describe the paranoiac) a little hypervigilant, rigid, suspicious, mirthless, and self-important? Paranoia's literal unmasking signals in distorted form the soul's need for depth, the visionary's insight.

In short, the roots of delusion and revelation are inextricable. There can be no clear distinction between them. All revelation contains elements of delusion, and vice versa. Even in Val of Peckham's case of "misidentification" we see that she was trembling on the brink of, from her point of view, a revelation and, from a "sensible" outsider's point of view, delusion. As long as we have religion, we will have revelations — and delusions. And we will also have committees of theologians, psychiatrists, etc., as fashion dictates, to decide where delusion ends and revelation begins. But, in truth, they exist on a continuum. The boundaries between them shift from person to person, from one age to another, from one culture to another.

8

Ladies

Our Ladies

In modern times the most attractive — and successful — cults are not those which spring up around mediums, channelers, or UFO contactees, but those which surround visions of the BVM (Blessed Virgin Mary). One researcher has established that there have been 230 alleged visions of the BVM between 1928 and 1975 — and these were only the ones acknowledged (but not endorsed) by the Roman Catholic Church.[1] There could easily be hundreds more visions which have remained unreported. Another writer on the subject estimates that more than 200 visions around the world have taken root — that is, they have become recognized sites of a Marian vision and places of pilgrimage.[2] About half of these are in France and Italy. They range from the world-famous site at Medjugorge where, to the delight of hundreds of thousands of pilgrims, Our Lady appeared regularly to six children from the 1980s onward, to small local sites such as the one at Gortneadin in the West of Ireland. Here, in 1969, Mr. McCarthy had the first of many Marian visions at a grotto established by his seventeen-year-old daughter at the behest of Jesus, seen in a vision the day before she died.

While each vision of the Virgin Mary is unique, it also contains typical or, perhaps, archetypal features. At the same time there are features which overlap with other, non-Christian, visionary experiences. For example, the following vision, which was granted to a fourteen-year-old girl at a natural grotto in 1858, could well be interpreted as a traditional encounter with, say, Mabh or Maeve, Queen of Fairy, in one of Ireland's wild places:

> ...suddenly I heard a great noise like the sound of a
> storm... I was frightened and stood straight up. I lost all
> power of speech and thought when, turning my head

toward the grotto, I saw at one of the openings of the rock a rosebush, one only, moving as if it were very windy. Almost at the same time there came out of the interior of the grotto a golden-coloured cloud, and soon after a Lady, young and beautiful...the like of whom I had never seen, came and placed herself at the entrance of the opening above the rosebush. She looked at me immediately, smiled at me and signed to me to advance, as if she had been my mother. All fear had left me but I seemed to know no longer where I was. I rubbed my eyes, I shut them, I opened them, but the Lady was still there...making me understand that I was not mistaken. [3]

In fact, the girl was Bernadette Soubirous, later to become a saint, and the place was Lourdes. Being a good Catholic, she automatically took out her rosary and knelt down before the apparition, who nodded approval and herself took up the rosary that hung over her right arm. However, when Bernadette tried to begin her rosary and to lift her hand to her forehead, she found that her arm was paralyzed — a frequent effect of daimonic encounters — and that it was only after the Lady had crossed herself that she could do the same.

There are several elements in classic BVM visions which show continuity with earlier pagan traditions and overlap with other non-Christian visions. Apparitions of the Virgin often take place in association with water — curiously, there is frequently rain about — and more particularly with springs. During her ninth vision at the grotto, Bernadette was told by the Lady to "drink from the fountain and bathe in it." There was no such thing; but, undaunted, the girl began to scratch at the ground, and, sure enough, a pool formed, later overflowing to become the famous healing waters of Lourdes.

The Virgin who appeared to twelve-year-old Mariette Beco at Banneux, Belgium, in 1933 beckoned her along the road outside her house and stopped at a "previously unknown spring" of which the Virgin said: "This stream is reserved for me." Subsequently she added that it was reserved "for all nations — to relieve the sick." During the thirties, some twenty "miracle cures" were officially recognized at the site.[4]

In this respect the BVM shows an affinity with the classical nymphs who haunt or, better perhaps, represent the spirit of a spring or stream. Tribal societies acknowledge such nature spirits, and they live on, Christianized, in the shrines which are dedicated to the Virgin Mary at sacred springs and holy wells all over Catholic Europe. Similarly, pagan cultures have always held that certain trees are sacred, inhabited by a female *numen;* and so we might expect Christian versions, Virgin Marys, to appear in connection with particular trees. In some cases they do. On 13 May 1917, for example, three children were tending sheep in a place called Cova da Iria near Fatima, Portugal, when a brilliant flash of light appeared out of a clear blue sky. Fearing a storm, they began to gather up their sheep and head for shelter when a second flash of light rooted them to the spot. Above the branches of a small holm oak tree there appeared "the most beautiful lady they had ever seen." She was "all in white, more brilliant than the sun, shedding rays of light."[5] At the beginning of December 1932, five children saw the Virgin appear beneath the arched branch of a hawthorn tree in the garden of a convent at Beauraing, Belgium. She looked about eighteen years old, had blue eyes and rays of light streaming from her head, and she was wearing a long white pleated gown which reflected a kind of blue light. In fact she had been seen five times previously in the vicinity by the children, but henceforth she always appeared under the hawthorn tree.[6]

The most interesting BVM vision from the point of view of an overlap with pre-Christian beliefs is probably the first to be extensively documented. It took place at daybreak on 9 December 1531, five miles north of Mexico City. A poor Aztec of fifty-seven who was called Singing Eagle but, as one of the first Indians to be baptized, had been re-named Juan Diego was on his way to Mass when he was arrested by a sound like a burst of birdsong. It seemed to come from a hillock on which had formerly stood a temple to the mother-goddess of the Aztecs. The shrill caroling ceased and in the silence he heard a woman calling to him from the rocks on the top of the hill, which were hidden by a mist. Juan climbed to the top and saw a wonderfully beautiful Mexican girl of about fourteen surrounded by rays of golden light. Whether or not his recent conversion had anything to do with it, the girl identified herself, not as the Aztec goddess, but as "the ever-virgin Mary, Mother of the True God."[7]

It is rare for Mary to identify herself so forthrightly. In *Les Apparitions de la Vierge,*[8] Emile Tizané examined fifty-seven well-substantiated Marian visions and found that in thirty of them the vision did not name herself and, in the remaining twenty-seven, she indicated by one means or another that she was the BVM. The cases I have already touched on are fairly typical. The startling tableau of figures which appeared outside the church at Knock remained silent (this vision, described briefly in the Introduction, is altogether atypical of BVM visions). The BVMs almost never call themselves "Mary." They usually remain enigmatic at first, anonymous. "I come from Heaven," said the Lady at Fatima; later, she called herself the "Lady of the Rosary." At Beauraing, the Lady merely nodded when asked if she were the Virgin; later she owned to being the "Immaculate Virgin." At Banneux, she said, "I am the Virgin of the Poor." At Lourdes, she only revealed her identity during the last vision at Bernadette's request: "I am the Immaculate Conception." It was supposed that a young semi-literate girl like Bernadette would not know such a theological expression, and so her report of these words was taken as emphatic proof of her vision's veracity. On the other hand, since the doctrine of the BVM's immaculate — sinless — conception had become dogma (that is, required belief) only four years before, she might very well have heard the expression. At any rate, we can say that where the BVM identifies herself, she is often enigmatic, not to say reticent, to begin with. Only subsequently, as the visions increase in number, does she positively (but never wholly unambiguously — "Queen of Heaven" can imply many things) identify herself, almost as if she were growing into the image, forming herself according to the cultural or religious expectations of the percipients.

The spinning sun

All Marian visions begin with what might be called a daimonic preface. It almost goes without saying that this is commonly a brilliant light. But, in addition, the BVM is sometimes introduced, as it were, by another daimonic figure. "He wore a long, seamless blue robe. He had fairly big pink wings. His face was small; it wasn't long, and wasn't round either. His eyes were black… He looked about nine years old. But, although he was a child to look at, he gave the impression of being very strong."[9] Conchita Gonzalez, one of four children who had around 2,000 visions of the BVM at Garabandal, Spain, between 1961 and 1965, gave this description of an "angel" that appeared to them more than once, before announcing the appearance of the

Virgin as "Our Lady of Mount Carmel."

The children of Fatima also saw an angel three times before the BVM appeared. On the first occasion, a strong wind shook the trees and above them a light appeared, "whiter than the driven snow. As it approached, it took the form of a young man, transparent and resplendent with light." He announced himself as the "Angel of Peace," amending this on the second occasion to "the Guardian Angel of Portugal."

Indeed, the visions at Fatima were beset by daimonic events. Moreover, they seem to be unique in that the Lady who appeared to Lucia, Francisco, and Jacinta on 13 May 1917 not only promised to return on the 13th of every month until October, but actually did so — unlike the false promises of so many daimonic figures. She had said as well at the beginning that she would reveal who she was and what she wanted only on her last visit, when she would also perform a miracle to convince everyone of her reality. As the word spread, a greater number of people arrived each month to watch the children communicate, in ecstasy, with their Lady. By the time of the penultimate visit, on 13 September, there were around 30,000 spectators. At noon, the appointed hour, the sun dimmed and the atmosphere took on the color of dull gold. Then "in the cloudless sky a luminous globe...suddenly appeared before the eyes of the astonished crowd. Moving from East to West, it glided slowly and majestically across the heavens while a light white cloud enveloped the oak tree and the children..."[10] At the same time a shower of white roses or rose petals fell from the sky and dissolved just before reaching earth. (Ufologists are eager to see the "roses" as "angel hair," a fragile gossamer-like substance which sometimes falls or drapes the surroundings in the wake of UFO apparitions.)

On the night of 12 October a terrible storm swept across Europe, making travel hazardous for thousands of pilgrims heading for Cova da Iria, the great natural amphitheater at Fatima where the visions were occurring. By morning, the storm had abated, but it still poured with rain, drenching the 70,000-odd spectators. Just after noon, the rain ceased and a flash of light heralded the approach of the Lady, who told the children: "I am the Lady of the Rosary." Her last message was: "People must amend their lives, ask pardon for their sins, and not offend Our Lord any more for He is already too greatly offended." Then, directing the rays of light from her hands towards the sun, she departed.[11]

It is difficult to arrive at an exact consensus of what happened next, but the general picture is clear. The Lady had promised a miracle and I see no reason to quarrel with her. The clouds parted to reveal the sun, or something which was where the sun was deemed to be. It was pale, like a silver disc, able to be looked at directly. It began to revolve like a Catherine wheel, spinning madly and throwing out great shafts of different-colored light — red, blue, yellow, green — staining the faces of the crowd with all the colors of the spectrum. Then it fell out of the sky towards earth. There was scarcely a soul in the arena who did not think it was the end of the world. However, the sun returned to its place in the sky and suddenly everyone noticed that, whereas a moment before they had been soaking wet, they were now completely dry. The sun had resumed its normal appearance.[12]

While there is clearly some continuity, then, between apparitions of the BVM and other traditional apparitions, I do not want for one minute to detract from the uniqueness, and the uniquely Christian nature, of her appearances. Perhaps because the visionaries tend to be children, or at least childlike people, they are able to remain aloof from the egoism and power hunger which disfigures so many UFO cults, for instance. It is true that the visionaries do usually have a leader of sorts, a dominant personality, such as Lucia at Fatima or Conchita at Garabandal; but these children add to the authenticity of the vision by remaining steadfast in the face of official persecution and, above all, humble. In the case of Conchita, who appeared on television some years ago (she now lives in the USA), one was left with an impression of serenity, radiance, and, frankly, a holiness which should put most of our worldly church leaders to shame.

The features peculiar to visions of the BVM may be summarized as follows: the visions are granted to children in a state of ecstasy or rapture. The Lady is always described as young and astoundingly beautiful; but, curiously, there are few details of, say, her face, and an abundance of details concerning her apparel — we hear of her veil, her white robes, decorated perhaps in blue and gold, the roses on her slippers, the stars embroidered on her hem, her crown, her rosary, and the rays of light which she emanates. We are reminded of a set cameo in which the Lady resembles nothing so much as the medieval courtly image of a Grail Knight's Lady.

Her messages scarcely vary. She asks for a shrine or chapel to be built for her. She imparts secrets to the children, which they do not reveal. If she prophesies, it is usually in general terms, more like vague warnings of retribution. She may imply that the world will end if we sinners do not reform — but she never makes the error, so common in spirit or UFO communications, of naming the day. However, her predictions, such as the blight of the potato crop (LaSalette) or the early death of Francisco and Jacinta at Fatima, came true. Her main, consistent message is an exhortation to repent, pray, make sacrifices, and there will be redemption. Miracles of healing always succeed her appearances.

The feminine principle

There is no surer indication of the daimonic nature of Marian visions than that they offend all parties except perhaps the most important party of all — the common people. They are certainly an affront to scientism which, if it notices the phenomenon at all, sends its debunkers to perform inhumane experiments on the ecstatic children, almost as if to punish them. The Catholic Church usually denounces the visions at the time and is later forced to backpedal and accept at least the more famous ones. It is no wonder that the visions are seen as subversive: since Our Lady comes to mediate between us and Christ or God, she undermines the authority of the priests to whom this role was exclusively assigned. But actually the Church should be grateful to the visions for counteracting its tendency to become too rigid and institutionalized, and for placing the miraculous back at the heart of religion. (Besides, the Lady rarely utters an unorthodox word — on the contrary, she urges attendance at Mass and so on.) To Protestants, for whom Christ is the only mediator, visions of BVM are regarded pretty much as the work of the devil. Finally, it need hardly be added that the BVM herself, let alone visions of her, is anathema to secular ideologies like liberalism and humanism, for which the mystical is simply gibberish.

C. G. Jung noticed the power that the BVM exerted over the European imagination for so many centuries and he diagnosed the popular movement to dogmatize her as "a deep longing in the masses for an intercessor and mediatrix who would at last take her place alongside the Holy Trinity and be received as the 'Queen of Heaven and Bride at the heavenly court.' "[13] The need for a feminine principle did not, of course, begin with the BVM. She was already present in the Old Testament as Sophia (Wisdom) or *Sapientia*

Dei (the Wisdom of God), who claimed: "I was set up from everlasting, from the beginning, or ever the earth was...when [the Lord] established the heavens, I was there..." (Proverbs, 8:22–4). In this she is clearly related to our *Anima Mundi,* and to the Shekhinah, the feminine principle of the Kabbalah, which shadows Judaism much as alchemy and Hermeticism shadow Christianity.

There is so little about the historical Mary in the Bible that her power and popularity cannot be accounted for except by recourse to psychology and to the idea that she answers this need for a feminine principle. The pagan religions, of course, all have their goddesses; Christianity did not. Thus a wealth of legend and folklore spontaneously accumulated around the figure of Mary. One striking story asserted that she was, like her Son, conceived immaculately — that is, without the taint of original sin. This effectively transformed her into the innocent state of a person before the Fall — into both a daimon who can mediate between mankind and God, and into a goddess in her own right. Another story told that she did not die like other mortals but was lifted bodily — assumed — into Heaven. These stories became beliefs which were so fervently held that they were finally elevated into the dogmas of the Immaculate Conception (1854) and the Assumption of the Virgin Mary (1950) — the only instances where dogmas were imposed on the Church by popular demand rather than being formulated by theologians.

The dogma of the Assumption meant that, psychologically at least, the BVM was well placed to reappear physically on Earth. Thus Jung, for one, was unsurprised by the increasing number of reports of her appearance — the Marian visions — which led up to the announcement of the dogma (they have not abated since). Nor was he surprised that so many children should receive the visions, "for in such cases the collective unconscious is always at work."[14] He saw the dogma of the Assumption not only as "the most important religious event since the Reformation,"[15] but also its social significance: the Assumption of the BVM to become the Bride of Christ recognized the equality of the feminine principle with the masculine. So, although he was writing in 1954, he was able, by monitoring the ground-swell of the collective unconscious, to predict the later waves of the women's movement.

Jung called apparitions of mysterious ladies the *anima*. As the personification of the unconscious, the archetype of life itself, as he called her, she is
not only an image *within* the soul but also an image *of* the soul. She can
represent the soul of an individual or of a particular natural object or of a
particular place. The BVM could be said to combine these features, and yet
she can unfold and develop, leading the witness on to the height of religious
contemplation. Thus did Dante pursue through heaven and hell the image of
Beatrice, who appeared first as a literal young lady of Florence and last as a
divine Marian figure, directing the poet's gaze towards the Godhead. She is
fairy-like, shape-shifting. In the Grail romances the fairy women who are
both so dangerous and so benevolent towards the questing knights became
increasingly Christianized until they fused with the image of the BVM. (M.-
L. von Franz suggests that, by seizing only on the positive aspects of the
ambiguous Grail *animae,* Christianity compelled the negative aspects to find
expression in witch beliefs.)[16] In Ireland the Queen of Fairy was poeticized
into Erin, the soul of the oppressed country; Shelley's early poem Queen
Mab transformed the fairy queen in later versions into the "Daemon of the
World"; Edmund Spenser's poem *The Fairie Queen,* derived no doubt from
Ireland where he lived for a time, also referred to Elizabeth I, who cultivated
an image of herself as Virgin Queen, so drawing on powerful and sacred
associations with the BVM.

The following visions of "ladies" are comparatively minor, but no less
suggestive. They mark that moment when, for the visionaries, a quest into
the Unknown is offered and it is up to them whether or not they accept.

White ladies

A girl of five or six was approaching the Aave Bridge near her home in the
canton of Bern, Switzerland, when she saw an odd apparition. It was
twilight. She often crossed the bridge on her way to meet her mother
returning from work. This is how she recalled the event sixty years later:

"Suddenly I saw before me the figure of a woman, not very tall and
snow-white. She floated in front of me, then by my side, sometimes a little
way off, then again nearer, hovering just above the ground. I could not see a
face; the figure was wrapped from top to toe in a very fine veil. I gazed at it,
wondering who the beautiful lady might be, walking about so late and in
such a thin dress, for it was rather cold…" She then heard her mother's

footsteps on the bridge and, hurrying to meet her, told her of the apparition, which was still visible. She pointed it out to her mother, but she could not see anything. The phantom moved away and disappeared.[17]

What was the girl looking at? A ghost? Possibly. But it is a distinguishing characteristic of white lady apparitions that they are not individually identifiable. They have deeper resonances than the shade of a historical person. The time and location are suggestive: a river and a bridge at twilight

Figure 2. In 1936 two men photographing the interior of Rayham Hall in Norfolk, England saw a figure in a brown dress coming down the stairs and quickly took this picture. (*Fortean Picture Library*)

provide a classic daimonic pattern, an hour and place of transition, of in-between. It is the sort of place where black dogs abound. (Perhaps white ladies are related analogically to black dogs — for example, ladies are to dogs as white is to black, as human is to animal.) If the child had been Catholic, would she have perceived the apparition as the Virgin Mary? It's possible, but I doubt it — this lady lacked the brilliance of the BVM. However, it is true to say that white ladies, like the BVM, do appear to many little girls and so may be intimately linked with their psychology; or rather, we should say that there is something about the psychology of little girls which enables this particular archetypal image to manifest. Aniela Jaffé suggests that white ladies such as this one represent the future fate of little girls — now veiled, soon to be revealed — a mysterious intimation of what they have yet to become, or a dawning consciousness of their own womanhood.[18] Unlike the BVM, white ladies do not speak. But their silence is eloquent. Their appearance is itself the message: enigmatic, often sinister, pointing towards the unknown.

If there had been an old house or castle nearby (perhaps there was), the lady might have been one of those many legendary white ladies who are said to *walk*. These are sometimes *gray* ladies. The one who haunts Denton Hill in Northumberland wears gray silk. She adds another face to the mystery because she is known as a silkie, a fairy woman, reminding us of the affinity between the people of Fairy and the shades of the dead.[19] At any rate, white or gray ladies are often ill-omened (like some black dogs), presaging a death.

A Swiss woman, who was in service with a Herr Gerber at Altdorf in the canton of Uri, recalls that a beautiful white woman was said to *walk* in the house before a death. The only person who knew nothing of this legend was a nursemaid in service with her. "One morning when I was sitting in the parlor with the Gerber family, [the nursemaid] was watching by the bedside of a sick child in the next room. Suddenly she burst into the parlor screaming with fear: 'Come here! Come here!' We all rushed into the next room, believing that the little girl was dying. But when we got there, the maid told us in terror: 'A beautiful woman in white came out of that cupboard and walked slowly to the bedside and looked at the child. When I cried out she glided behind the window-curtains.' A few days later the child was taken to the angels."[20]

Hauntings of this kind are mostly attributed to events long past. They have become legends, usually involving some crime or unexpiated guilt which has caused the ghost to *walk*. It may have been murder or suicide, for instance, but the ghost has to walk until the crime is pardoned. The crime usually connected with white ladies is a crime against love. She is the ghost of one who has suffered a breach of faith, such as adultery; or of one who had been shamefully abandoned or murdered. We might expect the guilty party to walk, but in fact it is the victim who walks. Jaffé suggests that this is because such crimes seem to break "archetypal laws of life…a divinity has been outraged"[21] — the feminine principle, if you like — and so it is not the actual ghost of the woman who walks but "an impersonal phantom, a deity."[22] In this sense, there is a certain continuity between apparitions of white ladies and visions of the BVM, who often warns us against breaking God's laws and calls us to prayer and repentance.

The banshee

There is another young and beautiful female apparition, arrayed in white, who is famous for presaging death. More often she takes the form of a frightful hag, who combs her hair and *keens*. This word describes her cry, an unearthly sobbing or wailing as of someone mourning a death. Unlike other white ladies, she is not attached to a particular spot, such as a bridge or tree (although she does have an affinity with streams, where she is seen washing something); nor is she attached to a house or castle. Instead, she is attached to particular families, and can follow them around, far from her native Ireland. My supervisor at Cambridge University, the Yeats scholar Tom Henn, heard her spine-chilling cry on a train to Manchester. He and another man in the compartment searched, shaken, for a cause (they wondered if a woman had fallen on to the tracks) but to no avail. Henn later learned that his elder brother had died at that moment in their ancestral home in Ireland.

I am talking, of course, about the banshee (*bean-sidhe,* meaning "woman fairy"). "Sometimes the banshee assumes the form of some sweet singing virgin of the family who died young," writes Lady Wilde, "and has been given the mission by the invisible powers to become the harbinger of coming doom to her mortal kindred. Or she may be seen as a shrouded woman, crouched beneath trees, lamenting with veiled face; or flying past in the moonlight, crying bitterly; and the cry of this spirit is mournful beyond all other sounds on earth, and betokens certain death to some member of the family..."[23]

One of Lady Gregory's informants, old Mr. King, saw her outside the window of the house where he was playing cards with six others. "She had a white dress and it was as if held over her face," he reported. "They all looked up and saw it, and they were all afraid and went back but myself. Then I heard a cry that did not seem to come from her but from a long way off, and then it seemed to come from herself. She made no attempt to twist a mournful cry but all she said was 'Oh-oh-oh-oh,' but it was as mournful as the oldest of the old women could make it, that was best at crying the dead. Old Mr. Sionnac was at Lisdoonvarna at that time, and he came home a few days after and took to his bed and died. It is always the Banshee has followed the Sionnacs and cried them."[24]

Between 1962 and 1979, Patrick F. Byrne compiled a column on ghost stories, submitted by readers, for the *Dublin Evening Herald*. One of many readers to describe the banshee was cutting timber just outside Newbridge, County Kildare in July 1912. Opposite the hut where he was staying was a derelict house owned by the Kelly family. He was awoken at three in the morning by the sound of keening. "It suddenly got louder, and it was like a woman or girl crying. I got up to investigate — the night was very dark — but I could see well through the huts and piles of logs... I plucked up courage and went out on the old road out of the wood. I could see nothing at first, but after a few seconds a most awful keen, more like a roar, came from about ten yards in front of me. I was frozen to the ground. Then I could see plainly a small woman. She was about four feet high, and I couldn't tell whether she was sitting or standing. Her clothes seemed to be the same color as the beech logs and her head was covered with a kind of cape. She was moving her hands up and down as she kept on wailing. I fled back to the hut. The following day I heard that Mr. Kelly, the owner of the old house, had died during the night."[25]

Phantoms of the road

Twenty-five years ago it was well known locally where I lived that a stretch of the London to Guildford road was haunted by a ghost. A fellow I knew knew a fellow whose uncle had picked up a young girl hitchhiking on this stretch of road — only to find that she had vanished from the car. I didn't know then what I know now, namely that this is a tale which is repeated all over the world, with only slight variations. The classic version can be represented by the following, told by a Toronto teenager in 1973:

"Well, this happened to one of my girlfriend's best friends and her father. They were driving along a country road on their way home from the cottage, when they saw a young girl hitchhiking. They stopped and picked her up and she got in the back seat. She told the girl and her father that she just lived in the house about five miles up the road. She didn't say anything after that but just turned to watch out of the window. When the father saw the house, he drove up to it and turned around to tell the girl they had arrived — but she wasn't there! Both he and his daughter were really mystified and decided to knock on the door and tell the people what had happened. They told them that they once had a daughter who answered the description of the girl they supposedly had picked up, but she had disappeared some years ago and had last been seen hitchhiking on this very road. Today would have been her birthday."[26]

In other variants of the story the girl is a woman. Sometimes she leaves some "physical evidence" behind in the car — a book, purse, sweater, scarf, etc. which subsequently identifies her as a dead person. She can be a girl to whom someone gives a lift home from a club or dance. She asks to be dropped at the cemetery and is never seen again. A popular American variant makes the girl a nun who cryptically predicts some event such as the end of a war before disappearing. In these versions she is sometimes Christianized, no longer a ghost but an angel. Sometimes she is a man, particularly (for some reason) if the driver in the story is a woman.

The "vanishing hitchhiker" is one of a family of stories which have become known as "modern urban folklore" or "urban legends," or even *foaf* lore (friend-of-a-friend lore). They are generally anonymous, circulating largely by word of mouth, and, while they vary in detail, always maintain a central core of traditional motifs. Otherwise it is difficult to say what these tales have in common, although they show a preference for the gruesome, macabre, slightly weird, often absurd or funny. Their shorthand titles give something of their flavor: the Killer in the Backseat; the Baby-Sitter and the Man Upstairs; the Pet (or Baby) in the Oven; the Spider in the Hairdo; Alligators in the Sewers. One story tells of a grandmother who dies while the family is abroad. They stash her on the roof rack. The car is stolen.

Another involves the invention of a car that runs on distilled water. A large company, such as General Motors, suppresses it. And so on.

After a while you begin to get the "feel" of such stories, even when they appear — as they frequently do — in the press, passing themselves off as news items. A friend of mine recently told me an embarrassing story concerning a friend of a friend of his who had gone to a posh country-house party where he had inadvertently sat on, and killed, the family's chihuahua. I expect to hear this again soon from another source. Attempts to "explain" these modern folkloric stories — as the result of "psycho-social" strains, as cautionary tales, as comments on the alienating effects of modern urban life, or whatever — seem to me to be rather thin. They have a more playful, gratuitous character — the sort of tale teenagers tell to make each other shudder or wonder or laugh.

These sorts of stories are not to be confused with the apparitional tales I have been recounting — the latter have an altogether different "feel," being first-hand accounts of apparitions with little or no plot, no neat twist, etc. — but there are overlaps. For, just as modern folk tales creep into the newspapers, into daily gossip and conversation, so they also infiltrate the peripheries of apparitional tales. For example, stories of crashed flying saucers, retrieved and stored in secret Government bases, have been widely recognized as having exactly the flavor of modern urban folklore. "A friend of mine met an ex-USAF officer who said he had seen a spacecraft in a hangar at —" but you can name your own airfield…

Such rumors abound in the wonderful world of anomalous phenomena. Lady Gregory remarked on them when she was investigating fairy sightings. "It is hard to tell sometimes what has been a real vision," she writes, "and what is tradition, a legend hanging in the air, a 'vanity' as our people call it, made use of by a story-teller here and there, or impressing itself as a real experience on some sensitive imaginative mind. For tradition has a large place in 'the Book of the People' showing a sowing and resowing, a continuity and a rebirth as in nature."[27]

By and large, modern folklorists, forced to choose between regarding folk-lore as fact or as fiction, have chosen to treat it as fiction. They have thereby enabled us to see through many stories which we would otherwise regard as fact. But they do us a disservice if they maintain that folklore is *only* fiction.

If it is fiction, it is fiction of a special kind. It is not, for example, fabricated by an individual, as literary ghost stories are.[28] Its origins are a great mystery. It appears, unauthored, from nowhere, as if thrown up by some collective mind. Much of its tenacity and power is due to its resistance to being categorized — not least being categorized as fiction. Folk stories depend on being viewed as factual accounts. Even a class of folklore students, on being confronted with a modern urban legend, will protest: *that* isn't folklore, it's true, it happened in our town, to the brother-in-law of our mother's hairdresser, etc.[29] I certainly believed the story of the chef who mistakenly microwaved his own liver, as I did the xenophobic tale of the couple who were served up their own dog in a Chinese restaurant.

The strange ambiguous nature of the folk tales as not-quite-fact, yet not-exactly-fiction is admirably encapsulated in the "friend-of-a-friend" convention which distances us from the alleged event, but not too remotely. It expresses the in-between nature of the tales — which sometimes turn out to be even trickier than we thought. For instance, just as we can definitely say that the "Vanishing Hitchhiker" is too widespread (it appears in many different cultures) to be "true" and, moreover, is certainly very old (it appears in the nineteenth century, where a horse and cart replace the car), we are confused by the story of Roy Fulton who, it seems, really did pick up a vanishing hitchhiker.

On 12 October 1979, Roy was driving home from a darts match in Leighton Buzzard, Bedfordshire. In an isolated spot, just outside the village of Stanbridge, he saw a man thumbing a lift. Roy pulled up in front of him so that he could be clearly seen in the headlights. The hitchhiker was wearing an open, white-collared shirt, a dark jersey, and dark trousers. He opened the door of the van and, on being asked by Roy where he was going, only pointed up the road. Roy drove for about five minutes before offering his passenger a cigarette. The man had disappeared. Roy braked, searched the van in vain and drove off as fast as he could.[30] He later reported the incident to the police (who subsequently confirmed his report to investigator Michael Goss — they had even sent a car to the scene). Roy later added to his description of the ghostly hitchhiker, saying that its face was very pale and unusually long but that it looked entirely real and solid — solid enough to open a van door.[31]

We cannot know whether the Vanishing Hitchhiker motif began with some apparitional event such as this, or whether such an event occurred because it somehow crystallized out of a current fiction, a "vanity," or "legend hanging in the air." We cannot know the truth as to whether folklore is fact or fiction because the truth does not lie in this distinction, but elsewhere. Like daimonic reality itself, "folklore is never literally true, but it may always be fundamentally true."[32] It eschews "either–or" distinctions and embraces the "both–and." It spans the gap between fact and fiction, just as daimons span this world and some other. Unlike myths which relate the archetypal deeds and patterns of a divine world, only touching upon our world where the humans are already semi-divine heroes, folklore's protagonists are ordinary humans who encounter daimonic persons or events, even including the macabre chef's microwaved liver and other "hilarious accident" stories. The traditional way of talking about such tales is in terms of imagination. And this is my third model — after the collective unconscious and *Anima Mundi* — for making intelligible the nature of daimonic reality.

9

Imagining Things

Primary and secondary imagination

In discussing imagination we must on no account confuse it with what commonly goes by that name — a stream of less than real images through the conscious mind. In a passage familiar to all students of English literary criticism, Samuel Taylor Coleridge dismisses such images as mere "fancy" which is "no other than a mode of memory emancipated from the order of time and space." Authentic imagination, on the other hand, is divided into two kinds, the primary and the secondary:

"The primary imagination I hold to be the living power and prime agent of all human perception, and is a repetition in the finite mind of the eternal act of creation in the infinite I AM. The secondary I consider as an echo of the former, co-existing with the conscious will, yet still as identical with the primary in the kind of its agency, and differing only in degree, and in the mode of its operation. It dissolves, diffuses, dissipates in order to recreate..."[1]

In order to understand this difficult utterance, it is worthwhile enlisting the help of another poet, W. H. Auden, who adopts — and adapts — Coleridge's definition of imagination as part of his own artistic credo. "The concern of the Primary Imagination, its only concern," says Auden, "is with sacred beings and events. The sacred is that to which it is obliged to respond; the profane is that to which it cannot respond and therefore does not know... A sacred being cannot be anticipated; it must be encountered... All imaginations do not recognize the same being or events, but every imagination responds to those it recognizes in the same way. The impression made upon the imagination by any sacred being is of an overwhelming but indefinable importance — an unchangeable quality, an Identity, as Keats said: I-am-that-I-am is what every sacred being seems to say... The response of the imagination to such a presence or significance is a passion of awe. This awe may vary greatly in intensity, and range in tone from joyous wonder to panic dread. A sacred being may be attractive or repulsive — a swan or an octopus — beautiful or ugly — a toothless hag or fair young child — good or evil — a Beatrice or a Belle Dame Sans Merci — historical fact or fiction — a person met on the road or an image encountered in a story or a dream — it may be noble or something unmentionable in a drawing-room, it may be anything it likes on condition, but this condition is absolute, that it arouses awe."[2] Aweful bedazzlement or dread is, of course, the hallmark, in varying degrees, of all the daimonic encounters I have been discussing. They are products of the Primary Imagination, which I will call simply Imagination. They are "sacred."

Auden recognizes that some sacred beings are, of course, sacred only to a single imagination — a particular landscape or building, say, or even a beloved childhood toy. Some, like Kings, are sacred only to members of a particular culture. Others seem to be sacred to all imaginations at all times — the Moon, says Auden, or "Fire, Snakes and those four important beings which can only be defined in terms of nonbeing: Darkness, Silence, Nothing, Death."[3] Such are the images which are entitled to be called archetypal. Lights in the sky fall into this category, while their differentiation into, say, UFOs *qua* structured spacecraft or witches depends upon the culture in which they appear. Sacred beings can also combine in action to form sacred patterns of events — myths such as the death and rebirth of the Hero seem to be universal.

The secondary imagination (which I will call imagination with a small "i") is of less concern to us here. It is the faculty which we bring to bear on the sacred beings of (the Primary) Imagination, from which, as Coleridge says, it differs in degree but not in kind. It is not creative — creation is the prerogative of Imagination — but recreative. It is active, not passive; its categories are not sacred/profane, but beautiful/ugly — that is, it aes- thetically *evaluates* the primary experience. Without its activity, our passivity in the face of Imagination "would be the mind's undoing; sooner or later," says Auden, "its sacred beings would possess it, it would come to think of itself as sacred, exclude the outer world as profane and so go mad."[4] This aptly describes, in a nutshell, the progressive psychic disintegration of those paranoiacs, false prophets, and doomed cult-leaders whom I touched upon earlier.

The struggle of the (secondary) imagination to realize the sacred beings makes art. But, in a different context, the same struggle can be purely psychotherapeutic. C. G. Jung used a technique he called "Active Imagination" to help his patients. He is nowhere as specific about this technique as he might be, nor is it particularly well-named since its purpose was to allow unconscious images — in the form of fantasies, for instance — to rise up into consciousness where they could be *passively* observed, as if in a waking dream. For this the patient obviously had to be in a relaxed, meditative state, perhaps even bordering on the hypnotic. The images could not truly be said to be made conscious, however, until they had been worked on, amplified, expanded through association, and finally assimilated — that is, integrated into the personality. Jung therefore recommended some quasi-artistic activity such as writing fully about the images or painting mandalas. There is clearly an overlap between art and therapy of this sort. We might say that they are the same in kind but differ in degree — perhaps the purely therapeutic image shades into the work of art at a point where it ceases to have predominantly private and personal significance, and takes on a public, impersonal, and collective significance. Therapy treats of *my* condition; art, of the human condition.

In this understanding of Imagination, we see another formulation of Jung's collective unconscious and of the Neoplatonic *Anima Mundi*. The sacred beings are the spontaneously appearing archetypal images. They are our gods and daimons. The advantage of Imagination as a model for daimonic reality is that it avoids the implications, however residual, of the term "collective unconscious" that it is somehow purely interior, within us — when, as we have seen, it is also external to us. Similarly, the model "Soul of the World" implies the opposite, emphasizing externality over internality. The idea of Imagination draws these first two models closer together. Like the collective unconscious it is the source of autonomous sacred beings; like the Soul of the World, it locates these sacred beings just as often in the world as in our psyches (as dreams, visions, etc.). "To the eyes of a man of imagination," remarked Blake, "Nature is imagination itself."

As I intimated earlier, when discussing alleged misidentifications of

UFOs and the inadequacy of "projection," Imagination is the key to understanding how everyday objects can be transformed into "sacred beings." In fact, this may be Imagination's usual *modus operandi:* a young girl, glimpsed on the street, can become the very image of Soul, as Beatrice was for Dante; an old man's shuffling footsteps can become the very image of Hell; before Val of Peckham's very eyes an ordinary planet becomes watchful, intelligent, takes on alien life; a log in a placid lake suddenly moves, grows monstrous. The whole world is trembling on the edge of revealing its own immanent soul. We see it in moments when our perception is raised by imagination to vision — poetic moments of joy and awe, terror and panic dread. We see it when, as Blake says, the doors of perception are cleansed and everything appears as it is, infinite.[5]

Imagination can operate quite ordinarily. Its images can come as sudden inspirations, patterns, ideas, flashes of insight, bolts from the blue; or they can come slowly, over the years, as we seem to grow towards a particular truth. Such images are no less numinous than the apparitions we encounter in dreams or on lonely stretches of road. Our lives do not have to be wrenched by weird entities. We do not have to be blinded, as St. Paul was, by a vision of Jesus on the lonely road to Damascus. Indeed, it might be argued that St. Paul's conversion in this way was a consequence of his former "blindness," his fanatical refusal to believe in Jesus, and the persecution of His followers. Imagination was compelled to employ a way of converting him as extreme and violent as his denial of it.

Such may be the case with all seers of apparitions: it may be their *lack* of imagination which compels Imagination to represent itself to them in spectacular, external manifestations. People who are commonly called "psychic" may be those who are unreflective, not especially well integrated, so that their daimons are experienced not as subtle influences, growing convictions, enlightening intuitions, and so on, but as external persons — spirits, for instance, who bring messages, make demands and predictions, issue orders. Similarly, people who "see things" such as phantom animals and UFOs are presumed to be "over-imaginative." Maybe the reverse is true: those who "believe in" UFOs, etc., and long to see them, notoriously do not. They have already imaginatively accommodated the daimonic. It is the people who have no conscious relation to daimonic reality who commonly "see things." If Imagination is denied autonomy and recognition, it is forced, as it were, to mount a stronger display — to body forth its images not only externally but concretely, because no more subtle approach will impress the literal-minded percipient. Those who have seized the daimonic through imagination do not need to be seized by it.

Alchemical imagination

Jung only begins to consider Imagination in depth in his alchemical writings. He had long understood that the Magnum Opus (Great Work) of alchemy was more than a primitive chemical attempt to synthesize an agent — the Philosophers' Stone — that could transmute base metals to gold. Rather, it was a unique combination of art and science, philosophy and ritual which was designed to transform the psyche of the alchemist himself. Unconscious contents were projected onto the substances and processes within the alchemist's cucurbits and retorts, producing among mists and vapors a wealth of exotic imagery. Chemical changes were described in terms of the conjunction of sun and moon, the marriage of kings and queens, their death and putrefaction; dragons, serpents, green lions expressed caustic reactions; a raven's head heralded Blackness, a peacock's tail Whiteness; sulphur, salt, and mercury were more like mysterious principles than actual elements; the Stone itself was no Stone — it was also the king's son, a hermaphrodite, phoenix, elixir, and so on. However, it was the alchemical notion of *imaginatio* which caused Jung to revise his view of "projection."

Martin Ruland's *Lexicon of Alchemy* (1622) defines *imaginatio* as "the star in man, the celestial or supercelestial body." (The word he uses for star, *astrum,* is derived from Paracelsus and implies something like "quintessence.") This "astounding definition," says Jung, invites us to conceive of the alchemical work *not* as a series of "immaterial phantoms" but as "something corporeal, a 'subtle body.' "[6] "Perhaps the most important key to the understanding of the opus,"[7] Imagination is now understood as "a concentrated extract of the life forces, both physical and psychic." In other words, Imagination is that "intermediate realm between mind and matter, i.e. a psychic realm of subtle bodies"[8] — the realm, that is, which is now familiar to us as daimonic reality. The images of the alchemical opus cease to be unconscious projections and become instead an archetypal drama enacted between the alchemist and his work. Their relationship is both collaborative and reciprocal. The chemical processes — conjunction, mortification, sublimation, even projection (the names are telling) — mirror the alchemist's psychic transformations, and vice versa. This is the intermediate, daimonic state into which we have slipped whenever natural objects, like the alchemical substances, unveil a hidden vibrant life: a monster in the log, a spaceship in the planet, a nymph in the tree, a heavenly host in the sun. Imagination sees into the inner life of things, reminding us that "there is always more to experience and more *in* what we experience than we can predict."[9]

Imagination and soul

The best of the post-Jungian psychologists, James Hillman, even criticizes Jung's concept of the unconscious for obscuring and detracting from Imagination. For to subscribe to the idea of the unconscious is to perpetuate both the error of Cartesian dualism, which posited a mind "inside" us and separate from the "outside" world, and also the erroneous notion of the unconscious as a container (Jung repeatedly refers to the *contents* of the unconscious). But the unconscious is not located "inside us," nor is it a "container" of archetypal images. It is not, in other words, a literal "place" at all, but a metaphor, a tool for deepening and interiorizing experience, a representation of the soul's richness, depth, and complexity.[10]

Hillman boldly and unequivocally relates Imagination to soul. In a sense he rescues soul from the theologians in whose hands it has fallen into disuse or disrepair. At the same time he restores to soul the religious importance accorded to the original Greek term, *psyche,* before it was taken up (or down) by modern secular, quasi-scientific psychologists. He reminds us that soul is not a "thing" in itself, not a substance (this is why I do not call it *the* soul); rather, it is the imaginative possibility in our natures, a set of *perspectives.*[11] Soul, that is, imagines; and the images it imagines are daimons that not only manifest as personifications, but also — invisibly — as perspectives. They are the many eyes that see through our eyes. We call the particular perspective of our daimon "the world"; but there are as many "worlds" as there are daimons. Reality is primarily metaphorical, imaginative, daimonic.

To imagine is to shift perspective, to see things entirely differently — from another person's point of view, for example, or, through that person, from another daimon's point of view. Now we can see more clearly the metaphorical nature of the "unconscious": it is really an unconsciousness of the perspective which is governing our viewpoint, our ideas, and behavior.[12] It is a lack of awareness of Imagination and its myriad possibilities in our conscious lives. The very fact that the notion of soul as a set of perspectives, as many ways of seeing, is so difficult to grasp bears witness to our unconsciousness of soul (we might even say our loss of soul). I am especially stressing this way of regarding soul because it will occur again towards the end of this book. Just as it is incorrect to talk about *the* soul, it is also, strictly speaking, incorrect to talk about *my* soul because soul is really only shorthand for *Anima Mundi* (Soul of the World) and, as such, is *au fond* impersonal and collective. However, this is not to say that it does not — paradoxically — also manifest itself personally, as individual souls. Imagination, then, is another way of representing *Anima Mundi* (or soul), as it is of representing the collective unconscious. Although all three terms are models for that reality I have been calling daimonic, they are not exactly synonymous with each other because they have been formulated in different cultural contexts and within different disciplines. *Anima Mundi,* for example, is more of a philosophical model (in the Neoplatonic sense), while the collective unconscious is psychological and Imagination aesthetic. We might say therefore that all three models are analogous to, or metaphors for, each other. Thus in future I will be using them interchangeably depending on the kind of emphasis I want.

It should also by now be clear that all three models for daimonic reality — *which is itself, of course, another model* — are inherently part of that reality. They are all, for instance, archetypal images of the collective unconscious *for* the collective unconscious, or, they are all attempts by Imagination to imagine itself. The reason why I have coined a new metaphor — daimonic reality — is to emphasize the power of Imagination (or soul, or the unconscious) to produce those concrete anomalies and, above all, personifications, which I have identified as daimons. I will be introducing another model, drawn this time from folklore studies, at the end of this section; but I would like to note here that this by no means exhausts the models by which daimonic reality has been traditionally known and described. One of these, for example, which is implicit throughout this book but nowhere elaborated, belongs, unlike the others, to a popular rather than an intellectual tradition. I mean the concept (although it never was a *concept*) of "fairy," which suggests most appositely both the intermediate nature of daimonic reality, and the hidden daimonic life "within" ("behind," "beyond," "below") all things. Nor, finally, am I able to include here the most fully elaborated of all models — the alchemical Mercurius — because it is so technical and esoteric that it would need a separate book to provide even an outline. (Fortunately, such a book exists in my own *Mercurius; or, The Marriage of Heaven and Earth*.)

Myths, stories, hypotheses

"…it would not be unfair to say that the nature of myths is still, in spite of the millions of printed words devoted to it, a confused topic…[13] there can be no common definition, no monolithic theory, no simple and radiant answer to all the problems and uncertainties concerning myths."[14]

Exactly so. Myths resist the explanations we foist on them. Theories of myth tell us more about the theorizers than about the myths. Rodney Needham, for example — professor of anthropology at Oxford University — rejects the various ideas that myth "reflects history, provides a social charter, responds to natural phenomena, expresses perennial human concerns, embodies a metaphysics, reaffirms eternal verities, copes with historical change, and so on almost endlessly."[15] Instead he prefers to try and discern what features myths have in common. He notices principally that the dramatis personae — gods, heroes, etc. — often change form, either to effect some positive action, or else to avoid restraint. In the latter case, it is usually space and time that are evaded. The ability to shape-change in order to avoid the restrictions of time and space, he remarks, is also characteristic of our imaginations and, as such, of art. And, he adds, of dreams. We might expect him to outline some such view of Imagination — commonplace enough among poets, for instance — as I have been struggling with over the last few pages; but, for whatever reason, he does not. He concedes that ethnographic comparison proves that there is a genuinely collective unconscious in the Jungian sense: "…the original structural components of the psyche are of no less surprising a uniformity than those of the body." Then, as if exhausted by this concession, he falls back on a feeble materialist position — this worldwide uniformity "is 'somehow' connected with the brain."[16]

What Needham (no less than the theorizers he gainsays) dislikes about the traditional stories we call myths is that they are a mystery, and so is their source. All we can say is that they arise spontaneously out of the mythopoeic — myth-making — Imagination or collective unconscious or *Anima Mundi* and they shape, whether we know it or not, the way we look at the world — shape, in fact, the world we look at. The origin of a myth is as mysterious as that of a "modern urban legend," from which it differs in degree but not in kind. We know only that the origins of both are remote — folklore is perhaps remote in space (told by a friend-of-a-friend) while myth is remote in time (handed down by "the ancestors"). But this remoteness is not literal; it is a metaphor which expresses the depth of the roots of myths which are constantly re-imagining themselves outside time and space.

The myths and folklore surrounding apparitions come from the same source as the apparitions themselves. UFOs, for instance, are embedded in the informal stories we call folklore. They approach the status of a more formal myth, especially when bodies of doctrine and belief congeal around them and cults come into being. The most convincing reason for attributing mythological status to them is that, like myths, they are capable of bearing an inexhaustible number of interpretations, no single one of which can finally explain them. But we should not overlook the fact that myth and folklore overlap with, and inform, works of fiction. The first "UFO contact," for example, occurred in a movie, *The Day the Earth Stood Still.* The widespread recognition of "flying saucers" in the late 1940s and early 1950s was preceded by popular fears of invasion from outer space — we recall Orson Welles's radio dramatization of H. G. Wells's *War of the Worlds* which, in 1939, caused panic in the streets.

Similarly, although the modern UFO era is usually dated to Arnold's sighting of some silver discs near Mount Rainier in 1947, it began in fact a little earlier, not with an actual sighting but with a fictional story. In 1944, Ray Palmer's *Amazing Stories* began to outline a strange UFO scenario; little aliens called "deros" had landed on Earth, living underground and molesting innocent citizens with rays that could penetrate walls. Palmer's stories were widely read and taken as factual, perhaps because he had tapped into a common vein of paranoia: many people who deny the inner influence of complexes, the independent partial personalities within the psyche, experience this influence as coming from outside, as invisible rays beamed at them by invading enemies. Interestingly, Palmer derived his stories from long, rambling, barely coherent letters about the "deros," written to him by one Richard Shaver, who was not a little paranoid himself and spent much of his life in and out of mental hospitals.[17]

Thus ufology had its roots in the fantasies of a paranoiac and in science fiction. But, really, Palmer's stories were not fiction as the term is normally used. They were not works of art, even of bad art. They were more like folklore which, although it is usually associated with oral tradition (and still flourishes there, as we have seen), now finds its way into popular writing. The mass of books and magazines on weird topics from UFOs to auras, leys, astrology, vampires, ghosts, etc. fall into this category. Ignored by "high" culture — artists, academics, literary critics — they are widely read and subscribed to by the populace in the same way as folklore is. It is a mistake to ignore them because such folklore displays more clearly, because more naïvely, the structure and working of Imagination than "high" art which is overlaid by so much sophistication, self-consciousness, stylistic variation, fashionable issues, and so on, that its archetypal foundations are obscured. (This is not true, perhaps, of the "highest" art which often, it seems, returns to the "simplicity" of myth; and, like myth, almost seems unauthored, anonymous.)

Modern ufology, then, arose out of an imaginative upsurge in which UFOs were, as Jung would say, constellated in the collective unconscious. UFO phenomena and their phenomenology are continuous, grounded alike in that Imagination which weaves history seamlessly with myths, and blurs the distinction between fact and fiction. (Consider the daimonic combination of history, myth, and folklore which, for instance, comprises the deeply resonant stories of religion, e.g. the four Gospels.) Imagination even underwrites those activities, such as science, which seek to exclude it. Scientific theories and hypotheses are also stories — some of them pretty tall. And just as myths can embody themselves in individual works of art — the idea of the individual arose comparatively recently, around the time of the Renaissance — so they can find expression in the minds of individual scientists. Newton's vision of a mechanical universe running like clockwork is, like all cosmology, primarily an image out of the mythopoeic Imagination. It replaced the Copernican–Galilean paradigm and is being replaced by modern post-Einsteinian cosmology whose fantastic universe of Dark Matter, Black Holes, Quasars and the like comes more and more to resemble some ancient Gnostic myth than anything that might be called "scientific fact."

Charles Darwin's theory of Evolution was also "in the air" — others were thinking along similar lines — before it crystallized in his mind. It represents a sterling contribution to the long history of mythology concerning Origins, one of Imagination's favorite archetypal preoccupations. If it masquerades as fact, this is only because it is part of the nature of scientism to present its myths as facts. But I am not saying that Newton's or Darwin's theories are untrue. They are, or have been (they are wearing out), just as imaginatively true as all visions of the universe or of man's origins. It is just that they are not, despite their protestations to the contrary, literally true. In time we will look back fondly on the theory of Evolution as a story, a superstition even, in which we no longer believe — just as we are already looking back with nostalgia at Newton's orderly image of a rational universe.

A note on lake monsters

There have been few in-depth, cross-cultural analyses of any anomalous phenomena, but one magnificent example is *Lake Monster Traditions* by the French folklorist Michel Meurger, in collaboration with Claude Gagnon. So much of what Meurger says about lake monsters bears directly on the problem of other anomalous phenomena, such as UFOs. For example, sightings of both UFOs and lake monsters have been reported worldwide, from Africa to Australia, Canada to Scandinavia, the USA to New Guinea, and so on. (Janet and Colin Bord list 300 monster-ridden lakes from around the world.) Both show a continuity with the past — modern sightings have precedents in legend, folklore, and myth. No two sightings of either are identical: there are as many different kinds, sizes, shapes, etc. of lake monsters as there are of UFOs, arguing against the actuality of such creatures no less than the actuality of extraterrestrial spacecraft. At the same time, there are a number of recurring motifs surrounding both kinds of sightings which Meurger calls stereotypical. They form a core of tradition, an imaginative matrix in which the sighting is embedded and from which it cannot be isolated.

In the case of lake monsters, Meurger established that the following motifs — he calls them "folklore beliefs" — are pretty much universal. Beginning with the lake itself, it is *bottomless;* it *interconnects* with other lakes or the sea; it is the scene of anomalous *luminous phenomena;* it is impenetrably *dark;* it has submarine *caverns;* it has strong currents and eddies or *whirlpools* which are caused by (or sometimes synonymous with) serpents; it is prone to unexpected *squalls;* it has swallowed up *divers who never return.*

Some of these features may be quite at odds with actuality. Many lakes are, for example, far too shallow or small to house the size of monster for which sightings are claimed. Lake Elsinore in California even dries up periodically but is still said to have a monster! In addition, the monster seems to adapt its nature to suit its surroundings. I remember the belief attached to a small lake near my childhood home, that it contained a spot which suddenly dropped to an unnatural depth where there lurked a very old, enormous pike which would have the leg off you if you swam over it. In a large lake the "pike" becomes the dinosaur-like creature of Loch Ness; and the beliefs which aggregate around such monsters are no less universal than those surrounding their habitat. For instance, the monster is mistaken for an *upturned boat* or a "living" log; it is really a *submarine,* itself mysterious; it has a *horse's head;* it has *humps* which *undulate* up and down; it moves at *extraordinary speeds;* it is really a *big fish* such as a sturgeon; or it is a *seal* or *serpent;* or a *dinosaur.*

Here, too, there are echoes of the UFO debate. Both lake monsters and UFOs move at unearthly speeds. Both are thought to be misidentifications of natural or man-made objects. In the "mystery submarine" legends, the monster becomes a technological vehicle just as UFOs become "spacecraft." Moreover, those who "believe in" lake monsters fall into two camps, just like the ufologists: on the one hand the crypto-zoologists believe in the literal reality of lake monsters, just as the extraterrestrialists believe in literal aliens from outer space. On the other, there are those who believe that lake monsters are supernatural creatures, phantoms, or spirits. Meurger rejects both of these beliefs: "I must stress that I do not believe that there exists an autonomous phenomenon in these lakes, be it an unknown animal or an occultist's ghost."[18] Instead, good folklorist that he is, he takes up a position not very far removed from our old friend "psycho-social strains." "In this study we will deal with the imaginative power of the human mind, combining an objective phenomenology — such as big fish, bizarre waves and floating tree trunks — with a subjective ideology such as that found in legends."[19]

Meurger seems to be saying that people who see lake monsters are carrying around an "ideology" composed of the various legends concerning the lake and its denizens, and this predisposes them to misperceive innocuous natural objects such as fish, waves, and logs. In short, they have imagined it all. Needless to say, he uses the expression "the imaginative power of the human mind" in almost exactly the opposite sense to that in which I have been trying to use it. He does not mean that an encounter with a lake monster is imaginative and real; he means that it is imaginary and unreal. But let us hear some typical accounts from misperceivers with overactive imaginations.

On a clear summer's night around 1972, Helen Hicks of Newport, Vermont, was out in a boat on Lake Memphrémagog in Canada when, according to her deposition, she saw "a creature which had the resemblance of a face somewhat like a horse, with two very red eyes and a body which was hard to judge as to length, about 75 to 100 feet long. The water around the creature...was iridescent. The neck appeared to be very long; the back of the creature had somewhat of an appearance like scales, large ones... A spotlight was put on it from the boat and then it started to come for the boat. It rolled over near the boat causing the boat to be very tippy. It shorted out the boat motor."[20] (Meurger, incidentally, says earlier that it "swamped the motor" — but she doesn't say that. It could be that the motor simply failed as motors so often do in the presence of anomalous events, especially UFOs.)

On 22 February 1968, farmer Stephen Logue, his wife, and five children watched a twelve-foot-long creature swim around Lough Nahoon near their home in Connemara, Ireland. It had "a pole-like head and neck about nine inches to a foot in diameter... From time to time it put its head underwater, two humps then came into view. Occasionally, a flat tail appeared... The thing was black, slick and hairless with a texture resembling an eel... Mrs. Logue...noticed two horn-like projections on top of the head."[21]

Okanagan Lake in British Columbia has a famous monster known to the Indians as Ogopogo and reported by the first white settlers to the area from 1860 onwards. It is similar to the Loch Ness monster, about 30 to 70 feet long, with a dark sleek body 1 to 2 feet thick, and with a horse-shaped head. Sheri Campbell, one of five young people waterskiing on the lake on 23 July

1968, saw "20 feet of Ogopogo floating on the surface… In her alarm she dropped the ski tow-rope and had to tread water while the boat circled to pick her up. By then Ogopogo had begun to move. 'His blue-green-gray scales glistened like a rainbow trout as the sun shone on him,' said Sheri. The group decided to try for a closer look and got within 'five feet' before the creature submerged and made off at high speed. 'When he swam beneath the surface, he made waves which streamed behind him in vee shapes.' They chased the creature in the boat, but at 40 mph could not keep up with it."[22]

I agree with Meurger that these monsters are neither "unknown animals" nor "an occultist's ghost." But are they really a combination of "ideology" and "misperception"? This explanation could itself do with explaining. It does scant justice to the experience of the witnesses; it does not go far enough or deep enough; it begs several questions.

For example: what is this "ideology" the witnesses are said to possess?

Figure 3. One of the earliest pictures of the Loch Ness Monster photographed 19 April 1934 by London surgeon R. K. Wilson. (*Fortean Picture Library*)

How conscious is it or does it have to be? Where did the myths which comprise it come from, if not from earlier sightings by indigenous people? How do we know that everyone who sees a lake monster possesses this "ideology"? How do we know that the early settlers, who saw lake monsters in America, knew about native legends or even about similar legends in their homeland? And what of the Japanese tourist who sees a lake monster in Scotland? Can the thousands of reported sightings of the Loch Ness monster *really* be accounted for in the way Meurger describes? How do we account for the sense of reality experienced not only by modern witnesses to lake monsters, but also by all the Native Americans, Australian aboriginals, Scandinavians, Irish, Scottish, Russians, etc. who, since time immemorial, have never questioned this reality? Why should their reality be less real than the reality Meurger never questions? And what of the other half of the equation — "misperception"? But I have already said enough on that score.

Meurger refers to the "folklore beliefs" which surround lakes and their marshes as stereotypic. But this suggests a set of beliefs which are worn-out, banal, dead. In fact they are still living, still powerful and compelling — not stereotypical, but archetypal, as different from stereotypes as truth is from truism. He is right to emphasize the collective nature of lake monster myths, but wrong to identify this collectivity with society or culture. In truth they are products of a collective Imagination. For, like almost no other natural feature, a lake provides a ready-made metaphor for the Soul of the World, a symbol of the collective unconscious, an imaginative nexus where individual perception (or "misperception") and collective myth meet. Regardless of the actual characteristics of the lake, it is transformed by the Imagination into a reflection of the unconscious itself, becoming a dark, impenetrable, bottomless kingdom which does not yield up its dead. Like an individual soul it interconnects at its deepest level with other souls, other lakes, or with the sea, the oceanic *Anima Mundi*. It is unpredictable and turbulent, prone to sudden squalls and impulses which trouble the surface of consciousness or eddy just beneath it.

The daimonic monsters are seen now as contained in the lake, now as another manifestation of it. Rising like archetypal images towards the light of consciousness, they are glimpsed in an instant of amazement before sinking back into the depths, their wake sending ripples into the far reaches of our minds. Or they shift shape, changing and merging, now tailed like a fish, now scaled like an alligator. The "water-horses" of European lakes from Italy to Siberia give way to immense humped serpents — which, in turn, reveal shaggy horse-like manes and blazing red eyes. "Fluid and elusive like the elements which shelter them, the lake serpents are, for the [American] Indians, beings which go through different metamorphoses. The waters where they live are endowed with the property of changing animals which drown into monsters."[23] Thus do traditional cultures recognize in their myths the power of Imagination to transform the ordinary into the uncanny, the supernatural. From Alaska to New Mexico the belief in a single huge, horned water-serpent is complemented by a host of hybrid beasts mirroring the animals of dry land — water-tigers, water-panthers, water-grizzlies, water-bison, water-dogs.[24]

Fairy glamour and pishogue

Sometimes the water-monster becomes personified, as if to step out of its natural element were to fix it in human shape. The Scottish water-horse, the Kelpie, emerges in the shape of a hairy man in order to drag passers-by back into the depths — "at Loch Barrachan in Sutherland, for example, only the clothes of two missing fishermen were found on the banks, surrounded by large hoof-prints."[25] In 1938, Kari Ivarsdotter saw a Nykkjen (a water-man) in the Myrkevatn ("dark lake") on the Norwegian west coast island of Hareidland. She thought at first it was an upturned boat moving through the water, but then the Nykkjen raised its head and shook the water from its dripping beard just as water-horses shake their wet manes. Kari fled.[26]

She had strayed from the usual well-worn path to the remote and wild mountain spot (she was looking for missing sheep). Thus one could say, along with Meurger, that her vision of the menacing water-man acted as a warning of the dangers that await those who trespass on the wilderness. This sociological reading of the event suggests that she misperceived some banal object because she was aware of having broken a taboo and so expected retribution. Her sighting was "group induced," an "act of social allegiance."[27]

Alternatively, one could say that Kari had strayed into a place of enchantment where for a moment her unconscious imaginative life had merged with that great Imagination which is congruent with the landscape. In this view of the world, the notion of subjective misperception is reversed:

the object itself is deceptive — altered, as the Irish were wont to say, by fairy "glamour" so that it suddenly appears uncanny, not *right*. Val of Peckham's planet was similarly transformed into an intelligent, watchful UFO; like Kari, she had strayed into the wilderness of a living myth. But the notion of glamour, the enchantment of the world, is complemented in fairy belief by the notion of "pishogue." The fairies put *pishogue* on us, altering our perception and making us see whatever they wish.[28] Thus the interaction between us and the world is expressed more elegantly and subtly than ideas like "psychic reality." Fairy belief recognizes that enchantment lies sometimes more with us, sometimes more in the world.

Further still, from the fairy perspective as it were, there does not have to be an upturned boat or log at all — these are really fairy creatures, pookas, or peistes (the word the Logan family used for their monster), which *take on the appearance* of boats and logs. Imagination precedes perception; daimonic reality is recognized as being prior to ordinary reality.[29] Accordingly, Meurger's postulated "ideology" is not necessary. It is true, of course, that our culture predisposes us to see certain kinds of apparitions or to see apparitions in a certain kind of way. But the remarkable uniformity of lake monster beliefs — and sightings — across the world suggests that they are as little determined by culture as, for example, "lights in the sky." Thus, in the case of early settlers in America who saw lake monsters, we do not need to insist, as Meurger does, that they were aware of native legends or that they brought lake monster myths with them from Europe. Lake monsters seem to be truly archetypal, less culturally based, as it were, than geographically based — certain lakes appear to contain the "autonomous phenomena" which Meurger rejects. These are not the literal monsters to which he is referring but autonomous daimons — archetypal images — which rise up out of the world-soul, briefly embodied by the lake. And this is why a Japanese tourist, let us say, who has no conscious or even unconscious connection with lake monster traditions, is just as liable to see one as anyone else — just as he might also see a black dog on a stretch of Norfolk road or a white lady in an old manor house. Popular belief, as so often, appears to be borne out: that there are enchanted places, none more so than lakes, where we can be spellbound — whether in certain moods or, as legend has it, at certain times of day, month, or year.

10

Daimonic Traces

A close encounter

There's no question but that daimonic events can have physical effects. Take the well-known case of Robert Taylor, a sixty-one-year-old foreman forester who, on the morning of 9 November 1979, was working in a forestry development near Livingstone, Scotland: rounding a corner on the forest track he came face to face with a dome-shaped object, about six meters wide, hovering silently above the ground. Almost at once he saw two spherical objects — between half a meter and a meter in diameter — rolling towards him. Studded with spikes, they attached themselves to his trouser legs, one on each side, and began to pull him towards the larger object. He was overwhelmed by an acrid smell and lost consciousness. After about twenty minutes he came round, but could neither speak nor walk. The objects had disappeared, leaving substantial marks in the grass. When he had recovered sufficient strength he stumbled home, where his wife contacted a doctor, the police, and Mr. Taylor's boss, who had the area fenced off. A thorough investigation ensued. There was no question about Mr. Taylor's honesty and integrity and no explanation for his clothes, which were torn in a way that was consistent with his story.[1] The physical traces at the site of the anomaly consisted of two parallel "tracks" about three meters long and three apart, with many holes about ten centimeters across.[2] (In February 1992 a plaque — the first to mark a UFO encounter — was erected to commemorate the event.)

Those who believe in the literal reality of apparitions — believe, that is, that apparitions are not apparitions — usually adduce two kinds of evidence. Firstly, they cite the presence of more than one, often many, witnesses — which is presumed to rule out the "merely psychological" (i.e. the "apparition" cannot be an individual illusion). I will be discussing this topic later on. Secondly, they cite various physical effects. These are, broadly, of two sorts. The first sort comprises the physiological and psychological effects on the witnesses themselves, whether, on the one hand, burns, scars, paralysis, etc. or, on the other hand, bewilderment, amnesia, feelings of depression or elation, etc. I will also be tackling these later on. For the moment, I will concentrate solely on the second sort of physical effect, namely those which appear as traces, marks, objects, and so on in the external world. They include such items as UFO "landing traces," photographs and radar evidence, Mr. Taylor's torn trousers, and a large range of strange objects.

A fairy shoe

For example, I have in front of me a photograph of a shoe.[3] It was found by a farm laborer on the Beara Peninsula, south-west Ireland, in 1835. It is black, worn at the heel and styled like that of an eighteenth-century gentleman. But it is also only two and seven-eighths inches long and seven-

Figure 4. The fairy shoe found on a remote path in Ireland. The shoe is under three inches, appears to be made of mouseskin, and seems to have a worn heel. (*Christopher Sommerville, Oxford*)

eighths of an inch at its widest — too long and narrow even for a doll's shoe. If it were an apprentice-piece, say, how did it come to be found on a remote sheep track? Why was it made in the style of the previous century? Why is it such an odd shape? How did it come to be *worn?* Who would possess tools fine enough to make such a curiosity?

The man who found the shoe assumed it belonged to the "little people" and gave it to the local doctor, from whom it passed to the Somerville family of Castletownshend, County Cork. On a lecture tour of America, the author Dr. Edith Somerville gave the shoe to Harvard University scientists, who examined it minutely. The shoe had tiny hand-stitches and well-crafted eyelets (but no laces), and "was thought to be" of mouse skin. Other shoes, equally odd, have been found in Ireland, not to mention other items of clothing, such as the coat found in a "fairy ring" by John Abraham ffolliott in 1868. It was only six and a half inches long and only one and three quarter inches across the shoulder. Fully lined and with cloth-covered buttons, its high velvet-trimmed collar was greased and shiny from, presumably, long wear, while other parts were frayed and the pockets holed and scorched as if from a tiny pipe.[4]

There is nothing that can be usefully said about these artifacts. They are like red herrings, deliberately planted to puzzle, provoke, amuse, baffle us. They polarize opinion, inviting ridicule and cries of "hoax!" from one party and, from the other, implicit belief in an actual race of little people who dress like us but always in a slightly older fashion. Further, more concrete, evidence of such a race is never forthcoming. Daimons not only leave red herrings — they *are* red herrings, leading us up blind alleys where we come face to face with mystery.

UFO relics

The situation is directly analogous to that of "UFO landings" where traces and remains are subsequently discovered. "Hundreds of witnesses" at Campañes, Brazil, on 14 December 1954, saw a gyrating disc dribble a stream of "silvery liquid" into the streets. Government scientists collected some of it and later announced that it was almost pure tin. The egg-shaped object which police officer Louie Zamorra saw landing outside Socorro, New Mexico, on 24 April 1964 left behind a metal-like substance on some rocks. It turned out to be silicon. In June 1965 a shiny disc was seen to explode over Texas, Maryland. Recovered fragments, analyzed at the Goddard Space Flight Center, proved to be ordinary ferrochromium.[5] And so on. The "remains" tease us and lead us on.

Again and again we hear of mysterious substances left behind by anomalous objects which either turn out to be quite ordinary or else disappear — on the way to the laboratory, in the post, at the research center, or whatever. The same is true of photographs. So many are mislaid or vanish that wild stories of cover-ups and conspiracies and suppression of evidence spring up. Yet these, too, are unfounded. It is exactly as if physical traces of daimonic events are, as the Cornish say, *pixilated*. This phenomenon of "vanishing evidence" is itself part of the daimonic scheme of things, as traditional folklore confirms: it is notoriously difficult to keep hold of anything which has passed, as it were, out of the daimonic realm and into this world. A widespread motif in folk-tales from Japan to Indonesia to Ireland concerns some reward for services rendered given by the fairies to humans who are forbidden to look at the gift until they reach home. Those who do peek inevitably find that what was gold immediately turns into withered leaves; or else they see only some coals which they throw away — only to discover that, had they kept them, the coals would have become gold. So much "evidence" for UFOs evaporates like withered leaves or, under the microscope, turns out to be common "coal."

Treasures

There are cases where treasure has not been handed over to the lucky recipient but merely pointed out — we remember our Apinayé chief who felt something hard with his foot at a place indicated by his sun-god, before he was called away. On 21 September 1821, an eighteen-year-old farm boy awoke to a vision in his bedroom near Palmyra, New York — a white-robed figure, surrounded by light and hovering above the floor, who identified himself as Moroni, a messenger from God. He told young Joseph Smith the location of a box which he was to unearth in six years' time. So, on 22 September 1827, in the presence of many witnesses, Smith dug up the box and found inside a series of gold leaves or plates on which many cryptic symbols were engraved. Smith took three years to translate the strange writing on the plates, whose existence was affirmed by formal affidavits signed by eleven friends and neighbors. However, once the translation was complete, the plates vanished — taken, said Smith, by the original messenger. His translation became the *Book of Mormon* and Smith the founder of the Mormon Church, whose members number in millions.[6]

Such tales of buried treasure can be trivial as well as exalted, but they differ, I think, more in degree than in kind. A boy of eight longed, as only small boys can, for a fishing rod which, in those days, cost 28 shillings and sixpence (£1.42½p). After accumulating money in every way he could — by doing small jobs, returning empty bottles, begging his parents for an advance on pocket money, etc. — he found himself still a half-crown (12 ½½p. short. He lay on his stomach on the grass verge outside his house on a hot summer's afternoon, idly prizing weeds out of the earth. He worked round them with his fingers, gradually loosening them until he could lift them out whole. As he worked, he wondered and wondered how he could get the half-crown. I dare say he wished for it. Lifting up a particularly large weed, he found at its roots, directly underneath, a half-crown coin. It was green with age, as if it had been there a long time. The boy marveled at the coincidence, or Providence, that had led him to dig at precisely that spot. He half-believed that the money had materialized there especially for him. At any rate, it did not turn to withered leaves because he bought the fishing rod, which was a disappointment in the end. (The boy, of course, was myself.)

Incidentally, there is a sequel to the story of the half-crown. Not long ago I came across this story in Lady Gregory's *Visions and Beliefs in the West of Ireland:*

"I met a woman coming out one day from Cloon, and she told me that when she was a young girl, she went out one day with another girl to pick up sticks near a wood. And she chanced to lay hold on a tuft of grass, and it came up in her hand and the sod with it. And there was a hole underneath full of halfcrowns, and she began to fill her apron. She called to the other girl, and the minute she came there wasn't one to be seen. But what she had in her apron she kept."

An alien exchange

There is every kind of trafficking between this world and the daimonic realm, each as ambiguous and inconclusive as the next. Not only do objects, as it were, pass over as rewards and gifts, but they are also stolen. "Narratives of the theft of valuables from supernatural beings are found the world over."[7] And a surprising number of these are drinking cups, horns, or goblets which, stolen from the fairies, sometimes become communion chalices. Rarer, but not unknown, are tales of *exchange,* for which Joe Simonton, a sixty-year-old chicken farmer living near Eagle River, Wisconsin, provides a notable example.

On the morning of 18 April 1961, Joe heard a strange noise outside his house and, looking out of the window, saw a silvery metallic machine alighting in his yard. He went outside and watched as a kind of hatch slid open in the upper part of the object to reveal three dark-skinned men, about five feet tall and wearing tight-fitting dark-blue uniforms with turtleneck collars and apparently knitted headgear, like balaclava helmets. None of them spoke throughout the encounter.

One of the men, if that is what they were, held out a shiny bucket-like object to Joe, who understood that they wanted it filled with water. He took it, filled it from his pump, and returned it to the silent man. He noticed that the interior of the machine was black "like wrought-iron," and that one man was busy at a kind of instrument panel, while the other was working at what looked like a stove. A pile of pancakes sat nearby. Joe said that he gestured towards them, whereupon the man with the bucket picked up four of the pancakes and handed them over. The hatch shut, the object changed its humming noise to a sound "like wet tyres on a pavement" and rose slowly into the air, making off towards the south. (At about the same time an insurance agent, Savino Borgo, who was driving along Highway 70, a mile or so from Joe's farm, saw a saucer rise diagonally into the air and fly parallel to the road.)

Joe dispersed three of the pancakes to UFO groups for analysis. They were made of cornmeal, hydrogenated oil, and salt, according to one account. According to another, there was no salt — which affirms the fairy nature of the tale (fairies hate and fear salt). At any rate, Joe took a nibble out of the fourth pancake and announced that it "tasted like cardboard."[8]

Gifts of the BVM

I can think of only two occasions when, among the many visions of the Blessed Virgin Mary, concrete objects have accompanied or resulted from the vision. The first that springs to mind is the Host — a small wafer, described as "luminous white" — which materialized on the tongue of

Conchita Gonzalez, the leader of the four visionary children who regularly saw the BVM at Garabandal.[9]

The second is the remarkable self-portrait of Mary given to Juan Diego in December 1531 at the remote spot about five miles north of Mexico City. Having seen her twice, and spoken to her, Juan failed to convince the local bishop of his vision; and so at the third vision he requested some evidence. Mary obligingly arranged some unseasonable roses he had gathered in his *tilma* — an Aztec garment like a long cape, worn in front and often looped up as a carry-all. When Juan delivered the flowers to the Bishop it turned out that a picture of the Virgin, just as Juan had seen her, was imprinted on the crude cloth of the tilma.[10] It is still venerated by the masses of people who subscribe to the cult of the Virgin of Guadalupe, as she subsequently became known.

Photographs

"There are tens of thousands of photographs of alleged UFOs in existence, but not a single one of them shows an unequivocal UFO clearly, in focus, and in juxtaposition to the ground, buildings or some other reference point."[11] Exactly so. And the same judgment may be made about photographs of all other apparitions as well.

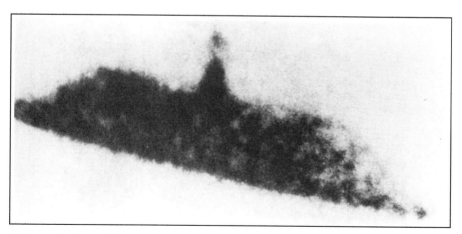

Figure 5. One of the most mysterious of the UFO photographs. Taken by Paul Trent in May 1950 at McMinnville, Oregon. (*Fortean Picture Library*)

At the same time there is no reason why daimons shouldn't show up on film. It's not as if they are "all in the mind," not as if they aren't — sometimes at least — *there*. Indeed they sometimes do show up on film. They even — I almost said especially — show up when they are not wanted. There are excellent pictures of ghosts, for instance, which intrude themselves on everyday scenes, appearing in the photo but invisible when it

Figure 6. A still frame taken from Roger Patterson's film of Bigfoot taken 20 October 1967 at Bluff Creek, California. (*Fortean Picture Library*)

was taken. Conversely, for every snapshot of an alleged UFO or a mystery animal, there is another where nothing came out; or, more interestingly still, where the entire film was blank or the camera jammed in the first place, just as guns can misfire and cars lose control in the presence of daimonic entities, lights, UFOs, animals, etc.

Photographs deepen rather than solve the mystery. The anomalous big black cat prowls in the distance, cat-shaped, too far away for any detail. We guess its size from adjacent shrubs, it seems bigger than a domestic cat, we can't be absolutely sure... The thing in the sky is dark. It might have a fin or a wing. Is it large and far away or tiny and close up? Is it flying or hovering, or is it something hung from wires and simply thrown in the air? Is it an insect on the lens? We can't be sure... We watch the famous film of the Bigfoot.[12] It is both impressive and absurd. It looks like a man dressed up — and yet it doesn't. Its strides are too long, its arms hang or move inhumanly. It pauses, turns, looks at the camera. It is a chilling moment. We imagine a penetrating, intelligent gaze, but its face is too distant to be sure. It ambles off. We are left not knowing what we have seen. We believe it is a Bigfoot, whatever that is; or we don't believe it. The film compounds, highlights, intensifies the mystery, but nothing is resolved. Cameras may not lie, but neither are they suitable for telling the truth. Photos can be blown up or analyzed until we're blue in the face; but the process turns the image into something else. Different processes achieve different results. We are forced to fall back yet again onto the evidence of our eyes. This picture's a fake, we say; this is genuine. Others see it differently. Believers and unbelievers pick and choose, or see the same photograph in opposite ways.

An air traffic controller stares at the dim glow of his radar screen. It is quartered like a mandala, inviting psychic projection. However, he is sure that the six blips which suddenly appear on the screen are not projections. But, then, neither are they ordinary aircraft, all of which are accounted for. This happens a fair bit. It happened to Sgt. William Kelly of Yaak, Montana, in the summer of 1953. He double-checked the blips, knowing that there is always interference on a radar screen, from birds, weather, atmospheric conditions, and so on. You have to interpret the data on the screen. The six blips changed direction five times, sometimes by as much as ninety degrees. It was tempting to interpret them as six very unusual craft. On the other hand, they were only blips. When the radar indicated that whatever the blips were, they were within visual range of the station, Sgt. Kelly and his colleagues had a look outside. They saw six objects flying in formation at an estimated speed of 2200 km/h. At the time the world airspeed record was only about half that.[13]

What did they see? They saw blips in the sky, here one minute, gone the next. Sometimes there are blips on the radar screen and nothing in the sky. Or vice versa. Sometimes they appear to be solid for a while — radar-detectable — and then they're not, just as UFOs are visible for a while and then not. Sonar soundings of Loch Ness sometimes produced a huge unidentifiable shape; more often, not. Something is there, and then not there, now material, now immaterial — a kind of blip reality. This is what daimons do: they blip, and we are left wondering.

Circular marks

One of the most common daimonic traces is the suspicious-looking circular or oval area of crushed (burned, depressed) grass (reeds, crops). These are usually, but not exclusively, associated with strange aerial lights, as members of a Russian biology team confirmed when they discovered and photographed an area of trampled grass by the side of Lake Khaiyr in eastern Siberia. They had rushed there after one of them, N. F. Gladkikh, had earlier seen a creature unknown to him, which he described as having a small head, a long gleaming neck, and a huge bluish-black body with a fin along its spine. Of course, by the time they arrived, the creature had gone, leaving only the customary enigmatic trampled grass — although three of the scientists did later see the creature's head and fin appear in the lake, whose waters were agitated by the lashing of its long tail.[14]

In the late sixties, Australia became famous for "UFO nests" — areas of flattened or swirled vegetation, often found after UFO sightings, and with no obvious natural cause.[15] More familiar are the regular "UFO traces," simple and suggestive circular marks on the ground with no fancy swirling pattern. We would expect these to appear in pre-UFO lore and, of course, they do — in accounts of fairy rings. It is not always clear what these are. We like to think they are only the patterns of greener grass caused by subterranean fungi; and it is true that these were attributed to fairy trippings at night. But there are indications that not all fairy rings were so simple. For instance, the sixteenth-century Swedish Bishop Olaus Magnus, who investigated these things, took it for granted that "they [the elves] make so deep an impression on the earth that no grass grows there, being burned with extreme heat."[16]

Whenever people in the past stumbled across such areas of flattened grass they found it difficult not to believe that fairies (or elves) were responsible, just as today we feel that similar flattened patches are proof of the literal reality of spacecraft. The same is true of the huge footprints or clawed paw marks we find after Bigfoot or big black cat sightings: the creatures in question really seem to have been *there*. But, as we have seen, each footprint is different, bearing different numbers of toes, or else there are no footprints where there "ought" to have been. Despite hundreds, possibly thousands, of examples of footprints and "landing traces," the evidence never gets any harder — no Bigfoot or cats are caught or shot; no spacecraft brought in and exhibited to visitors. There are stories in abundance, yes, of crashed "saucers" retrieved and stored in secret hangars. There are people who will swear to them. But we never get beyond stories or, rather, that curious kind of literal fiction, if you will forgive the oxymoron, which is called urban legend but deserves to be called a daimonic tale.

Slowly it begins to dawn on us that all the "physical evidence" is as ambiguous and elusive as the phenomena themselves, just enough to convince those people who want to believe in their literal reality — just too little to win over the unbeliever. "Physical evidence" turns out not to be separate from the anomalous event, as effect is separate from cause; it is an inseparable part, another aspect, of the anomaly. For "physical evidence," read "daimonic traces."

The question of causality has been highlighted in recent years by a new kind of apparition. It is unique in that it appears at first sight to lack a daimonic nature — to lack, that is, both material and immaterial aspects. It does not seem to be at all ambiguous or elusive; it is so wholly material, in fact, that many people doubt whether it is an apparition at all. However, all is not as it seems — I am talking about the phenomenon of so-called crop circles.

11

Circles

Crop circles

In the early hours of 12 July 1990, all the dogs around the Wiltshire village of Alton Barnes began to bark. Roofs shook very slightly and tiles rattled. A late traveler's car engine cut out. Dawn revealed an eerie sight: in a field below the neolithic barrow called Adam's Grave, an extraordinary configuration of circles, rings, lines, and "key-" or "claw-shapes" was imprinted on the corn. "They were perfect," said Mary Killen from the neighboring village of Huish, "as if they'd been made in one fell swoop, I mean there was no possibility of a human doing that, it was too geometrically exact."[1]

Simple crop circles had first appeared in 1979, mostly in the evocative, megalith-ridden landscape of Wessex, but also in other parts of the country. They occurred not only in fields of corn — wheat or barley — but also in oilseed rape, whose stalks, which cannot be bent without breaking, were nonetheless bent flat on the ground, with no sign of human or animal intervention.[2]

"Summer whirlwinds" were cited as the obvious cause of the crop circles. But it was equally obvious, on reflection, that no whirlwind could exert sufficient downward force to lay corn completely flat and swirl it perfectly in a clockwise or anti-clockwise direction. Nor could it overlay a swirl in one direction with a swirl in the opposite direction; nor carve such precise edges to the circles; nor — an intriguing feature, this — *plait* ears of corn together and lay them gently down.[3]

UFOs were invoked as a cause early on. The circles looked as though a large object had hovered above them and swirled the corn down with some powerful force, such as electromagnetism (helicopters were ruled out —

145

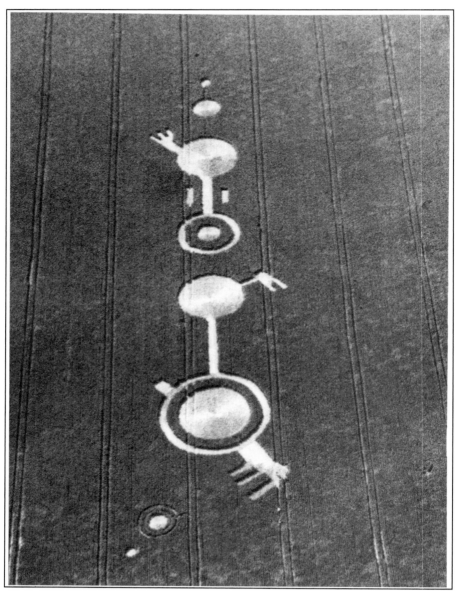

Figure 7. The Alton Barnes' crop circle from 12 July 1990, showing circles, rings, keys, and claws. (*Fortean Picture Library*)

they made a worse mess than whirlwinds!). In addition they often boasted smaller "satellite" circles, placed at equal distances around the main circle, which suggested round "feet" attached to "landing gear." At the same time, on nights before mornings when new circles were discovered, strange aerial lights were often seen in the vicinity.[4] In the summer of 1989, for example, a stone's throw from Wiltshire's Silbury Hill — the largest prehistoric man-made earthwork in Europe — a great globe of light, burnt orange in color with a lighter outer rim, was seen to descend on a field. It distorted like a soap bubble, pulsated, and then went out. A new circle with an outer ring was found in the field next day. In 1990, Pat and Jack Collins saw a huge circular object, like a carousel, hovering over Stockbridge Down, also in Wiltshire. "It had lots and lots of yellowy white lights all around the edge and more lights along spokes leading to the center of it," said Mrs. Collins. Next morning two separate "quintuplets" — groups of five circles — were found situated on a straight line from their sighting.[5] In 1992, a less spectacular year for crop circles than the two preceding years, lights seemed to be more in evidence than usual — I spoke to people who had seen a myriad small twinkling "fairy" lights; to people who had seen orange globes; and to a group who had seen a "structured craft" hovering, brightly lit, near Avebury. Thus anomalous lights and UFOs, if they do not actually cause the circles, are very much associated with them.

A few die-hards claimed that the circles were made by pesticides or fungi or animals (notably hedgehogs or rutting deer) — but careful analysis, to say nothing of common sense, disqualified such theories. No one, as far as I know, suggested that witches were the culprits, although they would be obvious candidates to many other cultures. However, fairies had their champions since, of course, any unnatural-looking circular phenomenon in Nature suggests their handiwork. In other words, as with all anomalies, it was a case of rounding up the usual suspects...

The scientists, naturally, kept well clear of the circles. They instinctively knew that they were faced with a can of worms they did not wish to open. The shining exception was Dr. G. Terence Meaden, an atmospheric physicist, who boldly claimed that a sophisticated kind of whirlwind was responsible for the circles: a vortex of air "ionized to the point at which it is better regarded as a species of low-density cool plasma producing a high-energy electro-magnetic field."[6] This hypothetical glowing plasma vortex could also explain UFOs. More than one newspaper announced that the mystery of the crop circles was solved.

But there were objections to the plasma vortex. It could not be proved to exist — indeed, it was as elusive as a UFO or a fairy. It did not create circles which straddled roads or boundaries, as a random meteorological phenomenon might be expected to do. Moreover, whereas it was just plausible as a cause of simple circles, it looked increasingly unlikely as a cause for the complex "pictograms." In June 1990 a great triple-ringed circle near Devizes was photographed from the air. Snapped again a week later, it was found to have acquired a fourth ring, perfectly concentric like the others, and over 1,000 feet in circumference.[7] Many people who had been skeptical of the plasma vortex's ability to create rings in the first place drew the line at a vortex which could make three on a Wednesday and return a week later to add another. Besides, if plasma vortices existed, crop circles should have appeared annually throughout history. However, apart from the testimony of one or two farmers who claimed to have seen them before, there was no record of them — not even in folklore, which is usually meticulous about recording any prodigy. The only phenomenon reminiscent of crop circles were the "UFO nests," swirled areas of grass or reeds which occurred principally in Australia during the seventies; and which, also associated with sighting of UFOs, were classed along with the kind of "landing traces" I looked at earlier.

Meanwhile the circles increased in number and complexity. By 1987, 75 had been reported; 1988 produced about 115; 1989, 300; 1990, over 400; 1991, about the same. There were reports of their appearance all over the country from Scotland to Kent. They were appearing overseas, too, in Italy and Germany, in the sorghum fields of America's Midwest, in the paddy fields of Japan. But nowhere approached Wessex, where circles came in threes and fours, linked by straight lines and sprouting rectangular shapes; where, in 1991, circles with antenna-like protuberances and "ladders" were dubbed "insectograms"; where fish- and dolphin-like designs appeared, and fluent script-like "curligrams." All but a few were beautifully formed. These were ascribed to hoaxers imitating the circle-makers, whoever and whatever they were.[8]

The fields thronged with believers in a supernatural cause and skeptics who did not. Ufologists jostled Japanese camera crews, American and

German tourists got in the way of dowsers who claimed that their rods went mad inside the circles. Instances of healing were announced; others claimed feelings of nausea, headaches, etc. Ordinary respectable citizens became obsessed with the circles; some of them developed mediumistic powers, "channeling" dire warnings from the "circle-makers" about the imminent ecological collapse of the world. Strange trilling noises were heard (and recorded in one case by the BBC) in the circles' vicinity.[9] Was it the rare grasshopper warbler or something rarer still? Two German students filmed an odd white sphere, the size of a football, which skimmed and swam through the ears of corn before diving out of sight.[10] In short, all the suspect usuals were in evidence...

Then, in September 1991, just as nearly all the circles had been harvested, two elderly men called Dave Chorley and Doug Bower stepped forward and claimed to have made most of the Hampshire circles over the last thirteen years, and no fewer than 200 in all. They remained cagey about which they had specifically made, and neither did their rudimentary tools — a plank, ball of string, and baseball cap from which depended a crystal "sight" — look very promising. But they made an "insectogram" at Ightham,

Figure 8. Another crop circle picture from Wiltshire. This one was seen on Milk Hill in 2001. (*Fortean Picture Library*)

near Sevenoaks, Kent, well enough to fool one of the crop circle gurus, who had been inveigled by *Today* newspaper into authenticating it. The subsequent article led, in the popular mind at least, to a widespread discrediting of crop circle "experts" and to the highlighting of Doug and Dave's hoaxes.[11] Once again the mystery was solved.

Crop circle enthusiasts, badly shaken at first, began to rally. Doug and Dave's demonstration hoax circle proved, on closer inspection, to be rough and ready, not at all like the "real thing." Suspicions arose that their effort had been a put-up job — by the press or Government or army, or worse. Disinformation abounded. The truth, as ever, receded into a cloud of accusations and counter-accusations, of half-truths and unsubstantiated stories. Meaden retreated, doubting now that plasma vortices could produce any but the simplest of circles. The rest, he said, were hoaxes. But others were not so sure: there remained features which still could not be so easily explained.

There were, for instance, the "grapeshot" circles, only two or three feet across, but perfectly swirled and scattered around the large formations with

Figure 9. A picture showing two grapeshot formations. This one is from Beckhampton, Wiltshire, 1989. (*Fortean Picture Library*)

seemingly no evidence of human or mechanical access. There were rings so narrow that they were faintly visible only from the air; the swelling of nodes on cornstalks within circles; malformation of grain; the number of circles appearing on the same night in different places within sight of busy roads, but with no hoaxers seen. On 28 June 1991, crop-watchers sealed off a field at Morgan's Hill with a battery of infrared cameras, radar, directional mikes, and anti-intruder alarms. Nothing could move undetected in that field — and yet, when the mist lifted in the morning, a small witty "dumb-bell" formation was revealed.[12] Above all, perhaps, there were the unquantifiable effects of the circles, common to contact with all anomalies, on those who had visited them: a sense of awe, strange symptoms, mystical experiences, odd sights and sounds — the aura of enchantment. The jury, it seems is still out in the case of the crop circles.

Causality and synchronicity

The phenomenology of crop circles entitles us to call them daimonic events. The only reason for balking at this description of them is that, far from being elusive and ephemeral like other daimons, they are indisputably *there*. We can measure, analyze, examine, and photograph them to our heart's content. But then, horrors, we find that instead of coming closer to unraveling the cause of them, we are sucked into a maelstrom of conflicting theories, arguments, and contradictions. The more we look into them the more elusive they become. They are as maddening as those daimonic traces — UFO "landing marks," Bigfoot's prints, scorched cars — which, we feel, must have something *behind* them but we can never discover precisely what.

Daimons commonly ignore those laws which constitute the pillars of the Newtonian world we inhabit: time, space, and matter. Crop circles obey these laws and so we have all the more reason to believe they obey the fourth: causality. We feel there must be some natural (e.g. meteorological) or human (hoax) cause of crop circles. Failing these, we turn to unnatural, or supernatural, causes such as UFOs or fairies. But since we cannot think in causal terms without thinking of a mechanism, which in turn depends on materiality, we have to imagine the fairies as physically exerting force on the ears of corn. Or we have to imagine the UFOs, as spacecraft, physically imprinting the corn or creating the circles with "rays."

There is much talk of rays and energies in crop circles. "Microwaves" emitted by secret military experiments, "rays" beamed down by aliens, mysterious "earth energies" which surge up and suck the crop down, and so on — they are all attempts to imagine a cause which is not quite material but is able to act as a mechanism. They are all attempts, that is, to bridge the age-old gap between spirit and matter, between the invisible and the visible — which is precisely the function of daimons, mediating as they do between this world and some other, between men and gods. "Rays" and "energies" are more or less materialistic metaphors for daimonic power.

In order to make the spiritual and the material worlds *continuous,* daimons are often mythically depicted as comprising a long chain stretching between gods and men. But no matter how many links are added to the chain, making the spiritual ever grosser, the material ever more attenuated, there is always a point of *discontinuity* at which the spiritual ceases to be spiritual and becomes material, and vice versa. This problem bedeviled the early theological debates about the nature of Christ: if he was God, he could not be man. Therefore he had to be a pure spirit who took on the appearance of a man. Conversely, if he was a man, he could not be God, and so he must be a good man who was divinely inspired. Both such views were declared heretical at the Council of Nicaea (325), which, to its credit, proclaimed the impossible, the daimonic dogma: Jesus Christ was both man and God. It asserted the centrality of paradox. And not the least of the daimons' paradoxes is that they are simultaneously continuous and discontinuous with this world.

Jung addressed the problem of daimonic events and causality with his concept of *synchronicity,* which he defined as an "acausal connecting principle."[13] An inner psychic event and an outer physical one could be connected by *meaning.* An example of such meaningful coincidences was provided by F. C. "Busty" Taylor, an aerial photographer of crop circles, who, flying over a field, was thinking about a recent "quintuplet" of circles and musing that it would be jolly if the satellite circles were to be joined by a ring to form a kind of Celtic cross. When he flew over the same field the next day, he found that exactly this formation had appeared, as if his wish had been granted. Such synchronistic occurrences are commonplace in the enchanted realm of anomaly research. (In extreme cases they get out of hand, occurring all the time, until everything seems laden with cosmic significance and paranoid delusions set in.)

Jung was able to abandon the mechanism of causation but could not quite bring himself to ditch causality altogether (he saw himself, after all, as a scientist). "Behind" synchronistic events there was, he said, an archetype which splits into two halves, one psychic, the other physical — an archetype, in other words, which, if it does not exactly *cause* the coincidence, at least "organizes" it.[14] A faint whiff of mechanism remains, doubtless because Jung still divides the world into outer and inner. He has not yet reached the imaginative, unified view of a world in which physical events simply have an inner meaning, as naturally as trees have their dryads, or in which psychic events such as dreams, images, and ideas have outer physical counterparts. Despite working on synchronicity with the nuclear physicist, Wolfgang Pauli, Jung did not see that daimonic events such as crop circles are to the ordinary world what quantum events are to the subatomic world — spontaneous, autonomous, and uncaused. They just *are*.

The idea towards which Jung was striving with his concept of synchronicity goes back at least to the Neoplatonists who were able to abandon causality and replace it with the "law" of *sympathy*.[15] This was expressed in two metaphors. The first, drawn from the model of the sun, said that the physical emanates from the spiritual as heat and light radiate from the sun. The second, drawn from music, said that the physical reflects the spiritual as the strings of a musical instrument resonate in harmony with another set of strings. Thomas Taylor puts it elegantly: "So in the universe, there is one harmony though composed from contraries, since they are at the same time similar and allied to each other. For from the soul of the world, like an immortal self-motive lyre, life everywhere resounds..."[16] This metaphor has been revived in recent years by the biologist Rupert Sheldrake and his principle of "morphic resonance."[17] The first metaphor (radiation, emanation) lies behind all the fantasies of mysterious "energies," "cosmic rays," and "alien beams" which are said to cause crop circles.

Sympathy and analogy

Most daimonic events are contradictory, both physical and spiritual, for example. As Jung said of his archetypes, they contain their own opposites. At first sight crop circles appear to be unequivocal because they are purely physical. However, on closer inspection, they are just as equivocal as all daimonic events: no one can agree on their nature or provenance; passions run high among materialists and mystics alike. The spiritual or immaterial aspect of crop circles manifests in the psychic response of the people who engage with them — in all the images, masquerading as explanations, theories, hypotheses, etc., that the circles provoke. They are not apparently contradictory in themselves, as UFOs are, say, or fairies; the contradictions are inherent in the human reaction to them, synchronistically.

If we are to understand crop circles — and this applies to all apparitions — we have to approach them in a Neoplatonic, *sympathetic* way. I suggested earlier that apparitions could be viewed as different manifestations of each other — that lights in the sky were alternative manifestations of fairies, for example, or that aliens were personifications, rather than occupants, of UFOs. It may equally be said that the putative supernatural causes of crop circles, among which fairies and UFOs are prominent, are really alternative manifestations of them; or rather, that crop circles are an impersonal manifestation of those personifications we call fairies or, as it were, solidified versions of those fluid phenomena we call UFOs.

However, none of this is strictly true: each image, each apparition is separate and cannot be identified with another. Instead, it is more accurate to regard them as analogous to each other. Thus, for instance: lights in the sky are to fairies as aerial is to terrestrial as impersonal is to personified. (This is formulaically expressed as lights in the sky : fairies :: aerial : terrestrial :: impersonal : personified.)

Or, fairies : aliens :: terrestrial : extraterrestrial.

Similarly, UFOs : lake monsters :: air : water.

But lake monsters : black dogs :: water : earth.

At once we can see a relationship between UFOs and crop circles:

UFOs : crop circles :: sky : Earth :: fluid : solid.

An alchemist would express it better perhaps as:

UFOs : crop circles :: Above : Below :: volatile : fixed.

Now, if you will bear with me, I will try and show that the "causes" of crop circles are images which are not only analogous to each other but which mediate between each other — and they include even the alleged natural causes. We will see that the true value of Dr. Meaden's plasma vortex is *not* as a scientific hypothesis but that it fills an imaginative gap in crop circle folklore. And this idea may be extended to all scientific "explanations" of daimonic phenomena (which, by definition, cannot be *explained*).

As we have seen, the hypothetical plasma vortex is a sophisticated version — a close relation — of the whirlwind. But whirlwinds are tricky. From the smallest eddy of air (to which the Irish used to doff their hats), to little Scottish whirlwinds by which fairies travel (according to Sir Walter Scott), to the full-blown affair, perceived as a wild rout led by a horned demon, maddening anyone in its path, whirlwinds have been immemorially associated with fairies.[18] The latter are, as it were, the inner meaning of whirlwinds, both equally capricious and unpredictable.

Even gods do not disdain to appear as whirlwinds, like the one Jehovah spoke out of to Job. Whirlwinds, then, can be said to mediate between plasma vortices and fairies, sharing characteristics with both. But fairies are also related to UFOs through their manifestation as aerial lights and through their family resemblance to UFO entities. So fairies can be said to mediate between whirlwinds and UFOs. In order to complete the circle, a mediator between UFOs and whirlwinds is needed — and plasma vortices are just the ticket. They are "whirlwinds" which are brightly lit and highly elusive aerial phenomena.

Theories of crop circles causation are therefore not isolated and competing; they are variations of each other, forming a kind of nexus of images which represent the imaginative attempt to reconcile by analogy such contradictions as natural/supernatural, aerial/terrestrial, and so on. For convenience, these contraries can be drawn up on the horizontal and vertical axes of a circular scheme as shown in Figure 10.

Daimons cannot be caught in a diagram, it's only for fun. But I can imagine other schemes in which, for instance, fairies, hoaxers, witches, and animals mediate between each other, falling under the rubric of such contradictions as human/inhuman, trickster/non-trickster, etc. Nor are crop circles necessarily central to the schemes. They can easily be moved to the periphery, relating to their opposite through a different set of contradictions, while one of the other phenomena takes center place.

I have lingered over crop circles (and will linger longer) because of the opportunity they provide to muse on daimonic phenomena generally. One of the main points of interest to emerge from a consideration of crop circle causation is that crop circles might be tailor-made to discredit the very notion of causation itself. The daimonic realm does not recognize, let alone obey, the laws on which the mechanistic and materialistic version of the

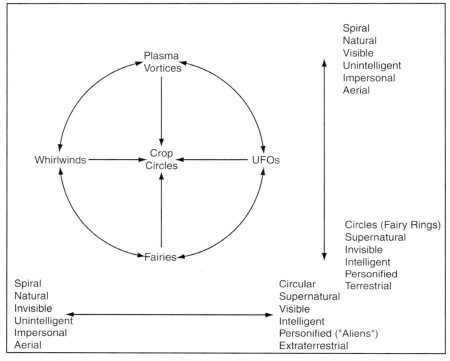

Figure 10. The connections between the possible causes of crop circles.

world is based.

It does not surprise us that apparitions and visions should have something in common, since they are all grounded in that great unknowable mythopoeic phenomenon variously called the collective unconscious, Soul of the World, and Imagination. What is surprising is that it looks as though such daimons and daimonic events are related to each other in a specific way: they seemed at first to merge and overlap with each other, but now we see that they are better described as analogical *variants* of each other. Even the hypotheses which set out to explain them — including the naturalistic and scientific ones — turn out to be variants of the daimonic event under analysis. To "explain" UFOs as plasma vortices is to say no more than that fairies are fallen angels. Thus a comparison of apparitions, while it can tell us nothing about Imagination in itself, might tell us something of its structure and mode of operation.

12

Structures

The structure of Imagination

My attempt to show how daimonic events, and the theories surrounding them, are analogically related owes a lot, of course, to structural anthropology, an approach pioneered by Claude Lévi-Strauss. In his four volumes of *Mythologiques,* he traces the development and interrelation of hundreds upon hundreds of myths all across the Americas. He wants to show "how myths think themselves out in men and without men's knowledge" ("...*comment les mythes se pensent dans les hommes et à leur insu*").[1] But his choice of the word *penser,* thinking, is not the best or most accurate word for describing the mythopoeic faculty of the human soul. He would have done better to say that myths *imagine* themselves in men without their knowledge...

However, whatever Lévi-Strauss's critics say, and whatever reservations I have about the details of his work (and about the application of structural analysis to fields outside anthropology), for my purposes here I want to draw attention to features of his method which have an important bearing on the daimonic realm.

First of all, Lévi-Strauss's studies of myth show that "what tend to change over time are the specific personnel or individual events; what remains constant is the relationship between one character or event and another, in short, the whole character of the tale. It makes little difference whether a myth is overtly about a young girl disobeying her mother, or a grandmother poisoning her grandson — the structure remains unchanged and is related to a conflict about generations, ultimately to its mythical resolution."[2] The elements that go to make up a myth do not have a fixed value, so to speak — what is significant is the underlying relationship between the myth's elements — its overt subjects — rather than the elements themselves. This can be shown, in a modest way, by considering the way "aliens" shift in value according to their context and relationship with other images, even reversing their value altogether:

aliens : UFOs :: personified : impersonal; but, aliens : humans :: impersonal : persons. Or, aliens : fairies :: extraterrestrial : terrestrial; but, aliens : UFOs :: terrestrial : aerial.

As the last quotation says, neighboring myths tend to be variants of each other. Superficially they may appear to bear no resemblance to each other, but when the structure is separated from the contents, they are seen to be akin but transformed according to certain archetypal rules, it seems, of symmetry, inversion, opposition, and so on. It would take too long to demonstrate these rules, requiring the structural analysis of several myths, but to give the flavor of them we can consider two brief myths of mankind's origins.

The first myth is devolutionary. It describes how we are descended from gods or god-like ancestors and our present state is fallen, a regression from the perfection of the past. We are inferior to our forebears.

The second myth is evolutionary. It describes how we have evolved from animals (apes) and our present state is advanced, a progress from the imperfection of the past. We are superior to our forebears.

We are used to calling the second myth history and fact. It is surprising to see that it is directly analogous to the first but with, as it were, all the signs reversed. We usually think of the second myth as having *replaced* the first, whereas it is simply an inverted version.

Although the second myth (or theory of Evolution) is opposed to the Biblical myth (Adam and Eve), it shares two important features with the Christian myth — it could, in fact, only have arisen in a Christian society. Firstly, it literalizes itself. Just as Darwin literalized the mythical ancestors into actual apes (or "hominids," daimonic creatures if ever I saw one!), so Christianity literalizes God into an actual man. (In all other cultures, gods appear among men — but never literally.) Secondly, it projects itself as intrinsically superior to, and truer than, other myths. Just as Evolutionists claim that their theory supersedes all other theories of man's origins, including the Biblical myth, so Christianity claims that it has superseded all other myths and religions. Whereas a religion like Hinduism recognizes and can accommodate other religions, Christianity outlaws them. They become heresies. But Christianity can be seen as a variant of such heresies. For example, the Christian doctrine that God descended into manhood to save corrupt men is an inverted version of the Gnostic doctrine that corrupt men have to ascend to the Godhead to save themselves. Christianity even contains opposite and inverted myths within itself: the beliefs surrounding the Virgin Mary are an example. Arising spontaneously among believers, it is as if they are trying to redress the imbalance caused by too great a concentration on a masculine God. At any rate, the following sets of analogies might be suggestive:

Christ : Mary :: male god : female human :: father : daughter :: immortal (bodily Resurrection) : mortal.

But, Jesus : the blessed Virgin :: man : goddess :: son : mother :: mortal (crucified) : immortal (bodily Assumption).

What is true of myths is also true of folklore, legend, speculation, theorizing — that they are variants of each other. So too are daimons. I have already mentioned that while apparitions of black dogs seem on the surface to be different from those of white ladies, there are considerable resemblances — both haunt the same specific locations, both presage death, both are part of fairy lore. They are analogous to each other (dogs : ladies :: black : white :: animal : human!). There may even be a connection between two such apparently disparate anomalies as crop circles and cattle mutilations. The latter is one of the nastiest mysteries around: thousands of cows, sheep, dogs, and horses have been drained of blood and had specific parts of their carcasses expertly removed — tongues, ears, sex organs. There are no traces or footprints around the bodies. No blood is spilled. UFOs and phantom helicopters are seen in the vicinity. So are Bigfeet. These are variously blamed for the slaughter. Other suspects range from vampires to secret cults of devil-worshippers. The mutilations probably peaked in America in the 1970s (175 were reported in twenty-one Colorado counties during four months in 1975); but they have been reported over the last 200 years and in countries as far apart as Sweden and Australia.[3] Can we say something like:

Crop circles : cattle mutilations :: vegetable : animal :: cultivation : stockbreeding :: benevolent : malevolent :: practical jokes : sinister plots :: Essex (England) : Midwest (America)?

At any rate, what Imagination does is to run through all the permutations of a given mythology. The structural elements remain more or less constant but they change in value and meaning in relation to each other, forming different patterns, producing different apparitions, telling different stories — just like the colored fragments in a kaleidoscope. (This is as true for the individual world of dreams as it is for the collective world of mythology. Jung approached this insight when he said that the unconscious acts in a *compensatory* way towards consciousness. In fact, dreams often simply take elements of our waking lives and reverse the relationships between them. Dreams, as it were, supply those permutations of our individual "myths" which consciousness excludes or ignores.)

Nature vs. Culture

What is Imagination up to? According to Lévi-Strauss, the aim of myths is to reconcile the fundamental contradictions by which our lives are rent, notably the contradiction between Nature and Culture. We have seen how the causal "explanations" of daimonic events such as crop circles are simply further daimons, and that includes scientific explanations. In other words, they are not explanations at all, but images — myths — posing as explanations. The sum total of the images surrounding crop circles — explanations, meanings, associations, allied phenomena, folklore, etc. — contributes to a body of crop circle "mythology" which, as my diagram suggested, is concerned with reconciling imaginatively such contradictions as natural/supernatural, spiritual/physical, visible/invisible, and so on. (In a sense these can be subsumed under the general contradiction continuity/discontinuity with which the argument started.)

But all contradictions remain, finally, irreconcilable. There can be no final mythical resolution any more than there is a primordial myth behind the variants. There can only be more, and more elaborate, variants. Some ufologists have seen a sort of development in daimonic manifestation from fairies to UFOs and aliens to crop circles. But historical chronology does not strictly apply to the daimonic realm. Each of these manifestations can happily co-exist and, indeed, feed into each other. It's just that, perhaps, one or another of them becomes fashionable, takes center stage as the imagination of the age dictates. The same myths can recur, as the recent spate of "gray" aliens (I am coming to these) repeats the 1940s' tales of "deros," or they can appear in different, variant forms. Fairies are often (mistakenly) thought to have died out, and it is true that they no longer enjoy their old prominence — in their original form, that is. But of course they are still present in other forms, in UFO and crop circle lore. UFOs themselves come and go in waves and the nature of aliens changes. Crop circles will doubtless peter out, only to be replaced by another, equally unlooked-for daimonic phenomenon. This will be hailed as new, and new explanations will be proffered as absolute truths. But it will not be new, and the explanations will not explain. Truth does not lie with this image or that but in the process of imagining; it is not an absolute but a way, transforming us *en route*.

We cannot know, therefore, what crop circles are or where they come from; we can only imagine and mythologize. We are entitled to wonder why the daimonic realm chooses to manifest in this particular way at this particular time — why *this* variant when so many others are possible. One of the most popular suggestions, for instance, is that crop circles are messages from Mother Earth (Dame Kind, Gaia, etc.) about ecological matters. They are a kind of cosmic graffiti signaling Nature's distress at being treated with pesticides and generally being polluted. I doubt that the message is that specific — and, besides, there are plenty of entities who are appearing to say as much in plain English. Crop circles are more enigmatic. Like most daimons, they do not bear messages — they are themselves the message. Circles, of course, are intrinsically evocative; they remind us of Jung's mandalas which, often appearing at moments of crisis in the psyche, are "attempts at self-healing." The native motion of the soul, according to Plotinus, is circular.[4]

Plotinus, perhaps the greatest of the Neoplatonists, also reminds us that "the configurations of the soul need containers."[5] Specifically he meant altars, shrines, and statues — vessels in which the daimons could be comfortably entertained and expressed and where men could encounter archetypal configurations, that is, gods. Examples of such shrines include the tumuli, barrows, stone circles, megaliths, and circular graveyards of places like Wessex. These daimonic places, superseded by churches and, latterly, by secular shrines such as power stations, fail to recognize the daimons who therefore have to provide their own shrines. Crop circles are perhaps their own shrines, as are the "spacecraft" containing "aliens."

Lévi-Strauss's Nature-versus-Culture is a fundamental contradiction, other metaphors for which are Consciousness v. the Unconscious (psychology) and Wilderness v. Habitat (anthropology). In the days when Wessex was a wilderness, congruent with the Unconscious and encroaching on man's frail conscious habitat, shrines were built in the wilderness. Half natural, conforming to the landscape, and half cultural, they were daimonic places where the supernatural could make its presence felt. Now that Wessex is tamed, the shrines mere obstacles in the tractor's path, the exiled daimons return by way of their own artifacts — crop circles — which are neither wholly natural, nor man-made, nor supernatural, but all three (according to the variety of competing theories). They no longer reconcile Nature to Culture, but heighten the tension between them. Like the incursion of mystery cats into civilized Surrey, crop circles re-introduce a kind of wilderness, the Unknown, to an over-cultured landscape and so return Culture to a Nature raised, as it were, to the second power.

Literalism as idolatry

We may also wonder, above all perhaps, why a daimonic event manifests itself so concretely. Crop circles are so much *there* that we find it hard to believe that it is daimonic at all — until we search deeply for a cause: then, animals, helicopters, hoaxes, UFOs, whirlwinds, earth energies...none of these are there when we need them. And yet we feel they *must* be there, just as we feel that spacecraft must be there when we find "landing traces" after a UFO sighting, or that Yetis are there when we find their footprints in the snow. Their daimonic signatures insist on the reality of their authors, but we find that the reality is paradoxical, metaphorical, poetic, symbolic, mythic. It is a daimonic, not a *literal* reality.

I have said this before and will doubtless say it again, if only because I don't know how else to put it. Literalism quite simply presents the greatest stumbling block to our understanding of apparitions and visions. It is especially evident when the apparition in question is something as physical as a crop circle. But to endow everything physical with only a literal reality is a folly to which our age is particularly prone. In fact, nothing physical is only literal. Imagination transfigures everything; soul is transparent to everything; "Everything that lives is holy." If we but cultivate "double vision," seeing through the eye instead of only with it, every object is informed with shining intelligence.

Literalism leads to idolatry.[6] Idolatry has traditionally meant the worship of false images, but actually it is the false worship of images (there are no false images). To treat our images — ideas, beliefs, theories of causality — as ends instead of means, as absolute instead of relative, is to become petrified in literal-mindedness and to obstruct the free play of Imagination essential for the soul's health. We become dogmatic, and even fanatical.[7] We become "fundamentalists" — Christians who treat Biblical myths and spiritual truths as historical facts and literal instructions; ufologists who insist on the literal existence of aliens from other planets; materialists who believe in the sole literal reality of matter; crypto-zoologists who believe that lake monsters are literal creatures; scientists who believe in the literal truth of their paradigms and hypotheses. All these people are united in reviling the daimonic.

It is to our discredit that in order to draw attention to their reality, the daimons have been compelled to become physical and fixed, like crop circles. By masquerading as — by parodying — literal facts, they answer our modern requirement for quantifiable effects besides which everything else is deemed illusory. In other words, their way of presenting their own metaphorical, mythical reality is to appear *not* as literal, but *as if* they were literal.

Hoaxes

To finish my prolonged musings on crop circles, I want to go back to the beginning and consider hoaxes, which have emerged as the only plausible non-paranormal "explanation." For perhaps the majority of the population — certainly for the majority of newspapers — hoaxes are the solution to the "mystery" of crop circles. However, as William James reminds us, imposture is always imitative. Just as "one swindler imitates a previous swindler, but the first swindler of that kind imitated someone who was honest," so it seems likely that hoaxers need "real" crop circles to copy. "You can no more create an absolutely new trick than you can create a new word without any previous basis. You do not know how to go about it."[8] Also there remain features of the circles, which, as I mentioned earlier, seem extraordinarily difficult, if not impossible, to fabricate. There *are* formations, of course, which have been man-made. These are usually distinguishable from "genuine" circles by their ineptitude — but not always. The same disputes occur over crop circles as occur over paintings which may or may not be forgeries. Experienced crop circle enthusiasts can often only authenticate a formation by its "feel" — real ones, they say, look as if they have been laid down by a single sweep of some artist's brush-stroke; hoaxes are almost too carefully perpetrated, too well-trampled, too mechanical.

This was a criticism leveled at all the competitors in a Grand Hoaxing Contest held at West Wycombe in August 1992. The aim was to discover just how good hoaxes could be. A complicated set pattern, incorporating many features seen in previous crop circles, was attempted by twelve teams. Some of the teams reproduced some of the features near-perfectly; no team reproduced them all. Even the winning team's effort, the five judges claimed, would not be mistaken for the "real thing." The experiment, then, was officially pronounced "inconclusive."[9]

Charges of fakery, lies, and hoaxing are leveled at all paranormal phenomena. I touched on this earlier in relation to Spiritualism. It is nowhere more true than in ufology, where debates run for decades about whether "contactees" really contacted aliens or whether they were lying. I suspect that, reality being what it is, they themselves don't know half the time. In other words, I prefer to see hoaxing as a daimonic quality inherent in, and continuous with, anomalous events — which are neither "genuine" nor "fake" but, in a deeper sense, *both*. To understand crop circles, then — and to some extent all anomalies — we need to grasp the complexity of hoaxes; and I would like to start somewhat at a distance by considering the relationship between daimons and gods.

Daimons and gods

Proclus tells us: "For many genera are hurled forth before the Gods, some of a daemonic and others of an angelic order, who terrify those that are excited to a participation of divination, who are exercised for the reception of divine light, and are sublimely elevated to the union of the Gods." (We note in passing that being scared witless is not necessarily a bad thing.) "But we may especially perceive the alliance of those fables [i.e., myths] with the tribe of daemons, whose energies manifest many things symbolically, as those know who have met with daemons when awake, or have enjoyed their inspirations in dreams, unfolding many past or future events."[10]

Proclus is writing here about the procedure attendant upon the Mysteries into which it was customary for the Hellenic intelligentsia to be initiated. The point which most concerns us is made more clearly in his commentary on the *First Alcibiades,* attributed to Plato, where he says that "in the most holy of the mysteries, before the God appears, certain terrestrial daemons present themselves...," and "about every God there is an innumerable multitude of daemons, who have the same appellations with their leaders...because they express in themselves the characteristic peculiarity of their leading God."[11]

Thus the daimons are like the preceding train of the greater gods, in whose nature they participate. Iamblichus distinguishes between "the ruling nature of the gods" and "the ministrant nature of daimons" who "put into operation that which the gods perceive, wish and command."[12] In another sense, says Proclus, the daimons can be seen as different forms of the same God; or they are appearances of the Gods who are in themselves "formless and unfigured."[13] This recalls Jung's archetypes which cannot be known in themselves; they can only be known through the archetypal images they assume. More recently, James Hillman has reminded us that "a God is a manner of existence, an attitude towards existence, and a set of ideas."[14]

In the light of these views concerning the relationship of the daimons to the gods, we may ask what god is behind crop circles — not behind in the sense of a literal cause, but in the sense of their archetypal background.

Demeter, goddess of fields and growing crops, is a good candidate. More fashionable is Gaia, who guards the earth just below Demeter's domain; she is the goddess of place and of the rituals that generate fertility. However, deities never come quite alone, unless it is their nature to be monomaniac like Jehovah. They are related to one another by blood or marriage. Both Gaia and Demeter are linked to the cold, infertile mineral depths of the Earth — the former through *chthon,* that shadowy quasi-deity who signifies the depths and the world of the dead (Gaia-*chthonia* was worshipped in Mykonos); the latter through her daughter Persephone, who was abducted by Hades, god of the Underworld.[15] Crop circles might be regarded as daimonic zones, sacred precincts, where Demeter–Gaia–*chthon* overlap, where green growing life is connected to black inert death. Yet, as circles in the ripe golden corn, crop circles are also emblems of solar deities such as Phoebos Apollo, perhaps, who presses down lovingly on Mother

Earth. Thus they connect the depths to the surface and the surface to the heights; they are symbols of middle earth, mediating between the sky world and the Underworld.

The Trickster god

Deities like Gaia and Apollo certainly play a part in crop circle mythology, providing the background to their latest New Age incarnations, "Energy" and "Higher Consciousness" — vague passionless abstractions which do scant justice to the precision and power of their prototypes. But I suspect that the god whose hand can be discerned in crop circles is the god who lies behind all anomalous events, whose very nature is to be more daimonic than the other gods because he scurries on winged sandals between the Olympic pantheon and Earth, bearing messages to the world of men. I mean Hermes.

Hermes is especially important for our culture, which has fallen increasingly under the aegis of Apollo, the archetypal principle behind consciousness, masculine detachment, rationality, clarity, purity of purpose, and so on.[16] Apollo is the god of Science. Hermes is his brother and a thorn in his side. He constantly subverts Apollo, stealing his cattle for instance (and mutilating them — he turns their legs around!) and then lying his way out.[17] I am reminded of an East African tribal saying, that although God is good and wishes good for everybody, unfortunately He has a half-witted brother who is always interfering with what He does.[18] But although Hermes may play the fool, he is fiercely intelligent. As the inventor of writing, he is the god of communication, wisdom, hermeneutics. But his communications can also be deceptions. Pompous high-flown Apollonic prophecies are hijacked by Hermes, who twists them and sows them with absurdities and untruths, seeking to restrain the single-minded, upward-striving flights of the spirit with the slow, ambiguous, downward-moving reflectiveness of soul.[19] His deceptions can, like Art, be dressings-up which entice us into a deeper truth. He misleads us, but often for our own good, leading us out of our ideas of truth — out of literalism, for instance — and into the tricky paradoxical twilight of the daimonic realm. Not for nothing is he venerated as the god of borders and crossroads where different realities intersect.

Like Coyote, Raven, and Hare — those North American Indian clowns-cum-culture-heroes — Hermes is a Trickster.[20] It is as difficult for us to countenance Tricksters as it is daimons: our monotheism, whether of Christianity or Science, has excluded them. So Hermes is forced to operate from the Underworld, to shadow Christianity in esoteric, "occult" Gnostic and Hermetic philosophies. As his Latin counterpart, Mercurius, he is the soul of alchemy. He returns to torment scientism with paranormal phenomena and maddening anomalies — *all* daimons are tricksters, as the fairies are; all are in the pay of Hermes–Mercurius. He unsettles our lives with all manner of impish tricks and pixilations; the more we ignore him, the more he bedevils us, until his tricks begin to look sinister. He becomes, in fact, the Devil.

The ancient Greeks were wise to keep Hermes in their pantheon, where the other gods could keep an eye on him. Similarly, the Norse gods tolerated Loki, "forger of evil," "slanderer and cheat of the gods,"[21] father of Hel (ruler of the dead), despite the fact that they knew he would lead the forces of destruction against them at Ragnarok, the "twilight of the gods." In Hindu mythology, Krishna displayed the full range of Trickster behavior, especially shape-shifting. Like the "little people," he was not above spiriting away the pots of curds while the milkmaids slept, stealing butter, and knocking things off high shelves;[22] and yet at the same time he can declare in ringing tones reminiscent of the alchemical Mercurius: "I am the Self, seated in the hearts of all creatures. I am the beginning, the middle and the end of all beings."[23]

Hermes–Mercurius is the god of hoaxes. A hoax aims to expose some flaw in society. For example, there are people (they may not be people — I'll come to that) who pass themselves off as social workers and knock at doors, asking to examine children. At a pinch this could be both comic and moral — as a satire, for instance, on a society which has become depersonalized, allowing bureaucracies to hinder right relationships. But if these people look as though they are out to molest or harm the children, the hoax becomes criminal and even diabolical. There is a sinister aspect to all hoaxers. They like to play god behind the scenes.[24]

Crop circles may or may not be hoaxes, but they are certainly *like* hoaxes in that they draw attention to our wrong relationship to Nature and mock our methods of investigation. Their perpetrators are like practical jokers whose satisfaction lies in seeing the look on the faces of those they have duped when the truth is unmasked. If crop circle hoaxers were asked why they did it, they might reply: "We wanted to bring self-knowledge to all the scientists and cranks who have a fantastic idea of themselves; to deflate their self-importance and de-intoxicate them from their illusions."[25]

Actually, apart from the fact that no hoaxers have stepped forward to claim the majority of crop circles, hoaxers often do not know why they did it. When asked, they shrug and say something like: "We did it for the hell of it." In a sense they are victims of their own hoax. While they were playing god, a god was playing with them — the arch-hoaxer Hermes, the devil who gets into all of us at times. Who knows whether the crop circles were perpetrated directly by Hermes or by him through the agency of human hoaxers behaving daimonically? (Personally, I suspect one of Mercurius's country cousins, Robin Goodfellow, who has traditionally been up to mischief in the countryside for centuries.)

Hermes–Mercurius does not unmask. He needs no satisfaction from the look on our faces. He forces us to unmask ourselves in the face of his emissaries — enigmatic marks on the cornfields, big-eyed aliens who abduct us into spacecraft, "frustrators" who dictate gibberish through automatic writing, entities whose revelations are delusions and whose delusions, if we persist in them, can lead to revelation. He manipulates us, knows our every thought — knows us better than we know ourselves. He is secretive, ruthless, impersonal, and inhuman. Like a psychopath. Like a god. He is less the Devil than Lucifer, who deceives both in order to destroy and in order to bring light. If we do not know ourselves — that is, know, discern, heed our daimons and demons — we are easy meat.

13

The Otherworld

Spatial metaphors

There are too many theories about the nature and origins of UFOs to enumerate, so I will only mention some of the more popular ones. UFOs are:

— Spacecraft built by the denizens of distant planets.
— Craft built by a superior race living inside the Earth, which is hollow.
— Craft built by humans or aliens in secret bases on the Earth's surface.
— Craft which have been developed by humans in the future and are traveling back in time.
— Craft which come from "other dimensions."
— Products of a subterranean "earth energy" which interacts with our psyches so that we perceive them as structured craft.
— "Purely psychological" projections of the unconscious mind.

While the proponents of all these separate theories are at loggerheads with each other, we are now in a position to see that, in one respect at least, they are strikingly similar: they are all literal readings of spatial metaphors. Each theory can be characterized by a preposition of place — UFOs come from beyond, inside, outside, next to, above, below, within, etc. Like crop circle theories, each theory is, of course, related to every other by analogy. For example: extraterrestrial theory : unconscious projection theory :: outer space : inner space :: physical : mental; but, extraterrestrial theory : "earth energy" theory :: above : below :: material : immaterial.

What I want to emphasize here is that Imagination always imagines itself spatially. Like my other two models, the collective unconscious and *Anima Mundi,* it is in itself non-spatial, just as it is timeless. Like the traditional definition of God, it is "an intelligible sphere whose center is everywhere and whose circumference is nowhere." But in order to talk about these models at all, we are forced to fall back on spatial metaphors, to talk about realms or domains, worlds or realities, oceanic repositories or storehouses of images. They invite such prepositions as "below" or "behind" — they "underlie" consciousness or "lie behind" our world — because the preferred metaphorical dimension of soul is depth.[1] However, there is a fourth model which is not imagined as being exclusively below, behind, beyond, above, within, etc., but which includes any or all of these dimensions. It is called, quite simply, the Otherworld. This is the usual term for daimonic reality among the folklorists. They employ it metaphorically and this is correct up to a point. However, when they assume that the Otherworld has no reality because it has no literal reality, they are incorrect.

The non-spatiality of the Otherworld is represented by multi-spatiality. It is, so to speak, everywhere and nowhere — and this is what the competing theories of UFO origins express. We have seen already that, in Celtic cultures, views concerning the origins of fairies did not so much compete as they were held simultaneously. The fairies were sometimes said to live underground and sometimes in the air; sometimes under the sea, sometimes on islands out to the West. These places also accommodated the glorious dead. Among the ancient Greeks, the land of the dead was imagined as Hades — underground but vast, and filled with air and light. Their Elysian fields was both an earthly paradise, accessible by sea, and a subterranean heaven, adjoining Hades. In the early centuries AD, the Pythagoreans and Stoics transferred the site of Hades to the air. "The whole air is full of souls," said Alexander Polyhistor, "who are worshipped as daemons and heroes, and it is they who send dreams and omens..."[2]

Hades was demonized by Christianity into Hell, while Heaven was promoted farther away from the living into some remote celestial sphere. For Christians, there was to be no other world anywhere near this one, unless it be some infernal region, and certainly not to the north or west where tribal cultures — the native Americans, for instance — often situated their afterlife paradises. In Norse mythology, Hel and Valhalla — the abodes of the undistinguished dead and the deceased heroes respectively — existed alongside other realms, whether of the gods (Asgard), of the daimons (Alfheim and Iotunheim for elves and giants respectively), or of humans

(Midgard). Here, as in all traditional cultures, the afterlife was conceived less as a place of reward or punishment than as continuous with this life. Indeed, the Otherworld could be entered while in this life, a belief which continued well into the Christian era. Dante, for instance, was pointed out on the streets of Florence, not as the man who had written *The Divine Comedy,* but as the man who had visited Hell.

The Otherworld as temporal

Instead of co-existing with us in some other *place* in the *present,* the Otherworld is sometimes imagined as having existed at some *time* in the *past*. Traditional societies locate the events which were decisive for their culture in the past, in the days of the ancestors or of the gods — *in illo tempore,* as Mircea Eliade says. Whenever the dispensation of a society is replaced by another, through conquest, say, or Christianization, its gods are said to have been vanquished, as if there were a time when they were active in the present but have now been destroyed or rendered obsolete. This is misleading. Gods are rarely thought of as being wholly active in the present; they always belong to a past Golden Age when, walking freely among men, they laid down the customs and laws of a society whose present state has always fallen away from an original perfection.

Analogously, folklorists usually assume that the "fairy faith" in Ireland, for example, has been progressively dying out and is now pretty much defunct. It is certainly true that the fairy faith is less widespread; but, at the same time, it does not do to take informants at their word. More than 1,000 years ago Irish monks were claiming that belief in fairies was on the wane. Peasants in the west of Ireland were saying the same thing 150 years ago. Two generations after that, Evans-Wentz and Lady Gregory found that it was still part of everyday life — although their informants, of course, asserted that the fairy faith had all but disappeared. It is still current today, despite embarrassed protestations to the contrary. In other words, the golden age of fairies, so to speak, has always — like that of the gods — been ascribed to former times. The fairies are always going, going — but never gone.[3]

Imagination, then, often represents itself as a past "before" there was strife, conflict, and contradiction, when gods walked among men in the cool of the day and heaven was still wedded to Earth. This pre-lapsarian state is expressed in myths of Edens and Arcadias which lie behind our nostalgia for the good old days, and for childhoods when things were more innocent, simpler, better. Soul's concern with, and rootedness in, the past is witnessed by psychoanalysis which seeks to uncover the moment in childhood when things went wrong. Jung's collective unconscious, too, is imagined not only as the domain of archetypes, but also as the repository of mankind's past experience, like a kind of race memory.

The reverse myth of the past Arcadia is the future Utopia. Mankind no longer dreams of a return to Eden but of a progression towards the New Jerusalem. This was another consequence of Christianity which re-imagined time altogether: it begins as it were at the birth of Christ (before which event — BC — it goes backwards) and advances inexorably towards the end of the world as we know it and the millennium. This myth lies behind all Utopias, including the dreams of scientism, which envisages a future secular and technocratic golden age. But there is always the reverse side of the coin: the dystopias beloved of science fiction and the prophets of doom. UFO lore contains both sides, pointing to a future when the extraterrestrials land either to conquer and enslave us, or to usher in a glorious new age via their superior technology. They constantly warn us about the consequence of nuclear recklessness or ecological folly. Unlike the fairies who belong in the past and appear only fleetingly in the present, UFOs and their "occupants" appear in the present and belong in the future. They are not, like the fairies, always going but never gone; they are always coming, coming — but never here.

The Otherworld as the Unknown

The Otherworld is always imagined as beginning at the edge of our known world. It can be the wilderness outside the city walls or the unexplored regions at the edge of maps labeled, "Here be dragons." It can begin at the brink of the ocean — or at the garden gate. As the boundaries of the Unknown are pushed back, the world largely mapped, the Otherworld is located in outer space. Early aliens claimed to come from Venus, Mars, or the Moon; later, when these planets seemed more local, less remote, they claimed to come from distant star systems such as Zeta Reticuli or the Pleiades.

Religion sets the boundary of the Unknown at the limits of human life. In traditional cultures, the other world beyond life, after death, is immanent

— another reality contained within this one. In Christianity, it is transcendent, a separate reality removed from Earth. Scientism recognizes no Otherworld, but, as I intimated in my "little history of daimons," daimonic reality has a way of subverting it. Thus scientism constructs its own literal versions of a transcendent and an immanent Otherworld. The former appears in the weird models of the universe articulated by astronomers and cosmologists; the latter appears in the speculations of nuclear physicists.

It is worth lingering a moment over the Otherworld of the nuclear physicists, if only because their discipline is widely held to be the doyen of sciences. They, above all, seek to establish the "facts" of matter. I would maintain, however, that their subatomic realm is merely another variant of daimonic reality. Everything that is predicated of it could, for instance, be applied with equal justice to the land of Fairy. Both worlds invert the cozy Newtonian world we inhabit: laws of time, space, or causality and, of course, matter are ignored. (Once past the "event horizon" of a black hole, say the astrophysicists, time slows to a standstill; or, once inside the black hole, it "runs backwards.") Subatomic physics introduces extra dimensions — "string theory" allows for ten, I think: our four, plus six more, compacted very tightly. Multi-dimensionality is a staple of science fiction and ufology.

The "daimons" of subatomic "inner space" are called particles, although strictly speaking they aren't — electrons, for example, are both particles and waves at the same time. They are paradoxical, both there and not-there, like fairies. Like UFOs they cannot be measured exactly: we can calculate their speed, or their position, but not both. This, roughly, is what Werner Heisenberg called the Uncertainty Principle, and it applies to all daimonic phenomena. We cannot know subatomic particles in themselves; we can only identify them via their daimonic traces. Like minute Yetis, they used to leave tracks in vats of detergent placed at the bottom of mines; nowadays they are more likely to leave their spoor on computer screens linked to particle accelerators.

They tease their investigators mercilessly. Each newly discovered particle promises to be the fundamental building block of matter. First there were atoms; then electrons, protons, neutrons; then quarks, their playful, even Mad Hatterish nature evident in their Lewis Carrollian name. I remember when there were only four quarks, daimonically named Upness,

Downness, Strangeness, and Charm (good names for UFO types). The last
time I looked into them there were more than forty. And counting. Ever
smaller, ever more impish and less substantial — the massless particles —
they recede from us like quasars, those enormous daimons said to be moving
towards the edge of the known universe at speeds close to that of light.

As with all anomalous entities, the very act of observing the particles
disturbs them. Observer and observed, subject and object, cannot finally be
distinguished.[4] Particles whose existence is predicted obligingly turn up. If
we didn't know better, we might almost say that they had been imagined into
existence. The so-called New Physicists smelled a rat long ago. They began
to compare the whole enterprise to oriental religion[5] or to suspect that its
reality is primarily metaphorical, not literal and factual.[6] This is not to say
that daimons cannot manifest concretely, as we have seen. In fact, the
smaller they are, the more powerful they can be, viz. the atom bomb.

Students of the daimonic — Spiritualists, ufologists and so on — excitedly invoke subatomic physics as evidence that other dimensions, other
worlds are possible and real. They are encouraged to believe that one day
their own favorite daimons will be acceptable to Science. But the subatomic
realm is not a literal world of facts from which they can derive support for
the literal reality of their own. It is simply another metaphor for the Soul of
the World. It is not even an especially good one: daimons prefer to appear as
persons, not as impersonal, quirky little particles. The subatomic Otherworld
has its own elegance and a certain stark beauty, as the physicists are keen on
emphasizing; but it is gray and meaningless compared to the world William
Blake saw in a grain of sand. Indeed, while special instruments, such as the
microscope and telescope, extend the quantitative range of perception
beyond ordinary sensory limits, they do not increase its qualitative depth.
They produce an ersatz vision, a shadow of that true imaginative vision
which alone reveals meaning.

The Einsteinian model of the universe — more like a great thought than
a great machine, said Sir James Jeans — reverses the Newtonian model.
They are variants of each other, images of a universe whose final reality can
never be known. The Otherworld mirrors ours. It can be benign, like the
paradises that reverse this world's suffering; or it can be uncanny, like the
realm some tribes ascribe to witches who walk or talk backwards, wear their
heads upside down, their legs back to front.[7] These characteristics are

sometimes attributed to the inhabitants of neighboring villages, reminding us that, to people of imagination, the Otherworld has always been in this one. For such people, to wake is, in a deeper sense, to fall asleep; to die, to live. There may well be an end to this literal world of ours, but there can be no literal end to it because it is continuous with that other world, without end.

Until now I have been dealing with relatively isolated or short-lived apparitions and visions. But I would like to turn to those visions which are no longer single events but whole dramas, and to the people who have journeyed into the Otherworld and returned like the intrepid travelers of old to tell their tales.

Part Three

Otherworld Journeys

"As I was walking among the fires of hell, delighted with the enjoyments of Genius, which to Angels look like torment and insanity, I collected some of their Proverbs…"

(William Blake: "A Memorable Fancy" in *The Marriage of Heaven and Hell*)

14

Missing Time

At the end of Chapter 1 we left John and Elaine Avis (these are pseudo-nyms), together with their three children — Kevin, Karen, and Stuart (aged ten, eleven, and seven) — driving towards their home in Aveley, Essex, one October night in 1974. They had been visiting relatives and were hurrying now to arrive in time to see a play on television. Kevin was the first to see the oval-shaped, pale blue light. He pointed it out to his parents, who thought at first it was an airplane, but decided that it could not be — they had never seen anything like it. The light passed over the car and disappeared behind some trees. As they drove on, they glimpsed it from time to time until it was hidden by bushes. They assumed that the incident was over.[1]

But then they noticed that an uncanny silence presided. They could no longer hear the car's engine, nor the sound of the tires on the road. As they rounded a bend, they drove into a bank of thick green mist. The car radio began to crackle and smoke. John pulled the wires out. The car's engine went dead, and the car jerked violently. Then there was a jolt — and they found themselves driving along the road again. Later, John was to say that when he first emerged from the mist, he had the peculiar impression that he was alone in the front of the car. However, they arrived home without further mishap and, switching on the TV, were surprised to find the screen blank. All the channels seemed to have closed down for the night. It was only when they checked the time that they realized it was after one o'clock in the morning. Having expected to arrive by ten-thirty, it was clear that, somehow, between two and three hours were missing from their lives.

As time passed, the Avises failed to put the event out of their minds. It was constantly being recalled by vivid dreams of unearthly occurrences and weird creatures. Their house was plagued by mild poltergeist-like activity which produced odd bangs and tapping sounds. Their lives were disrupted in other ways too, including a sudden revulsion on the part of all of them, except Stuart, for meat. Elaine could not even go near a butcher's shop, while John felt nauseous every time he smelled meat cooking. Eventually John had a nervous breakdown and lost his job. As a result of a local newspaper article and a local radio program on UFOs, he contacted a UFO research group. Andrew Collins and his colleagues began to investigate, soon enlisting the help of a London dentist, Leonard Wilder, who was proficient at hypnotism. Impressed by the Avises' obvious honesty and reasonableness, they decided to "regress" them through hypnosis in order to uncover whatever had occurred during the period of missing time. Elaine refused to be hypnotized, but she spontaneously remembered, as did John, many details of her otherworld journey. However, the main story emerged during three hypnotic sessions with John.

Later on, I shall be referring here and there to different aspects of the Avises' otherworld journey. For the moment, and before I relate their remarkable tale — we'll have a spot of suspense — I want to touch briefly on three interrelated themes. The first two provide an essential background against which all otherworld journeys should be read; the third — hypnosis — has a special relevance to the modern otherworld journey known as the "UFO abduction."

Remembering and forgetting

Periods of missing time — that is, lapses of memory — are not simply negative counterparts of remembered time. They are important occurrences in their own right, lacunae in the continuity of life which remind us of its depths. It was through the forgotten events in cases of hysteria, through the slips in everyday life, that Freud discovered the unconscious and so initiated depth psychology. Jung followed him down into the Underworld and discovered whole areas of philosophy and psychology — alchemy and Gnosticism, for instance — which had been collectively forgotten, as if history itself had suffered from a lapse of memory. Forgetting what we *think* is important may be a remembering of what *is* important.

In *The Republic* (II, 3), Plato gives an early account of what is now called a near-death experience. He called it the myth of Er, a soldier who was killed in battle but came to life again on his funeral pyre and who described the fate of souls in the Otherworld (which, unlike the Christian afterlife, exists before as well as after life). The souls who are queuing up to be born have first to drink the waters of Lethe, river of Forgetfulness, so that they will not remember anything of their previous existence during their lives in this world. Er was told not to drink in order that he might remember and so be able to remind mankind of the Otherworld and its disposition.

We are accustomed to think of forgetting crucial events as a function of trauma — the victim of a car accident forgets the moment of impact; the abused child represses the memory of its abuse; the "UFO abductee" cannot (at first) recall the horror of the aliens. But we should not overlook the fact that, as in the myth of Er, the injunction to forget is also an intrinsic feature of the Otherworld. In modern near-death experiences, the people who return from the Otherworld frequently speak of having been granted a tremendous revelation which, however, they cannot remember or which they were told they would not remember.[2] Budd Hopkins, who has dealt with hundreds of cases of abductions, remarks that the abductees are either warned not to speak of what has happened to them, or else "a kind of enforced amnesia can efficiently erase from conscious memory all but the very slightest recollections of such experiences."[3]

The idea that in knowing the Otherworld we have somehow tasted forbidden knowledge is an echo of the doctrine, found in Greek and Gnostic philosophy, in Buddhist and Hindu scriptures, that we have forgotten our essential natures. For Plato, knowledge consisted of *anamnesis* — a recollection — of this truth. A Talmudic legend says that a child in the womb learns the Torah backwards and forwards and is shown the secrets of the universe; but, at the instant of birth, an angel strikes it on the mouth to make it forget.

The elasticity of time

The motif of "missing time" is common in folklore. Hartland calls it "the supernatural lapse of time in fairyland."[4] It works in two opposite ways. Usually, those who enter the Otherworld spend what seems like a few minutes or hours there — only to find on their return that weeks or even years have elapsed, as in the Rip van Winkle legend (in the Avis case, hours were lost in the twinkling of an eye). On the other hand, a short period of clock time can seem like an age in the Otherworld. Even to peek into it — as when we watch a UFO, for instance — is to feel that "time is standing still." At the moment of death (or near-death, as survivors tell us) our entire past lives can flash before our eyes in an instant.

These two modes of experiencing time are analogous to sleeping and dreaming. Sleep can be long but seem short; dreams can be short but seem long. But in both cases we enter the Otherworld of the unconscious, regardless of whether we encounter it as unconsciousness or as another kind of consciousness. Thus the Rip-van-Winkle style of visionary encounters the Otherworld as timeless (it is like falling asleep, time passes unnoticed), while the near-death visionary encounters it as eternity (it is like waking to another reality, time stands still).

I might draw a further analogy. There are two situations which appear to be especially propitious for otherworld journeys. The first is driving a car, notably alone at night. The second is sleeping alone at home. Many, if not most, abductions by aliens take place under one or the other of these circumstances. In the case of sleeping, we wake suddenly to find that there are aliens — sometimes frightening, sometimes not — in the bedroom. We are not dreaming — at least, not in the usual sense — but the analogy with dreaming, and with the second kind of supernatural time-lapse, is there.

In the case of driving, it is remarkable how often we perform this complicated and potentially lethal activity without being conscious of it. We wake with a jolt after miles of driving without being able to remember any part of the journey. We were not asleep — at least, not in the usual sense — but the analogy is there. There is even a recognized psychological name for this phenomenon: highway hypnosis. It is supposed to be caused by the lack of "sensory input" while driving on long, straight roads at night. Unengaged by sights and sounds, the mind "switches off" and the motorist can pass through whole towns without remembering them.[5] It is perhaps during these lapses that we see a UFO or Bigfoot on the road; or that we embark on another, parallel journey, less monotonous than the literal one, into the realm of the daimons.

Hypnosis

No one knows exactly what hypnosis is or how it works. It induces a wide variety of altered states of consciousness, from the passive and receptive (but still conscious), to deep trances in which the subjects are unconscious of their surroundings. It is a shady business, hovering on the edge of scientific respectability. Some people think that "hypnotic recall" is nothing other than the ability to remember details of an event more easily in the relaxed atmosphere of a counseling room, say. Others claim that it is manipulated, consciously or not, by the hypnotist, who "leads" the subject, while in a suggestible state, to concoct the kind of story the hypnotist is after.

A good example of the latter case is the experiment conducted by Alvin Lawson, a professor of English, and William McCall, a doctor who practiced medical hypnosis. They hypnotized a number of subjects who were deliberately led into a UFO abduction scenario. The idea was to compare their stories with "real" abductions and so gain insight into any hoaxers that might be presented as genuine. But the experiment misfired: the subjects who had not been abducted produced descriptions of UFOs and alien entities which were indistinguishable from those of the "real" abductees.[6]

This result should not startle us. As I hope to show, "otherworld abductions" are archetypal patterns. They are myths which, by definition, can seize us and work on us; or they can find expression through us. Neither fact nor fiction, they participate in both through Imagination.

Jung used hypnosis a good deal in the early days of his private practice in order to plumb the unconscious and so reconstruct the "untold stories" of his patients' lives. But he found it an unreliable "groping in the dark" and soon gave it up in favor of dreams.[7] But, as I have mentioned, he later amplified dream work with "active imagination," in which patients entered a passive mental state and entertained, without judgment or restraint, whatever images spontaneously arose before their minds' eyes. Much regression hypnosis sounds very like this — sounds like a daimonic borderline state between sleeping and waking.

Jung did not imagine that his patients' recall of forgotten events in their lives was a record of facts. He knew that memory is an offspring of Imagination, changing, elaborating, even falsifying what we believe to have occurred. Hypnotic memories are no exception. They are as akin to dreams as they are to waking life. Hypnotic regression is not a straight re-enactment of past events, but a new journey into the same daimonic realm in which events that are past to our normal consciousness are still going on, still shifting like quicksand, and liable to suck us into the depths.

The abduction of the Avises

Regressed to the time of the unusual events on his car journey, John found himself "inside the UFO," standing on a "balcony" looking down into a giant hangar-like room. Below he could see a car whose occupants — two people in the front seat, more in the back — were all asleep or slumped over the seats. His wife was standing beside him. Elaine also remembered this consciously but recalls that Kevin, too, was with them. She also looked down and saw a car in the "hangar" — it was definitely their car because she could see John and Kevin standing beside it (although they were simultaneously with her on the balcony!). She was then separated from her husband and son, and led away.

John meanwhile remembered accompanying a tall figure, well over six feet in height, through a door that suddenly appeared in an otherwise blank wall. They passed along a corridor and entered an "examination room" furnished with a table and some apparatus. The tall entity touched him, and he blacked out. When he came to, he was lying on the table surrounded by the apparatus which was moving up and down over his body. Three of the tall entities were watching, but, to his left, were two other figures examining him with pen-like instruments. These entities were hideous. They had triangular eyes, a beaked nose, and a slit for a mouth; their ears were huge and pointed, their hands hairy and claw-like. But the feature which made them truly shocking was that they were wearing white surgical gowns, like a grotesque parody of doctors. The tall entities looked more human. They wore silvery one-piece suits which also covered their heads and, possibly, their mouths and noses (John could not remember seeing those features).

After the examination, John was taken down more corridors and was shown parts of the "craft" — a "rest and recreation area," for example, which contained sleeping cubicles — and then into a "control room" where he was made to lie down and watch a series of images on a dish-shaped screen.

Elaine also found herself in an examination room similar to John's, where she was strapped by her hands and ankles to a table and scanned by the grotesque creatures with their "pens." On getting down from the table at the end, she found she was wearing a long gown with a hood, although she had no memory of undressing or putting it on. She, too, was led to the control room and, like John, was shown images on a screen.

John's images were plans, drawings, and charts which flashed past too quickly for a clear view. He remembered a diagram of the solar system and pictures of Saturn. He was then taken to a three-dimensional image, like a hologram, which depicted some gray metallic cones under a lurid sky. It was explained to him that this was what Earth would look like after it had been destroyed by pollution. A robed figure appeared in front of this scene and held out a round glowing sphere which John was asked to touch. He did so, and felt a strange sensation on his arm. He had the idea that the hologram represented a kind of "shrine" for the tall entities.

Elaine's images consisted of stars in space which, she was told, represented "Home." There followed a "zoom shot" which concentrated on one star, then moved closer and closer until she could see the outline of the British Isles, then the Thames estuary, individual towns, streets, buildings and houses, until she was told that this was where she lived. Another screen flashed images at her as John's had done. It was "like having the contents of an encyclopedia pumped into one's head all in one go." She was also shown the hologram and required to touch the sphere held by the robed figure. She was told: "This is the seed of life, our past and your future, our whole existence. Accept this from us for yourselves, your children, and your fellowkind."

After his "show," John was told by the tall humanoid that it was time to leave. A few moments later he was back in his car but some hundreds of yards farther along the road from the last point he could remember. After her images and message, Elaine was conducted back to the car which was resting on a ramp in a kind of stepped amphitheater. "The children were already in the car, and John was standing by the door, about to get in. Suddenly the car vanished before her eyes, as if through the walls of the craft. Elaine became alarmed, but was told not to worry. Then she became aware of seeing the car moving along the lane, and of herself getting into it as it was still moving.

"With a sudden jolt the experience was over, and she was in the car sitting next to her husband."[8]

15

Supernatural Branding

The operations of the grays

So-called abductions by aliens have come to prominence in the last thirty years or so. Previously in the early 1950s people who claimed to have been taken aboard flying saucers went voluntarily. Their aliens were friendly and well-intentioned. Often tall, blond-haired, and noble-looking, they offered help, warning, or advice. Sometimes they intimated that they were representatives of an interplanetary council which was keeping a benevolent eye on us, rather primitive, Earthlings. The tall entities encountered by the Avises seem to have been akin to this type.

However, a different kind of entity began to be reported during the great wave of UFO sightings in France in 1954. Here, and subsequently across the world, small grotesque entities with disproportionately large heads, hands, and eyes were seen in the vicinity of a grounded "saucer." They usually appeared either to be repairing their craft or "collecting soil samples." Unlike the tall and handsome aliens, these creatures were indifferent to the witnesses or wary of them — sometimes downright hostile.

The early 1960s saw the beginning of many reports of abductions by entities nicknamed the grays (or greys) after their gray, rather spongy complexions. They are small — more or less child-sized — and skinny; they often have an irregular number of fingers on their hands, or webbed fingers; their noses and mouths are residual, hardly noticeable compared to their enormous eyes, which are often entirely black, i.e. pupilless, rather almond-shaped and which extend around the contours of the head like "wraparound" sunglasses. Typically, they remove people from their cars at night or, just as often, appear in their bedrooms, whence the unfortunate victims are "floated up" into a circular, evenly lit room, strapped to a table and examined or operated upon. Subsequently they are shown images of earth from space or pictures of alien landscapes before suddenly finding themselves back in their cars or beds, bewildered, horrified, or perhaps unable to remember a thing.

"Kathie Davis," to whose case Budd Hopkins devotes much of his book *Intruders,* sat up in bed one night in 1978 only to find herself face to face with "two strange gray-faced creatures," between four and five feet tall, with large heads, skin that was "dingy white, almost gray," and eyes that were "pitch black in color, liquid like, shimmering in the dim light."[1] It was only one of many encounters which she always referred to as dreams, albeit dreams which struck her as "real."[2] Her story began in a sense on the night of 30 June 1983, when she saw an eerie light in the pool house at her home in Indianapolis. At around the same time her mother noticed a strange round ball of light surrounding the bird feeder. Later that night while swimming in the pool with two friends, all three of them felt suddenly cold and then nauseous. Meanwhile the neighbors had seen a sudden flash of light in the Davises' backyard, followed by a low vibrating sound.[3]

Some seven months later, after she had contacted Hopkins, he tried to regress her through hypnosis to the events of that night. But as soon as she "returned" to the moment of seeing the light in the pool house, she became so frightened that she had to be brought out of the hypnotic state. However, she spontaneously remembered seeing an egg-shaped craft supported on four jointed legs in the backyard. A ball of light, two feet in diameter, irradiated her body, which she could not move. She was able to recall this light again in a subsequent hypnotic session "...the initial shock and pain [was] like a bolt of lightning hitting the center of her chest and then flowing all through her body." It occurred when she was going out to search the pool house. She also remembered someone touching her, and pinching her arm. Six "bullet-shaped things" in the yard formed a line and came towards her. Then there seemed to be only one. Something was inserted in her ear, which hurt.[4]

From these fragmentary beginnings an elaborate abduction scenario, some details of which I will give later, was revealed. Kathie was dogged by paranormal events over the years. She became prey to nameless fears at night. She could not sleep. Once she heard her name called out "in her head" and, on running to her mother's room, they both saw a small ball of light whizzing down the hall. Next morning, both women felt stiff in the arms and shoulders; there were tiny bloodstains on Kathie's pillow where her neck had lain. Her four-year-old son Robbie was terrified by a "man with a big head" who came through the wall and disappeared into the closet. "He kept going back and forth, and he wouldn't let me move," said Robbie. "And he had lights around his head...the man wanted Tommy [his younger brother]."[5] On another occasion, Kathie saw her little gray man while she was watching TV. He walked past the open door, taking no notice of her. A search of the house revealed nothing.

Virginia and the deer

I have to say that I do not find Budd Hopkins's interpretation of such cases as Kathie's wholly convincing. He is committed to the idea that she and others like her are being abducted and interfered with by extraterrestrials. This cannot help but be reflected in his kindly, sincere, but often misplaced readings of their experiences. Whenever he questions his abductees under hypnosis, the questions are rarely neutral; nor are his post-hypnotic discussions. He leads them towards his own hypotheses. Sometimes it almost seems as if he goes on hypnotizing them until they come up with a scenario which satisfies him. He sees the "physical operations" as "central,"[6] supporting as they do a sinister program being enacted by the aliens. He is concerned "to separate the signal from the noise," and for him the quasi-medical operations are very much the signal while the rest is noise. But are we entitled to be so selective? Let us consider the case of another of his subjects, a brilliant and happily married thirty-five-year-old lawyer pseudonymously called Virginia Horton.[7]

She came to Hopkins, asking to be hypnotized, in order to find out what exactly had happened to her at the age of six when, at her grandfather's farm in Southern Manitoba, she had discovered a deep cut, bleeding profusely, on the back of her calf. She could remember her fascination with it at the time, but nothing which might have caused it. When she asked her mother about the incident, she too could remember nothing — but she did remember another occasion when Virginia was about sixteen, which took place at a picnic on holiday in France, near the Rhine valley, about thirty to forty miles from Frankfurt. Virginia had gone missing for a short time in the woods. She eventually turned up, however, rushing out of the woods, with blood all down her blouse. She remembered only one thing about the event: that she saw "a beautiful deer in the woods...almost like a mystical deer...it was very strange."[8] She adds that "it was as though I had walked out of the woods and claimed that I saw a unicorn. There was that sense of excitement and wonder. And when I think about the visual memories that I had, there wasn't anything unusual about the deer, except that it was looking at me…in a very conscious kind of way…"[9]

Here, Virginia is describing the not uncommon experience of enchantment, when some natural object or creature seems suddenly instinct with profound intelligence and meaning. Magical deer are frequently found in fairy tales and in medieval romances where, like Hermes, they are psychopomps, guides of the soul — you hunt them and they elude your weapons, leading you deeper into the labyrinth of the forest. But, of course, you lose yourself in the dense forest of the soul only to find yourself: the deer has led you, as if inadvertently, to the enchanted castle where the lovely princess awaits you. You suspect she was in cahoots with the deer all along; you suspect in fact that she *was* the deer who, in other contexts, can not only talk but can proffer advice essential to the success of your quest, providing you ask the right questions.

Conscious of the deer's complexity, Virginia tentatively put forward the idea that she might have been hypnotized at the time and only *thought* she saw a deer in order "to make it easy to have a story to tell." ("Yes," says Hopkins firmly, "it could have been suggested.")[10] She was mindful of Hopkins's beliefs that the aliens are presenting themselves as a deer or are causing her to see a deer in order either to block her memory of what she was "really" seeing, or else to provide her with a cover story. But we know these aliens of old — they are the fairies who, as we saw in the case of lake monsters, masquerade as ordinary animals or cast their glamour on ordinary objects, or put pishogue on us to alter our perception.

Under hypnosis, Virginia talked more about the deer: "…I had a sense of personality inside this deer. There was a person inside this deer. That's what I know."[11] Imagination represents itself for preference as personified. The sense that there is someone behind phenomena is the sense of the daimonic, the divine even, in all things. To literalize this sense and to identify it with extraterrestrials who are getting at us is a touch paranoid.

Anyway, Virginia remembered that the deer "just sort of dematerialized, vanished" and, after looking for it a while, she returned to her parents with blood on her blouse. Under further, deeper hypnosis to explore this period, she at last came with something like the approved story:[12]

She is walking through the woods and sees a bright light which is round and roughly top-shaped, in fact "a ship like they have in the movies." She goes inside the "ship" and finds herself in the midst of a celebration, a party where everyone present is happy, especially the "old man" who originally contacted her on the occasion of her cut leg in her grandfather's farmyard, when she was six.

Virginia had already described the latter incident under regression hypnosis. She remembers lying comfortably on a couch. The light is soft and gray, and there is a clean smell as of ozone. She senses presences (but sees no one) who explain the reason for her cut as it were telepathically, but she does not understand. The main presence is loving and patient, very like her grandfather. He describes himself to her as having longer and skinnier fingers than humans, and more (or perhaps fewer) of them; as being grayer in color than humans; and as having different eyes, maybe more than two. He says he is very old. Virginia talks to him, it seems, all afternoon. She is asked her permission for them to take "a little teeny piece of [her] home," which she grants. The "old man" talks about all the wonderful places there are, including his own which is far away, and about endless beautiful things which, "no matter how long you looked or how far you went, you'd never get to the end of them."[13]

Now, meeting the "old man" again in the "ship," Virginia is struck by how ecstatic he is over his "research project" and over her condition "...it had almost a religious quality the way he felt about the research he was doing. It was like his own mission." At this point she casually mentions that they did, she thinks, take some blood from her nose via a small humming instrument, but she hardly paid any attention to it. She was too absorbed in the party, with all its talking, lights playing, and the sound of music which, though electronic-like, was not jarring but reminded her of wind blowing through a valley. While they talked to her by "thinking at her," the "aliens" talked among themselves in voices "a little clicky...and at a higher pitch than we talk."[14]

Virginia's alleged abductions are unusual, to say the least, in that they are without the horror and fear which govern most abduction reports. At the same time, the horror and fear is rarely unalloyed. Abductees often sense a helpful and protective presence in the midst of their ordeal at the hands of the grays. In the Avis case it was even dominant, the tall benign entities playing a more important part than their equivalent of the grays — those white-coated little horrors with beaks and claws and triangular eyes. Alternatively, once the initial shock of contact with the grays is over, they can appear on subsequent contact as less menacing, more ambiguous, almost benevolent.

Virginia's experience is also unusual in that it comes closer than any other abduction report I have read to a traditional fairy gathering. Inside their brightly lit raths or "forts" they feast, dance, and play music in an atmosphere of genial hospitality and joy which is like that within Virginia's ship — and quite unlike the silent, sterile theater of the usual uncommunicative grays. However, I do not want to force Virginia's story into the mold of a "fairy story." I am only saying that it fits her scenario at least as well as Hopkins's interpretation. He sees aliens "behind" the events, rather in the same way as Freud saw sexuality lurking behind most, if not all, dream images. Jung's approach was to stick with the image itself, allowing it to speak and, through its connotations and associations, expanding it rather than narrowing it down to a single, literal meaning. Thus the image of the deer clearly points to a magical, "fairy" reading of the event, not to an abduction by extraterrestrials.

On the other hand, the image of the wise "old man" who is personal (like her grandfather) and yet impersonal (like an alien) points to the archetypal image of the animus. Unseen, he introduces the child to the infinite delights of the soul's domain ("beautiful things...you'd never get to the end of..."), while later she is able to meet him face to face, when he is delighted by her condition — her successful transition from child to adult, perhaps.

Scars

Budd Hopkins's conviction that actual aliens are snatching people from their beds or cars in order to perform their inscrutable operations is largely derived from what he calls the physical evidence — the blood on Virginia's blouse, for instance, and the scar whose origins were shrouded in mystery. In fact many of Hopkins's abductees possess anomalous scars. Typically, they remembered suffering, in childhood, a deep cut to the leg for which there was no discernible cause. Under hypnosis they recollected being transported to the familiar evenly lit interior space where aliens operated on their legs. This was quite a surprise to the abductees who had entered regression hypnosis to discover what had occurred during a missing time experience, without suspecting that there had been a prior, childhood abduction.

More remarkably, four abductees who bore identical scars claimed that this first abduction had taken place in 1950, when all of them were seven years old. (Of these four, however, one refused to be hypnotized and one remembered only that the event connected with her bleeding leg was bound up with the attempt to catch a wonderful "hummingbird" — presumably a tiny winged creature — which she puts in a jar, but which, when she looks again, has vanished.) Over a period of five years, Hopkins made contact with twenty-seven further abductees with scars, a number of which were not straight like the leg scars, but circular shallow depressions. Kathie Davis, her mother, her closest friend, and her neighbor all carry similar scars on their lower legs, "all apparently resulting," says Hopkins breezily, "from earlier abduction experiences."[15]

Whatever the justification, or lack of it, for such a conclusion, we should not by now be altogether startled by these bodily marks. They are not caused by literal operations; they simply appear on our bodies synchronistically — sympathetically — with psychic events, just as UFO "landing marks" and mysterious foot- or paw-prints appear on the ground. They are marks of contact with the Otherworld, daimonic traces for which there are many traditional precedents.

The stroke

Seventy-three-year-old Neil Colton of County Donegal, Ireland, told Evans-Wentz of something that happened to him just before sunset on a midsummer's day when he was a boy. He, his brother, and a female cousin were gathering bilberries up by some rocks at the back of his house, when they heard music. "We hurried round the rocks, and there we were within a few hundred feet of six or eight of the *gentle folk* [i.e. fairies], and they dancing. When they saw us, a little woman dressed all in red came running out from them towards us, and she struck my cousin across the face with what seemed to be a green rush. We ran for home as hard as we could, and when my cousin reached the house, she fell dead. Father saddled a horse and went for Father Regan [i.e. the priest]. When Father Regan arrived, he put a stole about his neck and began praying over my cousin and reading psalms and striking her with the stole; and in that way brought her back. He said if she had not caught hold of my brother, she would have been *taken* for ever."[16]

This is an example of a fairy "stroke," a word which lingers on in medical usage. Fairies do not take kindly to being seen unless they expressly wish it. They can paralyze the intruder with a stroke or with a touch. A Galway man, Jackson Davis, told W. B. Yeats about an old, white-haired man who had appeared to him three times and then vanished. On the third appearance — perhaps as punishment for Davis's failure to pay sufficient attention to him? — the old man touched him with one finger on the side of the head; and the place remained forever after without feeling. Davis was lucky: those who are "touched" are liable to lose their wits ("touched in the head"). And this aptly describes many UFO contactees, who often report sensations of disorientation, dizziness, insomnia, amnesia, bad dreams, etc. — all signs that their lives have also been touched, turned upside down, whether for better or worse. They are often paralyzed or rendered unconscious, too, by beams of light, whitish or red or green, fired at them by UFO entities. These effects are identical to the "fairy blast" which can strike suddenly and invisibly in the form of a whirlwind laden with leaves and dust. (We should also remember the paralysis of St. Bernadette's arm when she first encounters the BVM.)

In Neil Colton's story, Father Regan uses the word *taken* advisedly. He does not mean "taken to God" — killed — but taken by the fairies — that is, abducted. While there can be no return from the Christian Otherworld, from the fairy Otherworld there can. The priest wisely acts, in his own fashion, as a tribal shaman might act, in order to retrieve a soul which has been lost or taken: he performs ritual incantations and homeopathically strikes the girl with his stole to undo the result of the fairy stroke. She would have been taken altogether had she not instinctively clung to the world of the living by grabbing her cousin.

Thus fairies are as likely to harm as to help us. It is dangerous to trespass on their preserves. The distinguished writer James Hamilton-Paterson, who has lived in the Philippines for many years, told me of a misfortune suffered by a friend of his there. The friend is a German missionary priest who has lived among the people of a remote village for forty-odd years. He decided one day to erect a radio aerial on a suitable tree.

As he climbed the ladder, he seemed to bang the top of his head on a hard flat surface — even though no such surface, such as a branch, was visible. The impact caused the priest to fall from the ladder with what he described as a *stroke* — he was suddenly paralyzed down one side of his body. For three days he lay helpless in his hut, unhurt by the fall but still paralyzed by the stroke. The local witch doctor visited him and pointed out that his mistake had been to interfere with a tree where *mu-mu* lived, without asking their permission.

(Incidentally, Hamilton-Paterson himself had come across these *mu-mu*, in whose existence he claimed not to believe, when camped out on an uninhabited mountainside with only a guide for company. He was woken in the night by the distinct sounds, not very distant, of a *party* — laughter, music, the clattering of dishes, etc. — which the guide nervously identified as *mu-mu*. Fairies everywhere have a fondness, it seems, for feasting and fun.)

The German priest was told that if he apologized to the *mu-mu* he would be cured. Reluctant to give in to pagan superstition, he was nevertheless desperate enough to try anything. He hauled himself to the foot of the tree and, feeling both foolish and unchristian, apologized out loud to the *mu-mu* for his presumption. His paralysis left him, as he said, on the instant.[17]

Elf-shot

It is worth mentioning, in passing, that fairies did not only inflict damage by touch or blast, or by the "green rush" which felled Neil Colton's cousin. They had their own counterparts of the technological "ray-guns" sometimes sported by UFO occupants. The Reverend Robert Kirk, who wrote the first "modern" study of fairies in 1691, describes the weapon as "a stone like to yellow soft flint shaped like a barbed arrowhead, but flying as a dart with great force...mortally wounding the vitall parts without breaking the skin, some of which wounds, I have observed in beasts, and felt them with my hands."[18] Kirk also describes the disorienting effect the weapon has on people who are pierced or wounded by it, making them "do somewhat very unlike their former practice, causing a sudden alteration, yet the cause thereof unperceivable at present: nor have they power...to escape the Blow impendent."[19]

Folklorists commonly identify these fairy weapons with the stone-age arrowheads which are strewn all over the British Isles. Be that as it may, the wounds inflicted by them were, it seems, invisible and inward. Cows damaged in this way were said to be "elf-shot," the Anglo-Saxon equivalent of the Celtic phenomena Kirk is reporting. (Charms against elf-shot are among the earliest written mention of fairy lore.[20]) If the cows died, their "aerial and aethereal parts" were taken by the fairies to live on.

The perennial interest, taken by daimons from Hermes down, in livestock (and especially cattle) calls to mind the puzzling epidemic of cattle mutilations. Again we are prompted to ask whether the invisible internal wounds from "elf-shot" — a metaphor for the indelible mark left on us by otherworldly contact — have become visible and outward, in order to persuade us, literal-minded as we are, of daimonic reality. And this may also be true of the increasingly unmetaphorical, unpoetic behavior of the inept, scar-inflicting alien surgeons.

Mr. Cunningham's near-death experience

One form of otherworld journey which has attracted a good deal of attention recently is the near-death experience, in which people who die revive — while in between they gain some knowledge of the afterlife. For example, the head of a distinguished Northumbrian family called Cunningham "died" and returned to report that he had left his body and had been greeted by a "handsome man in a shining robe," who guided him to a broad and infinitely long valley. One side of the valley was filled with burning flames and the other with hail and snow. Both sides were full of human souls who constantly jumped from one side to another as either the heat or the cold grew intolerable.[21]

Beyond the valley, Mr. Cunningham was shown a great pit from which masses of black flame arose. His guide suddenly disappeared, and he was left alone to watch more human souls being tossed high in the air like sparks in the rising tongues of flame, before dropping back into the pit. Then he heard the sound of a "desperate lamentation accompanied by harsh laughter": a throng of "wicked spirits" appeared, dragging five souls down into the dark burning chasm, where the men's weeping and the devilish laughter became indistinguishable. He was also menaced by a group of these "dark spirits" who emerged from the pit and surrounded him, their eyes glowing red, their mouths and nostrils breathing fire. They threatened to seize him with a sort of burning forceps but, although he was terrified, they did not dare, in the end, to touch him. He was saved from this ordeal by the return of his guide.

Cunningham was brought next to an infinitely long and high wall, without any sign of an entrance. All at once he found himself unaccountably transported to the top of it, from which vantage point he saw a bright, flowery meadow populated by hosts of men in white robes and happy people sitting together. His guide explained that the valley of fire and snow was a place where the souls of the dead were tried and punished, having led a more or less wicked life but repented at the hour of death. The pit was the mouth of Hell from which there was no deliverance. The meadow was where good people went, but it was not the Heaven reserved for the perfected. Reluctant as he was to leave the fragrant meadow, he was told that he must return to his body — which he does, waking up in the land of the living once more.[22]

Mr. Cunningham was so impressed by his experience that he joined a monastery at Melrose, where he was known as Brother Drythelm. His otherworld journey took place at the end of the seventh century and, having been reported by the Venerable Bede, set the pattern for most afterlife visions throughout the medieval period, culminating in the most profoundly imagined journey of all — Dante's *Divine Comedy*. The only major feature missing from Drythelm's journey compared to subsequent accounts is the Test Bridge — a tricky structure, slippery or narrow, from which wicked souls fall into Hell, but which righteous souls manage to cross into paradise. The invariable presence of a guide is clearly related to the Greek idea of the personal daimon, and to the Christian guardian angel. In several medieval accounts the guide is a saint rather than an angel; in contemporary near-death accounts, he or she is more likely to be simply a light or an indefinable Presence, or else personified as a friend or family member. (For Dante, of course, it was Virgil.)

We are reminded, too, of the tall alien encountered by the Avises, whose otherworld journey has perhaps more in common with traditional Christian accounts than with their pagan equivalents. In the latter, the visionary meets ambivalent daimons who are both dangerous and benign; in the former, everything is divided and polarized into fire and ice, light and dark, heaven and hell, angels and demons, etc. Like the Avises, a number of UFO abductees are faced with two sets of entities, one tall and benevolent, the other small and demonic. In addition, we can hear in the Avis case echoes of what was generally held to be the purpose of medieval visionary journeys, namely *conversion*. (For Bede it was a greater miracle to convert a sinner than to raise up a dead man.) And for the victims of "alien abduction" there is an analogous conversion: their lives are turned upside down and have to be completely re-evaluated.

Wounding and healing

It is axiomatic that, on returning like Plato's Er to their bodies, the medieval Christian visionaries are not only converted spiritually, but also altered physically. They have undergone what Carol Zaleski calls "supernatural branding." Fursa, for example, brings back a permanent burn mark on his shoulder and jaw from a flaming soul thrown at him by a demon. Gottschalk returns with three "witnesses" to his vision: a pain in the head, the side, and the feet. The monk of Wenlock, whose story was told by St. Boniface in the eighth century, was blinded for a week and suffered from amnesia; Orm lost the power of speech; Alberic is so stupefied that he cannot remember his own mother. Antonio Mannini entered the Otherworld at the famous pilgrimage site of St. Patrick's Purgatory, situated on an island in Donegal's Lough Derg. Shut up in a cave by the monks who controlled the rite, he passed through a doorway into the Otherworld and returned to tell the tale. "The bearer of this [letter]," he wrote to a friend, "will tell you how I came out marked, for I showed him so that he might tell you about it; and perhaps I shall carry the mark forever."[23]

On the other hand, the twelfth-century monk Edmund of Eynsham found on his return that an open wound on his leg had disappeared without a trace. "Old wounds are healed," remarks Zaleski, "or new scars appear."[24] But then, of course, instances of healing are commonplace in a Christian context, especially at sites of Marian visions, and accessible through prayer without accompanying visions. However, it is not unusual for the desperately ill to be comforted, and sometimes cured, by apparitions of Jesus, Mary, or an angel. A woman whom Hope MacDonald calls Jackie, for instance, prayed to God for help on the night before she was to have surgery on a face tumor — an operation that would disfigure her for life. She woke in the night to see a shining light at the end of her bed. The silvery form of an angel appeared, telling her not to be afraid and reassuring her that she would be all right. The next day, Jackie was taken for pre-operative X-rays. The tumor had disappeared, and did not return.[25]

But sudden gratuitous acts of healing can also occur outside a specifically religious context — we remember the clergyman's widow who suffered from an injured foot and was confronted in Regent's Park by a tiny man in green who promised that her foot would no longer pain her (and so it proved). But an even more remarkable case, brought to light by the well-known French ufologist Aimé Michel, concerns a doctor (called "X") who had been left partially paralyzed by a field mine in the Algerian war. A gifted pianist, he was then unable to play, and he walked with a limp. On 2 November 1968 he was woken at about 4 a.m. by his fourteen-month-old son, who pointed from his cot towards the window. Dr. X looked outside and saw flashes of light in the valley. Then he saw two disc-shaped objects, each emitting a downwards ray of light. As they moved towards him, they merged or fused into a single object which projected a powerful beam of light at him — before exploding into a cloud shape and dispersing.

Considerably shaken, Dr. X woke his wife to tell her about the event and she noticed that he was walking normally — both his limp and the pain from the war wound had disappeared. In addition, a wound on his ankle, incurred by a slip of the axe while chopping wood three days before, had also vanished. Dr. X went back to bed but, uncharacteristically, talked in his sleep. His wife noted the sentence "contact will be re-established by falling down the stairs on November the second."

The next day, the doctor remembered nothing of the previous night. But that afternoon he fell on the stairs and immediately recalled the entire "encounter." His war wound remained cured, and he resumed piano-playing as well as ever. However, he suffered a pain in his umbilical region, where an odd triangular mark appeared on the skin. A similar but circular mark, around the belly button, appeared on his baby son. Neither mark could be medically explained.[26]

Stigmata

The most famous type of supernatural branding is, of course, stigmata — that is, four or five wounds corresponding to Christ's nail wounds on the cross (both hands, both feet, plus one in the side from the soldier's spear thrust). The Italian priest Padre Pío was the best-known stigmatic in recent

times, but wounds similar to his have appeared on quite ordinary people —
though not, as far as I know, on people without some Roman Catholic
connection. Thus stigmata are not in themselves marks of special sanctity.
Padre Pío's likely canonization will not be for sustaining stigmata but for the
unusual holiness of his life and the miracles of healing claimed by people
who invoked his image during prayer.

Stigmata are daimonic marks associated with a peculiarly Christian
otherworld journey, which need not entail leaving one's body, as it does in
medieval near-death experiences. It is a spiritual and imaginative vision,
traditionally called *ecstasy* (*ekstasis,* "standing outside oneself"), which
especially enraptures Christians who for long years have visualized,
contemplated, and meditated upon — that is, *imagined* — the figure of the

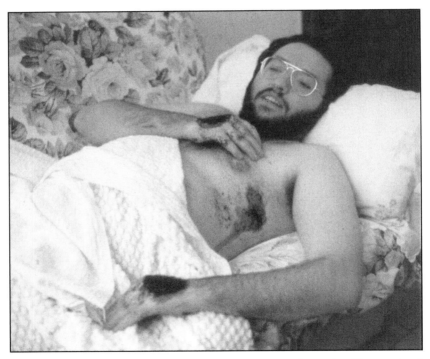

**Figure 11. Giorgio Bongiovanni is a modern stigmatic. He received
his stigmata when he visited the site at Fatima where the Blessed
Virgin Mary was seen. (*Fortean Picture Library*)**

crucified Christ. In my Introduction, for example, we saw how St. Catherine of Siena was ecstatically pierced by rays emanating from her vision of Christ, and how she thereafter suffered the exquisite pain of stigmata.

The first stigmatic, St. Francis of Assisi, isolated himself in a deep fissure in the mountains, fasting, praying, and (it is said) wrestling with the forms of Satan. He was visited by an angel who played a divine melody on a viol or flute, and he saw a ball of fire sweep through the heavens. On the morning of the feast of the Exaltation of the Holy Cross, he prayed that he might feel, as far as possible, the actual pain of Christ's Passion — whereupon a seraph with six flaming wings flew down towards him. As it approached, the image of a man on a cross appeared between the pairs of wings. The seraph came to rest in front of Francis and darts of flame imprinted on his body the wounds of Christ crucified — wounds which he carried for the rest of his life.[27]

In an ecstatic state whose ambivalence was so subtly sculpted by Bernini (it is both mystical and sexual), St. Teresa of Avila was also visited by a seraph which thrust a golden fire-tipped dart through her heart. The pain was "so excessive," wrote Teresa, "that it forced me to utter those groans, and the suavities, which that extremitie of pain gave, was also so very excessive, that there was no desiring at all to be ridd of it."[28] Like the wounds inflicted by the dart of the arch-daimon Eros who transfixes lovers, St. Teresa's wounds remained as invisible as elf-shots — but her heart carried God's scars for life.

16

Changelings

Da Silva's dwarfs

On 3 May 1969, a Brazilian soldier named José Antonio da Silva took time off to go fishing at a spot near Bebeduro, about fifty kilometers from his home town of Belo Horizonte. He camped overnight. The next day, at about three o'clock in the afternoon, he was surprised to hear voices and see figures moving around behind him. Suddenly his legs were burned by what felt like a blast of fire. Two stocky, masked figures then seized him and dragged him to an odd "craft," which he later described by putting a tumbler on a saucer, and placing another saucer on top, but upside down like a lid. Slanting tubes ran from the rim of the top "saucer" into the bottom of the "tumbler."[1]

Da Silva's captors were a little over four feet tall and of human proportions. Their heads were hidden by metallic helmets with eyeholes and with an apparatus which ran from the front to containers on their backs, as if it were a breathing device. A similar helmet was forced onto da Silva's head, but it fitted badly, chafing his shoulders.

He was bundled into the craft and seated on a bench which ran along one of the walls. These seemed to be made of a stone-like material. The lighting was like sodium light, but it came from no visible source. A third person entered and moved a small lever in the floor. There was a humming sound and the sensation of movement. A journey ensued, seeming to go on for hours. At last the craft stopped and da Silva was led outside, his eyeholes covered. Eventually he was made to sit down again, still wearing his helmet but able now to see his kidnappers without their "space-suits" on.[2]

Until now we seem to be dealing with a classic "UFO abduction" case; but subsequent events conjure up associations with an altogether different tradition, beginning with the appearance of the "aliens." They were dwarfish, with long beards and hair which fell down below their waists. Their faces had big noses and ears, very bushy eyebrows, and apparently toothless mouths. The room they were in appeared, like the craft, to be made of stone, and its illumination was once again indeterminable. On one of the walls there were pictures of earthly scenes — houses, buildings, vehicles, and animals. Beneath these was a wide shelf on which lay the dead and naked bodies of four men, one of them dark-skinned, another black.

The "dwarfs" began to rummage through the bundle of belongings which da Silva had hung on to throughout his ordeal. They took his identity card and one specimen of all the things for which there were duplicates, such as money, fishing tackle, and items of food. As they examined each article they jabbered and gesticulated excitedly, even at one point firing a weapon of the kind that had burned da Silva's leg, and making a burn mark on the wall.

The dwarf who seemed to be their leader tried to communicate with him by gestures and by symbols drawn on a grayish tablet. They looked like concentric circles. Da Silva interpreted them as representing days and years. He thought that they were proposing that he should stay on Earth for three more years, spying on their behalf, before visiting them for seven years in order to study their ways. He would thus be equipped to act as their guide when they landed on Earth at the end of the ten years. However, in spite of the baleful presence of the four corpses, da Silva refused the deal. He began to finger his rosary. The leader snatched it from him, spilling the beads all over the floor.

As if this were a cue for a change of scene, the atmosphere at once altered and, all of a sudden, a man materialized out of nowhere. He was entirely human, of average size, and wearing a long monk-like robe. Remarkably, he was not visible to the dwarfs. He spoke to da Silva in fluent Portuguese and gave him a message which, he said, should not be passed on for several years. When da Silva was later interviewed by the Brazilian UFO research group CICOANI, he was reticent about this message and even about the man's physical appearance, since, he claimed, the details of whatever had been revealed to him could be deduced simply from the description of the man — who, incidentally, vanished as abruptly as he had come.[3] There is an echo here of Marian visions whose recipients were given secrets; and, indeed, we can detect a strong Christian flavor, triggered as if in a dream by the spilled rosary beads. The man may well have been da Silva's personal daimon in the guise of a saint, or even of Christ Himself.

At any rate, he was taken off once more in the craft and left somewhere outside, sprawled semi-conscious on the ground. Recovering somewhat, he drank deeply from a nearby stream and caught a fish which he cooked and ate. Eventually he stumbled on to a road, where he asked directions from passers-by. He was amazed to find, firstly, that he was near the city of Victoria, nearly 200 miles from Bebeduro; and secondly, that four days had elapsed since his ordeal began. Exhausted, hungry, his leg hurting from the alien blast, his shoulders raw from the rubbing of the helmet, he at last found his way to a railway station, where he blurted out his story to an official who took him home for food and rest. On his return to Belo Horizonte, he repeated his story to senior officers at his barracks and, within a week, CICOANI sent a team to investigate.[4]

This extraordinary tale clearly owes as much to folkloric, and even Christian tradition as to ufology, demonstrating once more the underlying continuity between apparently diverse visionary experiences. The Otherworld presents itself imaginatively as a mixture of personal and impersonal elements, and as a combination of different traditions — in this case, some old and some new. The following case is similarly mixed; but it seems to combine modern ufological motifs with older themes drawn from the Native American tradition, almost as if the landscape in which it took place dictated the form of the visionary encounter.

The hunter's enchantment

On 25 October 1974, forty-year-old Carl Higdon, a petrol company mechanic in Riverton, Wyoming, set off in his pick-up truck to hunt elk in Medicine Bow National Park.[5] Being an intrepid sort of chap, and passionate about big game hunting, Carl decided to explore an area of the park little frequented by other hunters. He walked for some time through the forest, which, he noticed, was strangely silent. Then, seeing a group of five elk, he put his gun to his shoulder and fired.

Something strange happened. The sound of the shot was curiously muffled and the bullet seemed to travel so slowly that Carl was able to watch it in flight. It fell to earth some fifteen to twenty meters in front of him. It was completely crushed. Amazed, Carl picked up the bullet and put it in his pocket. Then, turning at the sound of a branch cracking, he saw a very tall man standing about twenty meters away in the shade of a birch. This man, or whatever he was, had yellow skin, bristling straw-colored hair, and was wearing a black costume. (He is oddly reminiscent of the "sungod" encountered by our Apinayé chief in the Introduction.)

He approached Carl and said, surprisingly, "How you doin'?" — to which Carl replied: "Pretty good." "Are you hungry?" asked the stranger. "Yeah. A little," said Carl. The man tossed him a package containing four pills, telling him to take one, which would last him for four days. Carl did take one, whereupon the man asked if Carl would like to go with him. "I guess," said Carl, and for the first time he saw a transparent illuminated "cubicle."

The next thing he knew was that he was sitting in this contraption. Two more men in black were seated alongside him, and behind him were five elk in a cage. His seat was a sort of armchair in which he was held by the sudden vertical acceleration which then took place. The trip went on for some time — Carl was vague about it — until they reached the men's "planet." Carl was not allowed to leave the vehicle, but through its transparent walls he could see "a sort of tower, surrounded by rotating lights, so unbearably bright that he complained." His hosts remarked that they would take him back since he was not any good for what they needed. Accordingly, after a short journey, Carl was returned to the forest and dropped out of the cubicle onto the rocky ground, which bruised his shoulder.

Bewildered, Carl found himself walking, gun in hand, along a cow trail that was unknown to him. By a stroke of luck he found a vehicle stuck in the mud, but with a CB radio, on which he called for help. After a while a police team arrived to rescue him. It turned out that the vehicle was, in fact, his own pick-up which he had not recognized owing to his loss of memory. It was bogged down in a place inaccessible to ordinary two-wheel-drive vehicles, and eight kilometers away from where he had left it.

He did not remember the full story until the following day. When the police arrived, they found him distraught, red-eyed, tearful, and (like the medieval near-death visionary, Alberic, who could not remember his mother) unable even to recognize his wife, who had come with them. He could only repeat the story of the pills and the men in black. His body was covered in scratches. The bullet, found in his pocket, was crushed and folded like a glove. He was taken to the hospital but the doctors found nothing wrong with him. His memory returned the next day and he was discharged, completely restored to normality.

Although Carl Higdon's story found its way into the UFO literature, it really belongs, as Bertrand Méheust has noticed, to more traditional folklore. To go hunting in the far reaches of the forest, it seems, is an archetypal activity which invites enchantment. A young Krahó Indian, for example, was out in the forest hunting deer, when a Xupé — a deity who protected animals — appeared to him and advised him to hunt elsewhere. Returning to his village, the young man was taken sick with a fever, and during the night the Xupé reappeared in the guise of a black man who inserted a substance into the Krahó's head, heart, and arms — a substance that not only cured him but also conferred on him the power to heal.[6]

A similar daimon, or deity, appeared to a Cuna Indian who was resting beneath a tree in the forest during an unsuccessful hunt. The daimon (the source says "spirit") put a pastille on his tongue — not unlike Higdon's pill — and announced that it would instruct him while the daimon himself would teach the Cuna man how to catch game.[7] (Higdon's men were adept at catching game — they had five elk in tow — but they may also, of course, have been protecting them.) In other South American stories, the guardian daimon even asks the hunter, as Carl's did, whether he is hungry, or stops his arrow in mid-flight, just as Carl's bullet was.[8] Nor is the "interplanetary" trip absent from such stories — it is a commonplace, as we shall see, for medicine men and shamans to embark on celestial journeys, either as part of their initiation or, subsequently, as part of their official duties.

Albert and the Bigfoot

We have already noted that the American Bigfoot or Sasquatch is not above behaving in a fairy-like manner, and this extends even to the abduction of humans. In 1871 a Native American woman claimed to have been kidnapped by a Bigfoot in British Columbia, when she was seventeen years old. It forced her to swim the Harrison River and then carried her to a rock shelter where she lived with the creature and its parents for a year — after which it took her home because she "aggravated it so much." She said that she had been treated kindly, however.[9]

Another tale of Bigfoot abduction in British Columbia surfaced in 1957: Albert Ostman announced that, while looking for gold around the head of the Toba inlet in 1924, he was woken at night by something picking him up. He was in his sleeping bag, fully dressed, and with his rifle to hand. He knew at once that it was "one of the mountain Sasquatch giants the Indian told [him] about." For about three hours Ostman suffered from lack of air and cramp as he was carried up and down hills, until at last he was dumped on the ground. At first light he saw that he was in a valley with only a single narrow exit, guarded by the largest of four Sasquatch, whom he presumed to be a father, mother, son, and daughter.[10]

Although I would contend, of course, that this was no literal kidnap, I have to admit that it is the least "otherworldly" journey I have come across, largely because of the compelling details that Ostman supplies, such as the sound of his belongings clanking about in the sleeping bag as the panting Sasquatch bore him uphill, and the pain caused by one loose hobnail boot sticking into his foot, and so on. There is also the detailed description he gave of the creatures. For instance, having coolly set up camp and eaten some food he had with him, he observed that the young male Sasquatch might have been between eleven and eighteen years old, seven feet tall, and weighing about 300 pounds. Its chest was about fifty to fifty-five inches, its waist about thirty-six to thirty-eight inches. It had wide jaws, a narrow forehead, a head that slanted upwards to a height of four or five inches above the forehead, and hair about six inches long. The hair on the rest of the body was shorter and thick in places. Ostman was only able to escape when the "father," intrigued by his snuff, gulped down a whole box of it and, becoming sick, rushed off to get water.

A number of people sternly interrogated Mr. Ostman, but failed to shake either his story or his dignity.[11]

The next case of abduction highlights in a modern context the age-old theme of fairy lovers, demonized by Christianity into *incubi* and *succubi,* who obsess us mortals and lure us, like Keats's Belle Dame Sans Merci, to our doom.

Alien sex

On the night of 15 October 1957, twenty-three-year-old Antonio Villas Boas was out on his tractor plowing a field at his farm in São Francisco de Salles, which is in the Brazilian state of Minas Gerais, near the border with São Paulo. At about 1 a.m. he saw a large red "star" approaching.[12] It was similar to a red ball of light that both he and his brother had seen the previous night, and which he had chased up and down the field but failed to catch. This second light, however, turned out to be an egg-shaped object so bright that the tractor's headlights could not be seen. It landed some ten to fifteen meters in front of him, on three metallic legs. Since his tractor would not start, Antonio jumped down and began to run away, but he was grabbed by three figures who dragged him into their machine.

He was led into a circular compartment where rubber tubes were attached to his chin, apparently to draw blood from him. His captors were dressed in tight-fitting metallic suits and round helmets which hid their faces except for their small, bluish eyes. Next, he was taken to another compartment, stripped, and laid down on a white plastic-like couch. One of the abductors began to wash him down with a sponge containing a clear refreshing liquid. Left alone, he suddenly noticed a pungent smell which caused him to be violently sick.

After a while a woman entered the room. She was blonde, small (about four feet eight inches tall), with a small mouth, nose, and ears but large slanting blue eyes, and unusually high, broad cheekbones. Also, she was naked. In spite of the circumstances, Antonio found her most attractive and became aroused by her sexual advances. They had sex, normal in every way, except that he was perturbed by the guttural barks the woman gave at certain moments, giving him the impression that he was lying with an animal. Before she left, the woman pointed at her belly and then at the sky — which Antonio took to mean that she intended to return and take him away to wherever she lived.

Antonio's clothes were given back to him and he was then returned to the first room, where three of the "crew" were sitting talking. After his attempt to steal a box with a clock-like dial on one face was foiled — he wanted it as proof of his experience — he was carried out of the craft and dropped in his field. He had spent four and a quarter hours in the hands of his captors. He was left with some odd wounds on his limbs (they became violet while they healed), and a scar.

In Antonio's sexual encounter, there is no suggestion of the attachment and even passion which characterizes fairy intercourse with mortals. If anything, it is marked by the kind of detached ruthlessness which gods like Zeus showed when they ravished women in the shape of an animal (a sinister hint of which is suggested by the alien woman's barks). However, Antonio does at least feel a certain attraction — an aspect wholly absent from the experiences of more than one of Budd Hopkins's male abductees.

"Ed Duvall," for example, had undergone a missing time experience in the early 1960s which had left him feeling uneasy ever since.[13] He was a mechanic at a mine, often working the nightshift. After the first hours of duty he would sleep in his truck with the motor running for warmth. On one occasion he remembered waking up completely paralyzed. Under regression hypnosis he recalled being engulfed by a brilliant light. He got out of the truck, only to be lifted up as if he were weightless and deposited in some kind of room, where two small round-headed humanoids helped him onto a table. They were about four feet tall, skinny but with heads too large for their bodies. They also had "weird eyes, with no pupils. You can't really see anything in the eye except that black thing looking at you."[14]

The entities examined his entire body (he had somehow become undressed), and then a "female of the species" was brought in. She was built more like a human, with breasts for example, but with no body hair. Her eyes were neither human nor like the other aliens', but rounded, as when "your eyes are wide open." She seemed to be "half in half." A "vacuum device" was stuck on to his genitals to induce an erection; the female mounted him; he had an orgasm. The "males" scraped the residual sperm off his penis and put it in a sample bottle. Ed had the impression that the aliens found humans attractive — his thick black hair, for example — and that they were trying to "upgrade their species." He felt nothing but shame and horror after his encounter — felt as if he had been simply and callously *used*.[15]

This is a complaint frequently voiced by female abductees, whose sexual molestation at the hands of the grays, if less graphic, is no less chilling.

Wise babies

Under hypnosis, Kathie Davis recalled seeing her first UFO in the winter of 1977.[16] The memory is disjointed, blurred, and discontinuous but, briefly, she remembered being parked in a car with two friends, when she was assailed by feelings which would later become familiar — a scared, tingly sensation of dread and uncanniness. She found herself paralyzed. She could see nothing, but she felt her legs being pulled away from her body, a feeling more unpleasant than painful. She then felt something hard being pushed into her uterus. At this point Hopkins persuaded her to take a peek at her surroundings. She was surprised to find that she was not, as she thought, in the car, but in a curved, lit room. She also saw the big-eyed gray alien who was by now familiar to her from other remembered abductions. (He was not always terrifying by any means; he often smiled, with his eyes rather than his mouth, and sometimes patted her reassuringly so that she felt happy and relaxed.)

Kathie thought that this event had taken place roughly at the same time as her first pregnancy, which had been confirmed by both urinalysis and a blood test, early in 1978. Mysteriously, however, she menstruated in March. Submitting to a second pregnancy test, she found, to the bafflement of her doctor, that she was no longer pregnant. She came to believe that during the episode in the car she had been impregnated by the aliens, who later came back and removed the fetus. This scenario was "confirmed" in later hypnotic sessions, and repeated by other abductees who contacted Budd Hopkins.

For example, another woman whom he does not name, to protect her identity, remembered having two operations — on her chest and back — with scars to match. She had also become pregnant at the age of thirteen, but without having had any sexual experience. However, she did remember having sex as if in a dream with a "real funny looking" man with no hair and "real funny eyes." She could not move during this act of sex — she just felt something sharp inside her vagina and a sensation as if her stomach was about to explode. A gynecologist found that she was pregnant, but still a virgin (her hymen was intact). She had an abortion — before the fetus, Hopkins remarked calmly, "could be removed by UFO occupants during a second abduction."[17]

As with all daimonic events, it is impossible to verify absolutely the "facts" of the matter, such as these puzzling pregnancies. Perhaps the best we can say is that the pattern of events described by Kathie and the other abductees conforms to an archetypal motif: all traditional societies recognize that there is traffic and intercourse between themselves and the daimonic realm, whether for good or for ill. Irish myths, for instance, tell us that humans enlist the aid of the immortal fairies in times of warfare, and vice versa. It might seem that the daimons would not need our help but, as Yeats has noticed, in all the stories of exchange, whether of warriors or wives, "strength comes from men and wisdom from among the gods who are but shadows."[18]

The notion that daimons need human strength lies at the heart of abduction myths. Irish fairies take especially handsome or strong young men and women to intermarry with; they take babies, leaving in their place "changelings" who are skinny and wizened like old men, and voraciously hungry (they are exchanging a healthy child for a defective one); they snatch young mothers to suckle their children. The motive usually assigned to fairies in northern, as opposed to Mediterranean, stories is that of "preserving and improving their race, on the one hand by carrying off human children...to become united with them, and on the other hand by obtaining the milk and fostering care of human mothers for their own offspring."[19]

This theme returns in modern "UFO abduction" stories, where, for example, Pam — one of Hopkins's abductees — dreamt about a baby which she is allowed to hold. She attached special significance to this dream, deeming it "real," because she had not long before gone for an abortion — only to find that there was "no sign of fetal tissue."[20] In the dream, the baby is given to her by a very small person in a long robe and with a "creepy" round head, who invites her to nurse (that is, suckle) the baby so that the person can watch and learn how it is done. Susan Williams, on the other hand, a psychotherapist who suffered missing time in 1953, had recurring "wise-baby dreams" in which a tiny, beautiful but very "old" and fragile baby addresses her eloquently and wisely. (In Jungian psychology, such babies, preternaturally "old" and wise, are often archetypal images of the Self.) We are asked to believe that, in these cases, the babies have been taken from their mothers — in line with advanced technology, they are taken before birth — and have been brought up by the aliens; that they are, in fact, half alien. Their purpose now is to improve the aliens genetically.

In the climax to the case of Kathie Davis, she spontaneously remembered — without hypnosis — an encounter with an alien child. Once again, the experience was "like a dream... But it was too real to be a dream" — an adequate description of daimonic reality. She was surrounded by the little grays, but they seemed pleased with her and, when they touched her, it was comforting. She was not afraid. Two of the grays escorted into the room a little girl who looked about four years old. She was "real pretty...like an elf, or an...angel." Her features were "just so perfect and tiny," her eyes very big and blue, her skin pale and creamy, her hair white and wispy.[21]

Kathie was unbearably moved by the sight of this shy, tiny creature whom she knew to be, in some sense, hers. She was told that she could not take the child with her because she would not be able to live — "you wouldn't be able to feed her" — and that she needed a father. The child is even dressed like an angel in "white silky stuff" which goes over her head and drapes down to the floor. Kathie remarked that, paradoxically, she could have been "really old" or "an infant." One of the grays says that the child is a part of her. When she asks where they are taking the child, they reply only that she is safe and always will be. The meeting is, for Kathie, full of sadness and loneliness, wonder and joy.[22] She subsequently met another of "her babies" in "a dream." In fact, there were nine in all, corresponding to the nine ova she claimed were stolen from her womb over a long period. The second baby was male: "He looked like an old man, and he looked so wise. I looked in his eyes...he was so...smart...more wise than anybody in the world."[23]

"And so there it was," concludes Hopkins, "the apparent answer to the problem of Kathie's mysterious pregnancy of 1977" — and he means that the aliens took Kathie's fetus as part of their ongoing genetic study and breeding experiment.[24] But her striking and, I suggest, archetypal child image can be seen in other lights. It might, for instance, be an image of Kathie's own soul, both partly hers (personal) and partly not (impersonal). It is fragile and vulnerable in relation to our literal reality (it cannot be brought into this world; there is nothing to "feed" it with); and yet it is powerful and numinous in its own right, both young and old — that is, timeless — but also perhaps growing, maturing, and realizing itself in the Otherworld, the unconscious, where its "father" is. It cannot be destroyed; it will always be "safe" — inviolable and immortal as daimons are and as the daimonic portion of ourselves, our souls, are said to be.

Moreover, there are links in the image of Kathie's child with the traditional *changeling* — the child left in this world by the fairies when they exchange it for a human child. However, whereas the fairy changeling is a reject — stunted, ugly, voraciously hungry — Kathie's child is angelic, beautiful, and unable to be fed in this world. But she is not a straight reversal of the changeling — the human child taken into the Otherworld — rather, a new kind of hybrid: she mediates between the worlds, not by the principle of exchange, but by the principle of synthesis, embodying both human and alien characteristics.

The midwife's journey

The idea that we have a reciprocal relationship with the daimonic world is nowhere better exemplified than in the host of folk tales which describe the otherworld journey — entirely voluntary for a change — of the midwife. Typically, she is visited at dead of night by a member of "the Gentry" — a fairy — and persuaded to go with him to attend an expectant mother. She is transported swiftly to a magnificent mansion "splendidly lit up with such lamps as she had never before seen" and conducted through opulent surroundings to the bedchamber of the mistress, whose baby she delivers. (The mistress sometimes confides that she is a human who has previously been abducted to the fairy realm.) The midwife attends the endless festivities which go on day and night — dancing, singing, feasting, and merriment. When at last she tears herself away, she is given a purse with instructions not to open it before she re-enters her own house. If she opens it prematurely, there is nothing in it but coal or withered leaves; if she waits until she is home, it is full of silver and gold.[25]

Jacob Grimm reported a Scandinavian story concerning a clergyman, Peter Rahm, who on 12 April 1671 had a solemn legal declaration drawn up. It testified to an event which had occurred eleven years before: he had been visited one evening by a little man, swart of face and clad in gray, who begged his wife — she was a midwife — to help his own wife who was in labor. Rahm, recognizing the man as a troll, prayed over his wife, blessed her, and bade her go in God's name with the stranger. "She seemed to be borne along by the wind. After her task was accomplished, she...refused the food offered her, and was borne home in the same manner as she had come. The next day she found on the shelf in the sitting-room a heap of old silver pieces and clippings, which it is to be supposed the troll had brought her."[26]

The midwife's passage to and from the Otherworld is comparatively easy because she is already a borderline, liminal figure. She was often a "wise woman" to whom a certain unearthliness attached, including at times a suspicion of witchcraft. But her special status stemmed above all from the fact that she presided over the rite of birth, when the ante-natal Otherworld draws very close to this world and the midwife, like a tutelary daimon, has to straddle the threshold. Young children are especially vulnerable to abduction for the same reason: they have not yet been officially received, or received back, into this world — they still have one foot in the other.

Supernatural food

One invariable feature of the midwife's visit to the Otherworld is her refusal to accept food and drink. She knows, and tradition confirms, that to eat fairy food is to be doomed to stay in the fairy domain. Indeed, the women whom she attends are often just such humans who have rashly succumbed to an invitation to feast and, compelled to stay, have married fairy, elf, or troll men.

The motif of supernatural food, its delights and perils, is as old as the gods, who are variously said to live on such substances as ambrosia or *soma*. Thus we are not surprised to find that UFO abductees are not infrequently asked or forced to eat and drink. Darren Sunderland, the younger brother of Gaynor who, as we saw in the Introduction, encountered some pink-eyed aliens near her home in North Wales, was taken from his bedroom by an orange globe and transported to a large "vessel," where he was seated at a long table. A red plate was put before him with a lump of yellow doughy substance on it. Although the prospect was less than appetizing, he knew he was expected to eat. The substance was sickly sweet, rather like honey (or, we might add, like ambrosia), but it seemed not to imperil him, for he was returned almost at once to his bedroom where he woke up feeling queasy.[27] The goblinesque abductors of José Antonio da Silva gave him a green liquid to drink from a small cubic cup made of stone. Even Albert Ostman was given some kind of grass to eat by his Bigfoot captors. It had long roots and tasted "very sweet."[28]

Otherworldly food is of course symbolic, not literal. It is the image of food — food for the soul — which nourishes us imaginatively. Eating is a way of assimilating the Otherworld, of becoming daimonized, so that there is part of us which does not return to this world or part of the Otherworld which stays with us, like the scars that are both reminders and conduits of that deeper soulful life underlying actuality. No human is immune to the power of supernatural food: we return dizzy, queasy, bewildered, converted, ecstatic from the otherworldly feast. But perhaps only those whose psychic condition is already precarious — midwives, unchristened babes, etc. — are compelled to remain there. Everyone, however, suffers to a greater or lesser extent from what tribal people call "loss of soul," by which it is meant that their personal soul-image, which dwells among others in the impersonal and collective Soul of the World, is disjoined from their individual mind and body, causing them to be overcome by sickness, lethargy, and even physical death. However, I shall be coming back later to the idea of soul loss, and to the specialists whose job it is to retrieve the soul in question.

For the moment, it is worth remarking that, unsurprisingly, soul food does not travel well. It is commonplace for those Irish countryfolk who feasted among the fairies to find themselves alone on a hillside the next morning, vomiting up dirt and grass — they had perhaps mistaken the metaphorical meat of their hosts for literal food. If we do not assimilate the images of the Otherworld, they come back to us as worthless and indigestible dirt, just as fairy gold translates (on contact with normal expectation and illegitimate curiosity) into coal and leaves. Traditional tales, especially Welsh ones, tell us that those who have been taken into the Otherworld and return long after their natural life-span remain intact and apparently not a day older — so long as they do not eat. But, alas, the moment a morsel of food passes their lips, their fragile daimonic existence is shattered and they re-enter the realm of literality — and crumble to dust. However, we should also remember that wherever the otherworldly images have been assimilated, the food of this world evokes a reciprocal repugnance and we are reluctant to eat, like the Avis family who could no longer abide even the smell, let alone the taste, of meat.

Reciprocity

Myths of sexual exchange, interbreeding, and changelings express the reciprocity of this world and the Otherworld. They metaphorically represent the mutual dependence of human and daimon. Likewise, an exchange of hospitality — of food and drink — maintains equilibrium between them. Well-ordered households across Europe used to leave out food at night (especially butter and milk) in order to propitiate the fairies, elves, or trolls. Few people expected such food to be literally eaten. Instead, it was said that the food had no goodness in it by morning — the fairies had sucked all the savor out, feeding on the food's essence rather than its substance. Thus folklore belief understood very well, and concretely expressed, the metaphorical function of food as a mediator between us and the daimons who, in return for the food, guaranteed an abundant harvest, healthy livestock, and plentiful springs or wells.

In a more formal, religious context, sacrifices and burnt offerings are an attempt to maintain right relationship with the otherworldly divinities. When sacrificial animals are burnt, the gods are said to feed off the savor which rises from them. The animal is "etherealized" — translated from flesh into spirit for which the ascending, aromatic smoke is a metaphor. (During the Reformation, no dispute was more bitter than that concerning the Transubstantiation: was the bread consecrated at Mass the actual, substantial — the literal — body of Christ? Or was it simply a symbol of His Body? To what extent can God penetrate the world and be digested by us? Our primal innocence was corrupted by the bite of an apple in Eden; it was restored by the sacrifice of Christ and the consumption of His Body and Blood. Eating is the first instinct, anterior even to sex, because it needs no other. It is supremely selfish. To give our food to others, human or daimon, is to recognize our interdependence. To give ourselves over to be eaten, as Christ does, is a symbol of supreme selflessness.)

It should be mentioned also, in passing, that otherworldly beings "feed" directly off us on occasions, such as when the fairies kidnap men to assist in their games or wars. The mere presence of humans seems to be a source of strength, as if daimons draw on our psychic energy to give themselves substance. In return, we receive the gifts of clairvoyance, healing, and occult knowledge — the skills, in other words, of mediums and shamans, "cunning men" and "wise women."

One of the traditional ways in which daimons are able to draw on our strength is through taking our blood. We remember the classic instance in *The Odyssey*: in order to speak with the shades of the dead, Odysseus poured the blood (of animals, in this case) into a trench from which the shades had to drink before they could become articulate. There is a touch of the vampire about the Otherworld. We recall Kathie's nosebleed, Virginia's bloody blouse, the alien device that Antonio Villas Boas felt to be removing blood from him. The aliens "need me in order to appear," said young Darren Sunderland. "I'm the ingredient they use to come here. They tap me."[29]

The daimons need and take — or exchange — our food, blood, power of procreation, and our offspring. In other words, they need what is most substantial and vital to us. They need our life. And this is why the Otherworld is also, implicitly or explicitly, the Underworld or afterlife.

Dancing with the dead

The mythic prototype — the archetype — of all "abductees" is Kore (Persephone), the daughter of Demeter (Ceres). She was gathering flowers one day in the sunlit meadows when the earth suddenly opened and Hades, god of death and the Underworld, seized her and carried her off to his abysmal palace. Knowing that she would have to stay there forever if she ate, Kore refused all food, until at last she succumbed to the temptation of eating seven pomegranate seeds — for which she was condemned to spend three months of every year in the Underworld.

This myth is more than a story about fertility and the origin of the seasons (Kore's three months in the Underworld represents winter, when Demeter's daughter — Nature's seed — is dormant underground). It also reminds us that all living things are continuous with, rooted in, death. The Otherworld is also Hades, both god and realm of the dead. Fairy lore is full of stories of visitors to the Otherworld who have seen, dancing among the fairies, people they recognize — people whom they know to have died. (We remember too the corpses seen by da Silva in the cave-like domain of his dwarfish abductors.) "Accordingly we need not be surprised if the same incidents of story attach, at one time, to ghosts, and at another to non-human creatures of imagination, or if Hades and Fairyland are often confounded."[30] In Brittany, the confusion becomes identity: everything predicated of the fairies in other Celtic regions is predicated of the dead. No less than the fairies, the dead even have to be fed — especially at Halloween when, impersonated by children, they have to be placated with candy if they are not to play tricks on us.

The dead are also, of course, the ancestors whom many tribal peoples revere as quasi-divine. The ufological equivalent of this myth is the belief that extraterrestrials visited Earth long ago, founded civilization, and even intermarried with humans. This belief — that the gods were "spacemen" — has achieved considerable popularity, to judge by the number of books which authors such as Erich von Däniken have sold. But it is mistaken. To call the gods "spacemen" is to literalize them, to read myth as history. If anything, the "spacemen" are gods.

Every journey to the Otherworld has connotations of death, for every Otherworld has something of the depth of Hades, the Otherworld beneath all other worlds. To encounter, however briefly, the Otherworld is to encounter a portion of death. No wonder we are suddenly numbed, paralyzed, scarred — our bodies are branded with a *memento mori*. Eating, drinking, sex, marriage, war — fundamentals of life — express our fundamental, mutual relationship to the Otherworld. But death, opposed to life itself, expresses the ultimate relationship: our bodies are taken for their strength and we are paid with soul's wisdom. "Dying each other's life, living each other's death" is how Heraclitus described the relations between mortal and immortal, human and daimon.[31]

17

Human Demons

Satanic ritual abuse

In 1987, some 121 children in Cleveland, in the north-east of England, were diagnosed as having been sexually abused. The prosecution of the alleged abusers — members of the children's families — relied on the evidence of doctors who claimed to be able to recognize sexual abuse from certain bodily signs or indicators. Although these doctors still have their supporters, their evidence was deemed insufficient and the prosecution cases collapsed.[1]

In November 1989 this kind of case assumed a further, more disturbing dimension when social workers in Rochdale abducted some seventeen children from their homes, on the grounds that they were not only being sexually abused, but that the abuse was taking place in the context of satanic rites. This was not an isolated case: similar accusations had occurred in Nottingham and would subsequently occur in the Orkney Islands, where even a minister of the church was implicated in the alleged satanic abuse. However, no evidence was found, the allegations of satanism were abandoned, the children were returned and the social workers were criticized. In Rochdale, the latter continued to insist that the children were suffering, at the very least, from neglect and might have been relating fantasies induced by hallucinogenic drugs — the children complained that they had been given strange drinks, fizzy or sweet, or suspicious foodstuffs, which made them feel woozy, odd, drowsy, helpless, etc.[2]

The sexual abuse of children is a tricky, emotive issue to write about. It undeniably occurs. But the addition of satanism complicates matters. Ritual magic, both benign and malign, *is* practiced; devil-worship *does* take place. But the connection between satanism and sexual abuse has not been established. Despite widespread belief in such a connection, causing fear and outrage like that of the medieval witch-hunts to sweep through whole communities, especially in the USA, conscientious police investigations have failed to uncover any hard evidence. The chief basis for accusations of satanism and sexual abuse remained the stories of the children concerned. Under questioning they spoke — more evocatively and vaguely than precisely — of strange "rites" which included sexual abuse by parents, incest, the drinking of blood, the killing and eating of children or of aborted fetuses. Such stories were substantiated by a number of adults who claimed to have undergone similar horrors in childhood. (We should note, however, that at least some of these adults seem to thrive on the attention given to them as "escapees"; many of them are "unstable," with a long history of neglect, abuse, and drug-taking — to say nothing of the reliability or otherwise of memory.)[3]

Two interpretations of the children's stories have been suggested. We will recognize at once that they are the same interpretations usually put forward to account for apparitions and visions. The first claims that the stories are literally true and that ritual sexual abuse actually took place. The second claims that the stories are, at worst, lies or, at best, "imaginary" — ritual abuse exists only in the minds of the children, who are either concealing a genuine sexual trauma behind fantasies of satanic rites, or constructing fantasies based on the leading questions of adults, in order to please those adults or gain their attention. I want to suggest that there is a third interpretation, which depends on understanding something of both the historical and mythological background to the children's stories. As we go along, we should also bear in mind the way myths tend to be variants — often complete reversals — of the same core themes and structures.

The image of the witch

The abducting, killing, and eating of babies is an archetypal motif. It is a myth. (It is, arguably, a reversal of fairy and modern UFO myths about the abduction, fostering, and feeding of babies.) Greco-Roman society accused Christians of such practices, and the Christians in turn accused the Jews. Everyone accused the gypsies. In medieval times, the Christians attributed the same diabolic acts to heretics, such as the Waldensians, and then to witches.[4] In other words, societies tend to demonize the aliens in their midst or the aliens who live nearby. Tribal societies are no exception. They commonly believe that there exist witches who eat children, practice cannibalism, and commit incest. Such reversals of right behavior are also predicated of neighboring tribes who are, therefore, witches. Other basic attributes which form the image of the witch include acting at night, wearing black, changing into animals, flying, emitting a fiery glow, and walking upside down, backwards, etc. — that is, behaving in some kind of inverted way.[5] Witches, then, are not only daimonic but demonic; their counterparts, to whom similar supernatural powers are attributed — but working for good rather than bad — are of course "witch doctors." But the unique characteristic of these figures compared to other daimons is that they are human.

The tribal image of the witch shares many features with that image of the witch which was established in sixteenth and seventeenth-century Europe at the height of the witch-hunts. Here, the witch was human and usually a woman who, during some crisis such as bereavement or destitution, made a pact with the Devil. He provided her with consolation or money, but he also terrified her, made her obedient and mated with her painfully (his penis was cold and scaly). He set his mark on her, typically by clawing with his left hand the left-hand side of her body. Thereafter the woman became a witch with the power to perform *maleficium* or occult harm, for example by inducing illness, impotence, and sterility, or by blighting crops and cattle.[6]

Witches specialized in the killing of babies and children in order to eat them or to use parts of their bodies in supernatural operations, such as the manufacture of potions for killing people, or of salves for flying. They flew to their Sabbats on demonic animals or else on sticks, spits, shovels, or broomsticks. Their spouses meanwhile slept peacefully, sometimes fooled by a stick laid in the bed which not only took the place, but also took on the appearance, of the absent witch.[7]

The initiation of women into witchcraft by the Devil obviously derived from Christianity. So did their Otherworld, the Sabbat, which was graphically described by the woman accused of witchcraft and identified by the Devil's "witch-marks." It contained the appearance of the Devil, a parody of the Eucharist — drinking blood and eating flesh or feces — orgies, incest, sodomy, and so on — a demonic inversion, in other words, of Christian values and practices.

But we should also notice that "Christian" witchcraft contains features drawn from or mingled with pagan traditions. The affinity of fairies with witches is an obvious example. Both could cause harm with a single look. Both are shape-changers (witches could turn themselves into black cats, hares, crows, etc.). The stick left in the bed by the witch is the counterpart of the log in the likeness of a body left by the fairies in place of the person they have taken. The Scottish witch Isobel Gowdie, we remember, saw the king and queen of the fairies on one of her trips.

The use of a broomstick to fly to the Sabbats reminds us of another tradition — that of shamans (I will be coming to them) who, in a trance state, travel into the Otherworld on a "horse" symbolized by an ordinary object such as a stick or a drum.[8] This, in turn, reminds us that the women who were demonized as witches may even have been the opposite — witch doctors or, as the Europeans preferred, wise women, seers, mediums, and so on. At any rate, they may have been shamanic daimonic figures, as midwives were often thought to be, who would be easily demonized by a Christian viewpoint, just as all daimons were. I might add that just as pagan elements infiltrate Christian otherworld journeys, so Christian elements appear in modern secular otherworld journeys, such as UFO abductions. Some of these are fairly explicit — I am thinking of the "angelic" entities — but might not the sensation of flying, the scars ("witch-marks") and the cold probing of the gray's tools (like the Devil's penis) be related to the Sabbat?

Witches, satanists, social workers

Lacking the category of the daimonic, the old Christian witch-hunters had to believe, however reluctantly, that the alleged witches' stories were literally true, while modern anthropologists and historians have to believe that they are not. Yet they still have to account for a phenomenon that is too persistent and prevalent, too drastic in its consequences, to dismiss out of hand. However, no matter how ingenious their theories are, we are somehow left with the feeling that they *have* dismissed it — that witch beliefs are pretty much "all in the mind," and in the minds, moreover, of peoples more primitive than ourselves. Witch beliefs could not exist nowadays, they seem to say, except in the minds of credulous peasants. But they do exist; and it is not only credulous peasants who believe in the literal existence of satanists, the modern equivalent of witches, who perpetrate age-old crimes against children.

(Margaret Murray provided a spirited attempt to account for witches by claiming that they were remnants of a pagan Mother-Goddess-worshipping cult.[9] Her opponents have — successfully, I think — debunked her theory, showing that it could not literally be the case.[10] They are scornful of the modern witch or "wicca" cults, calling themselves "revivals," which have sprung up in imitation of the cult Murray imagined. But they have not grasped the way in which theory, speculation, and hypothesis play the part that used to be played by legend and folk tales — that is, they do not see, as we have seen, how theories about daimonic events and the events themselves exist on a continuum, springing from the same imaginative source. Murray's theory is not literally true but, in a daimonic sense, it may be fundamentally true because, speaking as it does about the empowerment of women, it articulates a myth whose time, however modestly, has come.)

If I say that satanists are the equivalent of witches, I am not saying that no satanists exist. But I suggest that they exist in the same way as Murray's witch cultists exist. They are *acting out* a myth which, denied its own rightful daimonic imaginative space, takes possession of our (secondary) imaginations where it is duly literalized by the overweening, single-minded ego. At any rate, although I cannot prove it, I am willing to bet that there does not exist, as social workers have claimed (but equally cannot prove), a vast nationwide conspiracy of satanic cults dedicated to the corruption, and worse, of children.

Like medieval witchcraft, modern belief in the existence of satanism is largely a product of the Christian imagination. Many of the social workers involved in "rescuing" children from satanists had been influenced by Christian fundamentalist groups, originating in the USA, who spoke persuasively and doubtless sincerely about the actuality of satanic ritual abuse, and distributed lists of "indicators" by which it could be detected.[11] These indicators included nightmares, bed-wetting, dread of monsters and the supernatural, and an obsession with excrement and smells. "Given the nature of children," John Michell observed, "such indicators made the detection of satanic abuse a relatively simple matter."[12] Like the witchcraft myth which emerged during the inquisition of alleged witches and their interrogators, a satanic ritual abuse myth soon emerged from the interaction of the alleged victims and their rescuers.

The latter myth, harking back to witch beliefs, is far from new; but neither is it identical to the witchcraft myth. Rather, it is a fascinating variant, compiled by the mythopoeic Imagination and obeying the usual rules of reversal. For example, seeking to rescue the children, the social workers abducted them from their homes, often at night — exactly as witches were supposed to have done. The children's family demonizes the social workers, believing that their children have been abducted by people who will corrupt their children with sexual examinations and satanic tales. The social workers play the part of the witches. But they, in turn, demonize the children's family, alleging that they are the real satanists, but located in reverse, since the old witches were, by definition, aliens, wholly *outside* the family. The family plays the part of the witches. Meanwhile, the children are actually playing the role closest to the witches, but in reverse. It is they who visit the ghastly "Sabbat," but involuntarily instead of voluntarily. It is they who are helpless and harmed, instead of being given occult power to harm. It is they who are examined for physical signs of sexual interference, just as the witches were examined for physical signs ("witch-marks") of their pact with the Devil. The witches' victims play the part of the witches.

Like the ancient ambiguity of hunter and hunted who take on each other's attributes, the (Christian) social workers took on the (demonic) attributes of the very phenomenon they were trying to uproot. And it is this aspect of the complicated set of reversals which seems to have appealed most to the collective Imagination. I say this in the light of a strange and unexpected development in the story of alleged ritual abuse.

The curse of the bogus social workers

On 30 January 1990, two smartly dressed young women claiming to represent the National Society for the Prevention of Cruelty to Children called on twenty-four-year-old Elizabeth Coupland at her home in Parkhill Flats, Sheffield. They asked if they could examine her children, aged two and five months. Mrs. Coupland allowed them to do so. One of the children was partially undressed. Two days later (other sources say six days), one of the women returned with a man, saying that they had been authorized to remove both children. Mrs. Coupland resisted their demands, threatening to call the police. The "NSPCC workers" left.[13]

This visit, or visitation, formed a pattern which was to be repeated in many parts of England over the coming months. Reports poured in to the police, describing "health workers" or "social workers" who called to examine or take away children, but who hurriedly left when the householder became suspicious. The visitors were mostly one or two women, but sometimes a woman and a man. The women were typically in their late twenties or early thirties, heavily made up, smartly dressed and of medium height. They carried clipboards and, often, identification cards. "They looked professional," said one witness. "Like doctors." Few of them had local accents. Some even telephoned in advance to make appointments.[14]

Twenty-three separate police forces combined to launch Operation Childcare, dedicated to tracking down the bogus social workers. By May, the incidents were so widespread that police feared that up to four organized gangs were involved. (On 6 May there were three separate incidents in Nantwich, Cheshire, alone.) They were thought to be gangs of pedophiles. But clearly there were signs that the matter was far from straightforward: the pedophile theory was weakened by the involvement of so many women, who are rarely implicated in pedophilia (except in cases of alleged satanic ritual abuse.) Perhaps to account for this, it was hinted more than once that one of Mrs. Coupland's two "women" visitors had been a man in "drag."[15]

Far from deterring the bogus social workers, the police operation seemed only to encourage them, as did the increased publicity (the *News of the World* offered £10,000 for their capture).[16] The number of reported visits rose sharply. At the same time the prospect of arrests being made seemed to recede, as none of the culprits could be traced. By early July, the number of reported incidents had reached 173; by early August, 251. The baffled police grew dispirited. Only eighteen cases were judged worthy of investigation — those when the visitors were said to have actually examined the children. (Some of these may well have been genuine social workers.) No child was ever taken away. Since no obscene touching of the children was reported, the pedophile theory lost further ground until it was more or less ruled out. Instead, it was vaguely suggested that the visitors were either scouts for a group of pedophiles, on the lookout for victims, or members of a vigilante group looking for evidence of sexual abuse. Neither theory stood up to close scrutiny. The police began to talk of "social panic." No suspects were arrested; no charges brought against anyone. The whole affair petered out.[17]

The bogus social workers were, I suppose, daimons. It is especially hard to believe this because they are so mundane, so like ordinary human women.

We expect our daimons to be larger than life. But then again, witches or the image of the witch isn't; and bogus social workers are clearly related to the witch archetype. At the same time they are not credited with any supernatural powers, except perhaps the ability to evade capture. Instead, their outstanding characteristic is their Trickster-like quality. They might almost be perpetrating a practical joke or a hoax in order to discredit social workers or to satirize their activities. In this they are like the perpetrators of crop circles, as I pointed out in Chapter 12. I also suggested that hoaxing was a daimonically driven activity, continuous with "authentic" daimonic events — in other words, the Trickster myth not only acts *on* humans, but is also enacted *through* them. We would therefore expect to see hoaxers acting out the daimonic pattern of the bogus social workers. And indeed they have: in October 1992 a man was arrested for posing as a social worker and attempting to interfere with a child.

If Christianity had not excluded Tricksters, forcing them to merge with the only image it has of supernatural duplicity, the Devil, demons would not appear. Like evil witches, bogus social workers are products of our demonizing imaginations. As it is, we were lucky: they remained more mischievous than actually harmful. All daimons are by nature Tricksters. If we continue to deny them their own space, I cannot help wondering whether they might not become out of necessity more demonic, more literal, until they really do hurt us — either directly or through those humans who, like hoaxers, are momentarily possessed by their spirit. Will we open the newspapers one day to read that the police have found the remains of a child in the house of a satanic cult?

Before I leave this nasty but intriguing subject, I ought briefly to mention one other, quite common, form of "human demon" which crops up from time to time in the ufological literature. In fact, at least one of our female bogus social workers sounded very similar. Mrs. Pat Crotty of Battersea, London, entertained her on 13 May 1990, and described her as bland, official-looking, well informed about matters she could not logically know anything about, but also prone to making the odd slip — for instance, calling Mrs. Crotty Mrs. *Crosby* and referring to her *four* children instead of three.[18] This description fits the peculiar kind of alien-like "officials," who threaten UFO contactees, but finally do no harm. They are usually called Men in Black.

Men in Black

On 16 July 1967, two men called on Robert Richardson of Toledo, Ohio. They questioned him about an incident in which he had apparently hit with his car a UFO that had landed on the road. He had returned to the scene of the crash and retrieved a small piece of metal, which he sent to a UFO investigation group. The men spoke to Richardson for about ten minutes. Later, he was surprised that it had never occurred to him to ask them for any identification. He noticed that they left in a black 1953 Cadillac, whose number he wrote down. When he checked the number, he found that it had never been issued.

A week later, two different men turned up (in a current model Dodge). They were dark and wore black suits. One of them had a foreign accent. At first they seemed to be trying to get Richardson to admit that he had not had any kind of UFO encounter. Then they asked him to hand over the piece of metal, about which no one could have informed them. When Richardson explained that he had passed it on, the men said that he had better get it back "if you want your wife to stay as pretty as she is..."[19]

This sort of stilted utterance is typical of Men in Black and in keeping somehow with their old-fashioned, fifties-style suits and cars. They are B-movie demons. They appear in the aftermath of a UFO sighting, often before it has even been reported, usually when the witness is "by chance" alone. They wear white shirts with their smart black suits; they appear foreign or "oriental"; they have dark skins and slanting eyes. They behave stiffly, formally, speaking without expression, like robots. Witnesses accept them as normal at first, as when we see a ghost, but when they reflect on the men, they do not seem to have been quite human. The Men in Black sometimes wear uniforms, like Air Force officials. If they offer names or identification, these turn out to be false. They know details about the witness's life which they could not possibly know in the normal course of things. Like the bogus social workers, their visits are sinister — they even issue threats and warnings — but these come to nothing.[20] They are not, like other daimons, more real than life; they are merely life-like. They do not inspire horror or awe; they merely induce mild paranoia. They are, needless to say, never traced. They are unpleasant Tricksters who belong at the same imaginative level as second-rate science fiction.

18

Daimonic Humans

Rites of passage

The abduction of children is an institution in most tribal societies. At around the time of puberty, they are snatched from the safety of their homes by tall entities with extraordinary faces — slit mouths and noses, large eyes, for example — and carried off to a dark place, sometimes narrow and subterranean like a grave, where they are left for days at a time. Deprived of food, exhausted, they are periodically visited by the entities, who torture them, slashing their penises and scarring their faces. At the same time they are given amazing knowledge — secrets they must not reveal — before being returned to their villages in a blaze of lights where their families no longer recognize them.

I am, of course, roughly describing quite usual puberty rites in which the candidates are taken away by the masked and painted elders of the tribe, penned up in the fetish house or buried in the bush, and subjected to ritual operations such as scarification, circumcision, or clitorectomy. They know what is going on in one sense, but, in another, they really are in fear of imminent death from the adults they once knew, but who are now transformed into alien beings like the spirits of the ancestors. The children are themselves painted to resemble ghosts — that is, assimilated to the dead — for their former childish selves have to die through the initiation in order that they can be reborn into new adult selves. Thus, when they return to their homes in a blaze of torchlight, newly instructed in the secret and sacred tribal lore, their relatives pretend not to know them. Indeed, like all abductees, they hardly know themselves.

Christianity retains vestiges of puberty rites in the ceremonies of First Communion and Confirmation; but these have abandoned any pretence to the same imaginative and transforming power. Above all, they lack the fear and pain which seem to be necessary elements of initiation. We may wonder what the consequences are of losing effective official rites to render our biological changes significant and to stamp us with the mark of adulthood. Isn't there a danger that we remain childish, selfish, dependent, mere victims of whatever life throws at us? Many people, of course, are unwittingly initiated by the exigencies of their lives, such as family catastrophes, bereavement, or even by the ordeals of schooling. Initiation depends less on the experience itself than on what we make of it, how we use it for self-transformation. But without traditional rites that both induce and channel suffering, it is difficult to use it correctly — we are encouraged instead to seek a *cure* for it.

However, tribal societies universally recognize a type of person who is initiated *spontaneously* — not by socially organized puberty rites, for example, but by direct supernatural experience. It might even be argued that this spontaneous initiation is the model on which all initiation is based and which is imitated — literally re-enacted — by the tribal elders who are charged with initiating their children. The type of persons I am referring to are witch doctors, medicine men (or women) or, as current fashion now calls them, *shamans*.

The shaman's tradition

While a shaman may attain his position through heredity, he is just as likely to receive it by spontaneous vocation. There are several signs of such a vocation: sudden illnesses, fits or fainting spells; a "big dream"; or, above all, an unexpected state of trance or ecstasy. While in this state, the recipient undergoes a visionary experience whose contents invariably include one or more of the following features: a dismemberment of the body by "spirits" (daimons) or by the souls of dead shamans; a purging or scraping down of the body which is then reconstructed with new organs or "iron bones"; an ascent to the sky, followed by a dialogue with gods or spirits; a descent to the Underworld, followed by conversation with subterranean spirits and the souls of dead shamans.[1]

Once the future shaman, or shamaness, has been clearly chosen by such a primary initiatory experience, they undergo further daimonic experiences, usually under the supervision of an existing shaman, in order to acquire the help and protection of familiar spirits (often animals) and tutelary spirits (human, often a dwarf). Such spirits can possess or speak through the shaman, but this is not the determining characteristic of shamanism (anyone can be possessed) which is, rather, the ability to make the heavenly ascent or subterranean descent at will, controlling the sacred itinerary which is structured according to the tribe's cosmology. For instance, among the tribes of northern Asia, such as the Tungus of Siberia — who gave us the word "shaman" — the shamans climb a symbolic world-tree which connects the Above to the Below, ride their drums like horses into the sky or climb down through the smoke-hole into the yurt, to retrace the heroic, celestial, and subterranean journeys of former shamans.

The spirits' ritual operations on the prospective shaman have their parallels among UFO abductees. For example, on 26 August 1975, Sandra Larson saw a number of glowing globes descending towards her on the drive to Bismarck, North Dakota. She could not account for an hour of her journey. Under hypnosis she described a classic UFO abduction during which her captors scraped the inside of her nose with some kind of instrument and then, opening her skull, removed her brain and replaced it.[2]

On 6 January 1976, Mona Stafford, Louise Smith, and Elaine Thomas encountered an enormous object with multiple lights while driving to Liberty, Kentucky. When they arrived, they found that a period of one and a half hours was unaccounted for. Under hypnosis, their stories concerning the events which were presumed to have occurred during this missing time partially confirmed one another. They had been abducted by small, gray creatures whose slant eyes, the only features visible behind a kind of visor, fixed on them in an unnerving gaze. The three women were separated and taken to a sort of cave which was stiflingly hot. Like Antonio da Silva, they were pinned to tables and had a hot sticky liquid poured over them. Then their arms and legs were twisted as if being tested to see how much stress they could stand. Mona's eyes were removed from their sockets, examined, and replaced.[3] (A Yakut shaman, Pyotr Ivanov, reported that his initiation entailed the disjointing of his bones, and the scraping away of his flesh and the tearing of his eyes from their sockets.)[4] We remember, too, how Kathie Davis found herself lying paralyzed in her car after the first UFO sighting she could remember. Then she felt her legs being pulled away from her and something hard being pushed into her uterus. Both she and another abductee,

Susan, describe "things…being moved around, like organs."[5]

Another recurring motif in UFO abduction lore is the "implant." Abductees claim that their abductors insert through their noses and the side of their heads some kind of tiny object whose purpose is unknown (extraterrestrialists speculate that it is a kind of transmitter, enabling the aliens to monitor their victims). This is reminiscent of an almost universal motif in shamanism, of which the practice of the Aranda in Australia provides a typical example. The initiate is lanced through the neck by a "spirit," while sleeping at the entrance to the initiatory cave. He is then carried into the cave by the spirit, who tears out his internal organs and replaces them with new ones. Fragments of quartz are inserted into his body. Then he is returned to life but, for some time, behaves like a lunatic.[6] The quartz crystals are supposed to bestow powers on the shaman, notably the power to fly. They are imagined to be of celestial origin and only quasi-material, like "solidified light."[7]

These beneficial, power-bestowing "implants" have their malevolent counterparts in the magical objects which are inserted into a person's body by a sorcerer, demon, dead person's spirit, or malign shaman. Next to "loss of soul," these magical objects are the most widespread cause of disease (throughout the Americas, for instance), and have to be sucked out by a shaman who then displays them as, for example, a thread, insect, lizard, or stone.[8]

When we consider too that UFO abductions contain the equivalent of the shaman's celestial journey, teaching or revelations from the spirits, and even an echo of the initiatory cave in the circular, evenly-lit "interior," it seems likely that they are related to the kinds of experience which tribal societies recognize as initiatory.

Death and rebirth

The essence of initiation, for abductees no less than shamans, is death and rebirth. In puberty rites, the childish self dies that the adult self may live; the shaman is dismembered and resurrected, dying to his old bodily perspective and rising again with a new daimonic perspective. Many tribal peoples sanction "secret societies" whose purpose is to initiate adults into the mystery of death and rebirth via rites which are the same in kind as, but less extreme in degree than, shamanic initiations. This was the norm also in ancient Greece, where everyone who was anyone was initiated into the Mysteries which took place at Eleusis. The wisdom of Socrates and the philosophy of his pupil, Plato, cannot rightly be understood without taking into account their initiation into the Eleusinian Mysteries. Since it was forbidden to speak of these, we know little about them; but, significantly, they were thought to revolve around a re-enactment of the Demeter–Kore–Hades myth — the classic myth, in other words, of death and rebirth.

In his treatise *On the Soul*, Plutarch specifically compares initiation into the Mysteries with the experience of death. For the soul at the point of death, he tells us, "has the same experience as those who are being initiated into the great mysteries." At first one wanders to and fro in the dark; then one encounters terrors which induce "shuddering, trembling, sweating, amazement," until at last "one is struck by a marvelous light" and received into "pure regions and meadows, with voices and dances and the majesty of holy sounds and shapes."[9]

Proclus tells us that "in the most holy of mysteries, before the god appears, certain terrestrial [i.e. chthonic] daemons present themselves, and fights which disturb those who are to be initiated, tear them away from undefiled goods, and call forth their attention to matter." The daimons here distract us from the higher symbolic purpose of initiation and redirect our attention back to the physical or, better, the literal world. Clearly these daimons are among Plutarch's terrors, for "the gods exhort us not to look at these, till we are fortified by the powers which the mysteries confer. For thus they speak: it is not proper for you to behold them till your body is initiated."[10]

We will recall that in January 1984, Kathie Davis was hypnotically regressed to the moment when her bizarre series of experiences (and her memory of even earlier experiences) began: the strange light she saw in her pool house. She was so frightened by the memory which began to surface that she had to be brought out of the hypnotic state — she had heard a voice in her head telling her that if she remembered any more she would die. And, indeed, she reported that her body "felt like it was going to die."[11] She did not say that *she* was going to die, only that her *body* was.

In fact, as it turned out, she did in the end recall the events of that night and, frightening as they were, her body did not die. Thus we should perhaps think of her sensation of impending physical death as the kind of death

associated with initiation — that heart-stopping sensation of having one's
bodily perspective dismembered and turned around, of being wrenched out
of literal reality, out of this world and the attachments to it. This can be a
more painful death than physical death because it is the death of everything
that we think of as ourselves. It is also the beginning of a new kind of self, a
rebirth.

Like initiates into the Mysteries (like abductees), all shamans stress the
terror of initiation, including even the encounter with their helping or
tutelary spirits, who can appear fearsome. But, as an Australian shaman
advised, power can be gained from the spirits as long as we are not
intimidated into panicking.[12] There is no indication, in other words, that fear
and pain are bad or wrong, as modern secular ideologies and
psychotherapies tend to suggest. Dreams are full of fear and pain. So are
myths. So are religions. (Consider only the Crucifixion as a model of
initiatory death and resurrection: the heroic God-man prays that the bitter
cup be passed from Him. It is not. He is scourged, crowned with thorns,
pierced by nails and by a lance in His side; He is hung from a cross and left
to die; He descends into Hell and, on the third day, ascends into heaven
when He sits at the right hand of God the Father.)

In Mr. Cunningham's (Brother Drythelm's) near-death experience,
which set the pattern for most subsequent Christian otherworld journeys, we
remember that pain and terror were inflicted on him by demons in the
intermediate realm of Purgatory. Initiation is here Christianized into
punishment for sin, while rebirth is translated into *conversion*. Something of
this Christian influence — this demonizing influence — lingers on in
modern abduction myths. The first fully recorded abduction by the now-
familiar "grays" was perpetrated in September 1961, on Betty and Barney
Hill, while they were driving along a deserted road.[13] Both victims were
subjected to the usual examination-cum-operation: while Barney had a cup-
shaped device placed over his genitals — it left a ring of red marks — Betty
remembered (under hypnosis) having a needle pushed through her abdomen.
This, of course, is a traditional torture employed by demons in Christian
iconography — the same operation can be seen, for example, in the
fifteenth-century *Kalendrier des Bergiers,* in which demons are depicted
torturing damned souls. Thus Christian fundamentalists, who are particularly
voluble in the USA, are not wholly unjustified in regarding the grays quite

simply as demons in the service of Satan.

Another approach, secular this time, which has become fashionable in America, is to treat the alleged abductees, not as sinners being punished by demons, for example, but as *victims*. They are diagnosed as suffering from "post-traumatic stress disorder," which regards them separate from any belief about their trauma's origins, in the same way as rape victims or the survivors of war. In other words, their experience is medicalized and so stripped of its profound, initiatory, not to say religious, potential.

Orpheus

The principal function of the shaman is healing. But since the prime cause of illness among his patients is believed to be "loss of soul," his cure consists of traveling into the Otherworld, retrieving the lost soul, and restoring it to the patient's body. Souls can be lost by accident, as it were, wandering off during sleep, for example; or they can be taken — abducted — by spirits of the dead, witches, and so on. The shaman is uniquely equipped to retrieve them because, in a sense, he has retrieved his own soul, taken from him in his original initiatory trance. The shaman, then, mediates between this world and the Otherworld. He is a daimonic figure, a daimonic human.

In Greek mythology, the archetypal shaman was Orpheus, who by the sweetness of his lyre-playing and songs — the shaman learns his songs from otherworldly daimons — charmed Hades himself into returning his dead wife, his soul-image, Eurydice (although he lost her again by breaking the injunction not to look back just as they were approaching this world). Orpheus is also credited with having initiated the Eleusinian Mysteries. As such, Orpheus was the first theologian, as well as the founder of poetry and music — and shamanism (he also suffered ritual dismemberment). In other words, shamans combine the functions of doctor, priest, poet, and expounder of tribal lore. All these activities were understood to originate in the Otherworld — that is, in the same daimonic realm, the Imagination. Our culture has divided up these functions in accordance with its division of the human organism into separate parts such as mind, body, spirit, and soul. Psychiatrists tend the mind, doctors, the body, and priests, the spirit. Soul, which, rightly understood, binds these together, mediating between them, has been lost. It has been subsumed under, or made synonymous with, spirit, which is by definition wholly immaterial and transcendent, whereas soul is both material and immanent as well. (More accurately, we might say that soul, having no substance in itself, being both everywhere and nowhere, manifests now as spirit, now as matter, depending on context and perspective.) The neglect of the daimons, who pertain to soul, led to their return as psychic (i.e., soul) disorders. Psychology was born to deal with them. Unfortunately, psychology itself divided into schools that believed soul could be reduced to mind or medicalized into an offshoot of the body, or left to a purely spiritual monotheistic religion (soul, as we have seen, is inherently polytheistic). Only a Jungian style of psychology does justice to the depth and complexity of soul in its own right — recognizes, that is, that soul needs the care of a shaman-like figure who combines (as Jung did) a knowledge of medicine, theology, mythology, philosophy, Art, together with first-hand experience of the Otherworld and its denizens.

Dream initiation

We cannot know with certainty whether otherworld journeys, such as abductions, occur spontaneously because the recipient has been deprived of a traditional, social initiation (such as puberty rites), compelling the unconscious to generate images of its equivalent; or whether these otherworld journeys are truly extraordinary initiations, vouchsafed to those who possess the equivalent of a shamanic vocation. I incline towards the latter viewpoint, if only because it seems that our otherworld travelers, such as abductees, usually have a long history of paranormal experience. They are people whom we recognize nowadays as "psychics" (I use the word in the popular, not the Jungian, sense). And, although we also recognize that most of us are capable of some psychic ability, however small, at certain times, we grant the persistent psychic, so to speak, a special status — much as tribal societies grant a special status to shamans.

I will be taking a closer and longer look at the relationship between the psychic and the shaman in the next section, but, to finish this section, I want to observe that there is one entirely natural form of initiation which, although it is highly developed in the shaman, is also open to us all. In fact, I might argue that since we lack effective formal rites to accommodate and structure spontaneous daimonic experiences, the latter would occur more frequently and be more overwhelming, more potentially maddening, were it not for this form of initiation. I am referring to dreams.[14]

Dreams initiate us into the Otherworld by taking the people, things, and events in our conscious waking lives and translating them into images, deliteralizing them — daimonizing them. Conversely, daimonic images linger on after sleep, haunting us, adding another, deeper dimension to our lives, asking us to attend to them, understand them, incorporate them. Like the daimons who inhabit them, dreams offer us wisdom in return for our strength. Unhappily, we too often coerce them with interpretation, drag them into too harsh a light, and harness them to the ego in order to strengthen its perspective. No wonder we forget dreams — they resist recollection because they do not wish to be pressed into the ego's service, to be literalized and, alas, demonized. The strength they seek is not of this kind. Even Jung was perhaps over-zealous in his insistence that we make unconscious contents conscious (after all, daimons have their own consciousness, often "higher" than ours).

What the daimons in dreams seek is our ability, through reflection and pondering, through all our making and doing, to give shape to their dynamic shape-shifting; to order and discriminate their chaos; to body forth their ethereal volatility; to express *their,* not the ego's perspectives. This is the "strength," the substance they seek. It presupposes that we recognize, accommodate, and even revere them; for, if they can only know themselves through us, it is only through them that we can know our own deepest selves.

In the old days, dreams were held in high regard. We have tended to suppress them, to be suspicious of them, scanning them for signs of madness. No wonder they come with difficulty, with distortion. It is our turn, perhaps, to abandon our egoistic daylight world and go to where they are, in the dark, even if we have to bend over backwards. For dreaming may be the only method of initiation left to us: each night brings a "little death" by which we acclimatize to the Otherworld, rehearsing the journey that all souls have to take in the end.

The psychic and the shamanic
Police Constable Alan Godfrey, whose missing-time experience, hypnosis, and abduction scenario I touched on in the Introduction, began subsequently to remember previous periods of missing time. At the age of eighteen, for example, he was driving with his girlfriend at 2 a.m. when he hit a woman

pedestrian with a dog. She just stepped out in front of his car. When Alan got out to take a look, no one was there. Arriving home, he found that two hours were unaccounted for. On another occasion, he was walking his brother's dog in the park when it suddenly went berserk and ran off (the dog motif recurs with the "horrible" big black dog he saw in the "craft" during his "abduction.") Alan thought he could make out a figure in the bushes. It turned out to be a friend with whom he conversed for some considerable time. When Alan was long overdue to return, his brother set out to look for him, and found him wandering alone. He reminded Alan that he could not have been talking to his friend because the man in question had died some months before.[15]

Belief in the literal existence of extraterrestrial spacecraft on the part of many UFO investigators has led them to neglect investigation of the witnesses. When such an investigation has taken place, witnesses such as PC Godfrey are invariably found to have a history of "psychic" experiences, often stretching back to early childhood. Moreover, the experience, such as an abduction, which has appeared in the foreground, is often surrounded by other paranormal events which, unlike the private and personal abduction, appear to be public and impersonal. For instance, Kathie Davis's strange dream-like abduction experiences are embedded in a matrix of weird external happenings — tiny lights whiz down her hallway; little men are seen walking out of the bedroom walls; she receives, every Wednesday, telephone calls in which a voice moans and mutters incomprehensibly. Her neighbors also see lights, hear loud noises, suffer power cuts. Kathie's abductions, as we have seen, were reminiscent of shamanic initiation ordeals. Moreover, she seems to have displayed the shamanic temperament, which is often characterized by sudden or chronic illness (Kathie suffered everything from high blood pressure, hepatitis, and pneumonia to allergic reactions to medicines, asthmatic attacks, irregular heartbeats, anxiety, and insomnia).[16]

Thus it may well be that those people we call "psychic" have a shamanic vocation. But since our culture lacks a shamanic tradition, a daimonic framework to shape and channel psychic abilities, they remain undeveloped, untrained, and uncontrolled. Modern ecstatic otherworld journeys are rarely recognized as opportunities for self-transformation and rebirth, but are merely frightening, mystifying, and open to misinterpretation. At the same time, acting as conduits through which daimonic powers can flow unchecked into this world, untutored psychics are shocked by the intrusion into their lives of uncanny events — what Jung would call unconscious contents which, unable to be integrated into consciousness, are projected onto the external world. The shaman learns to control and manipulate such events — we call it magic or sorcery — but modern psychics are often simply like lightning conductors that unwittingly draw daimons out of their clouds of concealment. Small wonder, then, that other members of their families, and even innocent bystanders, are drawn into their circle of enchantment. In their presence we see things we never thought to see.

This phenomenon accounts for many "multiple-witness" UFO sightings, for example, which — along with such "physical evidence" as bodily scars and landing traces — are held up as evidence for the literal reality of spacecraft. But they are no more literal than any other sighting: UFOs are simply more likely to appear, and with greater objectivity, in the presence of certain people — and, as we have seen, at certain places. The combination of the two is irresistible. I have met people who had never seen anything odd in their lives until they ran into a real old shaman-style figure called Arthur Shuttlewood, who was at the center of a famous UFO "flap" in the late 1960s and early 1970s. He used to take parties of UFO spotters up to the summit of a strange tor, sculpted in the Iron Age, called Cley Hill near Warminster, Wiltshire. UFOs appeared, practically to order. Similarly, Anthony "Doc" Shiels, a self-styled psychic, wizard, and "surrealchemist" (*sic*) used to delight in "monster-raising" rites at promising coastal sites and lakes. The monster Morgawr, an old denizen of Cornish coastal waters, was seen shortly after one such rite, while Doc's photographs of the Loch Ness monster are still the best known.

It is not hard to see that those rare cases, like the Avises', of "multiple abduction" can be accounted for in a similar way. Psychological interpretations of such cases talk vaguely of the phenomenon known as *folie à deux* (or *à trois*). But this begs the usual questions. Instead, using the notion of daimonic reality, we can imagine how two or more people might be enveloped by the same enchantment. One of them is likely to be the chief catalyst, the shaman figure, while the others (they are usually psychically linked to him or her by close emotional ties) are drawn into his or her otherworld journey. The unconscious, after all, is very fluid, especially at a level beyond the personal. Individual souls interconnect in *Anima Mundi,* at the impersonal and collective level. We are always liable to meet in Imagination, sharing the same daimonic space.

The simplest example of this is telepathy. We tend to think of it as "thought-transference," as though one person were transmitting images by a conscious effort of will. Actually, it is more like a relaxation where one person enters daimonic reality and imaginatively establishes links with another, at the psychic level they hold in common. We should regard this as normal rather than otherwise, just as it is normal for members of a tribe — Kalahari Bushmen, say — to communicate over long distances. This is simply an extension of their normal mode of consciousness, which is daimonic by nature and primarily tribal (collective), rather than narrowly literal and primarily individual, as ours is. In the late seventeenth century, the Rev. Robert Kirk noticed similar abilities of telepathy and clairvoyance among Scottish Hebridean Islanders, all of whom he reckoned seers. They were, of course, by his and our standards; by their own, they were merely exercising faculties we have lost — our sharply focused, willful ego-consciousness isolates us in our own individual units and, under normal circumstances, blocks out that more diffuse, twilit, daimonic consciousness which is able to connect naturally with others of its kind, with other times and places. However, we are always liable to slip into their type of consciousness, notably when we sleep (and dream), but also at moments of crisis in our lives, whether emotional (bereavement, for example) or biological (puberty) — or simply when we are driving alone late at night on deserted roads.

Having touched on the way paranormal phenomena can plague a shaman-like figure such as Kathie Davis, and even plague those in proximity to her, I am led to consider another form of initiation. It is difficult to describe — indeed it may not be appropriate to call it initiation at all since it does not apparently involve the death and rebirth experience of the shaman's subterranean and celestial journeys. But it does involve a change, sometimes dramatic, in the recipient, usually in the form of an expanded awareness of the Otherworld and a greater degree of wisdom in encountering it.

Unlike the shaman's experience of the Otherworld as a daimonic realm entered during altered states of consciousness, this different kind of initiation happens the other way around: the Otherworld enters this world. Our everyday reality becomes heightened, full of extraordinary synchronicities, significances, and paranormal events. People who investigate the daimonic are particularly prone to these — although they can happen to anyone who is engaged on a search for some sort of knowledge or truth (every scholar, for instance, knows how the very book he requires can fall off a library shelf at his feet!). In other words, it is a goal-oriented kind of initiation and, as such, might be called a *quest*.

John Keel's quest

A quest can perhaps be imagined as an extroverted version of the shaman's introversion — perhaps they are the outside and the inside of the same Way. Unlike the shaman, who is passive in the face of the dismembering otherworldly beings, the quester is active, single-minded, even obsessive. To draw mythological analogies, he is less like Orpheus, the archetypal shaman, than like Odysseus, Jason, and Aeneas, whose journeys took place through this world while beset at every turn by intrusions from the other. (In Christian terms, the quest becomes the pilgrimage while the shaman's journey becomes the mystic's ascent to God.) The danger for the shaman is that he might travel too far or too badly prepared into the Otherworld and so lose his soul; the danger for the quester is just the opposite — the Otherworld is too close to him, threatening to overwhelm and possess him. Even as he clings to his this-worldly perspective, which the shaman is compelled to give up, he is bombarded by the otherworldly. The song of the Siren lures him towards the mind-wrecking rocks. Paranoia is always just around the corner. He is particularly vulnerable to that mixture of delusion and revelation I discussed earlier.

But let me give an example of a modern quest, undertaken by the pioneer anomaly researcher John A. Keel. Although I have to abbreviate his account considerably,[17] I will nevertheless quote more lengthily than usual in order to give some idea of the quest's distinctive flavor.

"Within a year after I had launched my full-time UFO investigating effort in 1966," writes Mr. Keel, "the phenomenon had zeroed in on me, just as it had done with the British newspaper editor, Arthur Shuttlewood, and so many others. My telephone ran amok first, with mysterious strangers calling day and night to deliver bizarre messages 'from the space people'. Then I was catapulted into the dreamlike fantasy world of demonology. I kept rendezvous with black Cadillacs on Long Island [New York], and when I tried to pursue them they would disappear impossibly on dead-end roads... Luminous aerial objects seemed to follow me around like faithful dogs. The objects seemed to know where I was going and where I had been. I would check into a motel at random only to find that someone had made a reservation in my name... I was plagued by impossible coincidences, and some of my closest friends in New York...began to report strange experiences of their own — poltergeists erupted in their apartments, ugly smells of hydrogen sulphide haunted them... More than once I woke up in the middle of the night to find myself unable to move, with a huge dark apparition standing over me. For a time I questioned my sanity..."

Mr. Keel was indeed close to madness. This is what daimonic reality can seem like when we approach it in a manner that is too rational, too intent on explaining, too this-worldly — when we approach it, that is, in the archetypal style of Apollo. But the Apollonic attitude, as I have already said, constellates that of his brother, Hermes, the patron of daimonic reality itself. As god of borders, roads, and travelers, he is particularly evident on quests; as a trickster deity he specializes in teasing us beyond endurance, leading us beyond all rational limits. He delights in baiting Apollonic consciousness by producing physical phenomena which seem like evidence for the literal reality of the daimonic — only to leave us grasping at thin air. He parodies Apollonic prophecy by sending us predictions which turn out to be unerringly accurate at first. Then he springs the Big One on us — the date of the end of the world is a favorite — and it turns out to be false.

Yet, in another sense, it is true: our own little worlds are ending forever as they are engulfed by the otherworldly deluge. Keel received a great many Hermetic messages, not only from alleged UFO entities, but also from trance mediums and "automatic writing." The startling accuracy of their predictions persuaded him to believe the sudden spate of forecasts, from several of these sources, that a cataclysm was about to destroy New York City. He fled. The disaster did not occur. He had been had. He began to understand that the messages from the extraterrestrials and spirits should no more be taken literally than these entities themselves. Indeed, he began to realize that they were not what they claimed to be — not, for example, from other planets, but from some other order of reality inherent in this one. He called them "ultraterrestrials" or "elementals." He goes on: "I developed an elaborate system of checks and balances to preclude hoaxes. Unrelated people in several States became a part of my secret network to that 'other world.' I wasted months playing the mischievous games of the elementals, searching for non-existent UFO bases, trying to find ways of protecting witnesses from the 'men in black.' Poltergeist manifestations seemed to break out wherever I went. It was difficult to judge whether I was unwittingly creating these situations, or whether they were entirely independent of my mind."

But it is not a case of "either–or"; it is a case of "both–and." And it is not merely difficult to judge, it is impossible. Any attempt to pin the daimons down only makes them stronger, like Antaeus who drew strength from his mother earth every time Heracles threw him. If we hold them to be "only in the mind," they appear outside us, complete with apparently objective evidence; if we hold them to be outside us, they appear in dreams, fantasies, and as voices in our heads. Even as Keel pursued them single-mindedly, believing in their literal existence, they reflected that literalness back at him, seeming to be literal but all the while evaporating under his grasp, leading him up the garden path, driving him insane until he began to get an inkling of their ambivalence.

"Now, in retrospect, I can see what was actually taking place," Keel continues. "The phenomenon was slowly introducing me to aspects I had never even considered before. I was being led step by step from skepticism to belief, to — incredibly — disbelief." He means, of course, disbelief in the literal existence of his tormentors. He believes in them all right. But he has learned that they are not as we think they are — nor as we would have them be: reliable, spiritual, pure Beings who purvey higher wisdom. And yet, "when my thinking went awry and my concepts were wrong, the phenomenon actually led me back on to the right path. It was all an educational process and my teachers were very, very patient. Other people who have become involved in this situation have not been so lucky. They settled upon a single frame of reference and were quickly engulfed in disaster."

Here we see the other side of Hermes–Mercurius, not the Trickster but the psychopomp or guide of souls. His tricks not only confuse, but also lead us towards the truth; his messages are not only misleading, but are also "messages from the gods" whose messenger he is. He is also, we remember, in charge of dreams, another form of divine message which features prominently in quests.

"Educational process" is a mild way of describing Keel's quest, but it is apt. For the characteristic that most distinguishes the quest from the shamanic initiation is perhaps the emphasis on *learning*. In the course of their quests among magical islands and Keel-like supernatural antagonists, Homer's hero Odysseus and Virgil's hero Aeneas both visit the Underworld where they might be expected to have been shamanically initiated. In fact, they went there simply to consult the dead and learn from them.[18] If all questers showed their willingness to listen and learn, to pay deep attention to daimonic phenomena instead of either fighting them off or trying to fit them into a rational framework, then they would learn, like Keel, to walk the narrow sword-bridge between one kind of madness and another.

The first is the madness that confines the Otherworld to "a single frame of reference," and so cuts us off, not only from daimonic reality, but also from our own souls, like dogmatic over-rational ideologues. The alternative madness is to lose *all* frames of reference and to be confined in the Otherworld alone, like the poor souls who eke out their days conversing with spirits in the lunatic asylum. Keel learned the sanity of "double vision," the ability to believe and not believe. He learned to recognize and name the daimons for what they are, in all their ambiguity. If he constructed frames of reference, they were provisional and relative ones that safeguarded his reason without doing violence to the infinite richness and complexity of the daimonic realm. Above all, he learned that the quest does not lead to some final solution, some absolute truth; it is itself truth. We are transformed by the Way we take, at home with Hermes on the road which has no end in this world, nor even perhaps in the next.

The wise fool

The heroes of mythology embody different styles or ways of approaching the Otherworld; and it is to this vital question of how we should broach the Otherworld (and especially the Underworld which, in our time, is the most crucial because most neglected spatial metaphor for the Otherworld) that I shall be devoting the last chapter. However, to end this chapter, I want to note that, if any single attribute is indispensable for a successful otherworld journey, it is humility. "All visions, revelations, heavenly feelings," wrote St. John of the Cross, "are not worth the least act of humility, being the fruits of that charity which neither values nor seeks itself, which thinketh well, not of self, but of others...many souls, to whom visions have never come, are incomparably more advanced in the way of perfection than others to whom many have been given."

The humility which is essential to the mystic has to be exercised equally by the shaman and learned painfully by every quester, from the Grail Knights to John Keel. But all these great ones would have done well to have taken a few tips from that hero of a thousand folktales, who quests for the Treasure (of truth, of wisdom) or the Princess (of his own soul).

Typically he is the youngest of three brothers and, significantly, he is not really a hero at all in the accepted sense. He is foolish, dismissed as useless by his father, fit only to look after pigs; he admires his elder brothers who treat him with contempt. They are more conventionally heroic — well-favored, clever in the intellectual sense, dressed in fine clothes, handsome, accomplished, and so on. They expect to win the hand of the Princess (together with her father's wealth) without much trouble. Thus they set out on their journey with every expectation of success. They are single-minded, so intent on traveling with all speed that they brook no obstacle on the way. They are haughty, brushing aside the old woman who attempts to give them directions at the forking of the road. They ignore, or do not hear, the advice of talking animals. They may well reach the Princess by sheer force of will, as it were — only to find that she is unimpressed by their intelligence, self-importance, and humourlessness. They bore her. She laughs in their faces when they ask for her hand in marriage.

The youngest brother, on the other hand, is a fool in the eyes of the world — but not such a fool as he seems. He is thought to be an idle daydreamer. He passes no exams. He has no accomplishments, except perhaps trivial ones such as being good with animals or able to play a wooden pipe he has carved himself. He decides to set out, too, and is ridiculed by his family. Even he has to admit that he stands no chance of success compared to his brothers. He lacks their confidence. But he has some sort of belief in himself, no more perhaps than a vague feeling that he might be lucky. Besides, he reckons that it is a good day for a journey — the weather is fine and there is the possibility of adventure — and so he sets out to enjoy it for its own sake, regardless of the outcome.

He is unfailingly courteous to beggars, old women, and talking animals, to whom he pays deep attention, gaining useful tips, and, often, talismans to help him on his way. He is not sharp or suspicious; but he is not unwary. He takes no nonsense from deceivers, seeing through their schemes to delay or obstruct. If he encounters ogres, he does not quail before them or try to defeat them by brute force, as his brothers might fatally try to do. Instead he outfaces and outwits them, often acquiring some powerful magical attribute in the process. He is ingenious, adaptable, even cunning. He is witty and full of good humor; and the Princess accepts him at once, if only because he makes her laugh.

19

Soul and Body

Souls

St. Paul mentions an ecstatic experience in which he was "caught up even to the third heaven," but, as he says, "whether in the body, I know not, or whether out of the body, I know not; God knoweth."[1] And this is the dilemma confronting many otherworld journeyers.

It is, I think, too easy to dismiss the conviction of many of them that they were physically lifted into another realm, such as an alien spacecraft. This, after all, is what it felt like; and it is a conviction shared by members of traditional cultures — although, as we shall see, with an important difference in viewpoint. Thus, although I do not share the conviction, I want to stress that it is ancient and respectable and, I think, nearer to the truth of the matter than not to believe in any kind of otherworld journey at all. However, using the model of daimonic reality I have been outlining, it is possible to make otherworld journeys intelligible, without recourse to a belief in an actual, physical experience. To do this, I will briefly consider the relationship between soul and body, beginning with a few elementary remarks about different kinds of daimonic states.

In order to journey into the daimonic realm, the shaman goes into a trance or semi-trance in which he is either unconscious of the ordinary world or only dimly conscious of it, respectively. In other words, in the state of trance (or ecstasy) the Otherworld constitutes his only reality; in the semi-trance he retains one foot in this world, enabling him to relay his otherworld itinerary to an audience. His procedure is analogous both to that of modern mediums, who either allow spirits to possess them fully or who act as intermediaries between spirits and audience, passing messages between them; and to that of hypnotic subjects who are either fully "asleep," in which case, like the trance medium, they have no memory of what they have said or what was said through them, or only partially "asleep" — in which case they are able to describe, and remember, what they (or some part of themselves) are experiencing. It is a measure of the shaman's superior control over his journey, that he is able to remember all that befalls him while in a full trance, that is, while he is dead to this world. However, all these states are more or less controlled, if only (in the medium's case) by his or her "spirit guide" or personal daimon; or in the case of the hypnotized, by the hypnotist who, like a guide, sets the agenda for the session and intervenes if the daimons grow too importunate.

Spontaneous, involuntary, and uncontrolled journeys into the Otherworld can be highly successful. They can result, for example, in mystical revelations which enhance the lives of the recipients. But they can also be highly perilous, resulting in one of two undesirable conditions which used to be called "loss of soul" and "possession by spirits." The first, analogous to what we now call neurosis, occurs when we lose touch with the Otherworld; the second, analogous to psychosis, occurs when we are too much in touch with the Otherworld, becoming overwhelmed by it. (The nature of both these conditions will become clearer in the course of this chapter.)

The use of the word "soul," and "loss of soul," is rather different from the way I have been using the word. Hitherto, I have taken "soul" to refer to two distinct, but related, images. Firstly, soul is synonymous with the daimonic realm itself, the realm of Imagination, and is really an abbreviation for the collective *Anima Mundi,* or World-Soul. Secondly, soul refers to whatever image the World-Soul itself uses to represent itself. Archetypally, this image is usually feminine and appears, for example, as a female daimon or goddess who, as Jung would say, "personifies the collective uncon-scious."[2] Now the third use of "soul" refers to the image by which we, as individuals, are represented in the World-Soul.

Traditional views of human nature have always allowed for (at least) two "souls" of the latter kind.[3] In ancient Egypt, for instance, they were known as the *ka* and the *ba;* in China, *hun* and *p'o.* One of these souls inhabits the body and is the equivalent of what, *faute de mieux,* we call the ego.[4] I will call it the *rational ego* to distinguish it from the second soul, variously called, in other cultures, the shadow-soul, ghost-soul, death-soul, image-soul and dream-soul, for which our culture has either the word "soul" or else no word, because it is not generally believed to exist. However, it does exist and can also be thought of as an ego, in the sense that it confers identity and individuality. It enables us, that is — like the rational ego — to say "I." But it is an ego, not of consciousness, but of the unconscious; not a waking, but a dream ego; not a rational, but an irrational ego.[5] I will call it the *daimonic ego*. Like the rational ego, it has a body — not a physical one but a dream-body, a "subtle" body such as daimons are imagined as having, an "astral" body as some esoteric doctrines say: in short, a daimonic body.

The combination of rational ego and physical body is not directly analogous to the daimonic ego and daimonic body because the latter are not, strictly speaking, experienced as separate. The daimonic body immediately reflects the daimonic ego, and vice versa. It is an imaginative body, an image, as we know from dreams, when it can wear whatever clothes it wishes and can even change its shape altogether. Suddenly it can shift from a position of observing someone to becoming that person — that is, it embodies the way in which the daimonic ego shifts its point of view, looking out of the eyes of a person whom the moment before it was watching, or feeling the emotions of someone in whom it was previously inducing those emotions.

Thus it is this daimonic ego-body, so to speak, which is the "soul" that can be "lost," the soul that, in the shaman, takes otherworld journeys. It is this which leaves the physical body in "out-of-the-body" experiences or in fashionable "near-death experiences" when, typically, we "die" on the operating-table, only to find that we are floating above our bodies, able to observe what is going on and to hear what the surgeons are saying (they are startled to have us tell them their words later, when we recover). It is this soul, too, which can be seen by us, or others, in those cases of "bilocation" when our *doppelgängers* (doubles) appear mysteriously.[6] It is this soul which, in Christian mystics, ascends towards the Godhead, sparking the debate as to whether it remains intact during mystical union (as a sense of identity) or whether it is, finally, dissolved in, or subsumed by, God.

The daimonic and rational egos are not as separate as, for the sake of convenience, I have made them out to be. They constantly flow into each other, just as our waking lives and dream lives influence each other. The daimonic ego can at any time dispossess consciousness of its rational ego as, for instance, when we are absorbed in some imaginative activity or when we are seized by a visionary experience. Conversely, the rational ego can traduce the daimonic, carrying over into dreams and visions those "daylight" attitudes which are wholly inappropriate to the twilight world of the daimons. Naturally, the rational ego is often frightened by the irrational images it encounters there. It tries to run away or lash out — only to find that it cannot move, because such literal muscular actions have no power to move the daimonic body.

Similarly, when we wake in the night, as abductees so often do, to find "aliens" in the room, we cannot move because our physical bodies are asleep and only the rational ego has woken. Actually, I ought to say that it is the daimonic ego which "wakes"; but, since we do not recognize or understand it, we imagine that it is the rational ego — the latter is so robust, so adamant, that it *imposes* its rational viewpoint on the daimonic ego so that we come to believe that the nocturnal events are literally occurring. The fact that we seem to wake in our bedrooms is a metaphor for this literalizing activity of the rational ego; for, in fact, we wake up in the daimonic realm on which the *image* of our familiar, daylight, "rational" bedroom has been imposed. When the aliens, intruding into this image from the daimonic side, "float" our bodies up into their "spacecraft," this is not only the daimonic body leaving the physical body, but also the daimonic ego leaving the image of the literal bedroom and entering daimonic space proper, where it is increasingly pressured to give up its rational, literalizing standpoint. But this, precisely, is initiation: the threatening and, finally, dismantling of the rational standpoint by the alien daimonic world in order to instate its own, daimonic ego.

It should now become apparent that the division I have made between the two kinds of ego is only a manner of speaking. In reality, there is only a single ego, but with two *perspectives:* the waking, conscious, rational, literalizing ego is simply another aspect of the dreaming, unconscious, irrational, daimonic ego, as if they were two sides of a single coin. But the shape-shifting daimonic ego can assume any number of different perspectives, all more or less daimonic, all members of the same family as it were, like the heroes of Greek mythology. Only the rational ego promotes its own single, literalistic perspective as the only perspective, while simultaneously denying — demonizing — all others.

Bodies

One of the things a study of otherworld journeys teaches us is that we cannot imagine life without a body. We cannot exist as bare discarnate egos, even in the "life to come." "It is sown a natural body"; wrote St. Paul, "it is raised a spiritual body."[7] And we cannot help but envisage this spiritual body as something like the "subtle" — the daimonic — body which can separate from, and survive, the physical.

Paul was writing, of course, long before the Church Council of 869, which officially decided that we humans are divided into two parts — a body and a spirit (thus losing the category of "soul"). He still conceived of life, including spiritual life, as bodily; and the word he uses for "body," whether "natural" or "spiritual," is *soma*. He contrasts this in his Epistles with another kind of body, for which he uses another Greek word, *sarx*. Sometimes translated as "flesh" (as in "the sins of the flesh"), *sarx* referred exclusively to the evil possibilities of bodily life. *Soma,* on the other hand, referred to all the possibilities of bodily life, good or evil. The key point here is that neither word referred exclusively to the physical body. Rather, *soma* referred to all perspectives on bodily life, of which the physical was only one; *sarx* referred solely to the literal perspective that would reduce all bodily life to the physical, to mere flesh.[8]

In my scheme of things, the daimonic body (*soma*) is no more separate from the physical body (*sarx*) than their two kinds of ego — they are simply two different perspectives. And this confronts us with a disconcerting idea: that our physical bodies are not necessarily literal. (We should not be too disconcerted — we have, after all, been prepared for this conclusion by all those daimonic traces, culminating in crop circles, which also, though physical, turned out to be far from literal.) The sense that our bodies are literally real is a construct of the rational ego which, while it does not identify itself with the body (it sees the body as its vehicle), nevertheless allies itself so closely with the body as to impose its perspective on the body. It makes our physical reality the only reality — makes of our physical reality a literal reality. This leads to the erroneous belief that, with physical death, we cease to exist. But our physical death releases the daimonic body. Moreover, if we undergo initiatory death, which destroys the rational ego's literal perspective, the physical body is deliteralized, freed from its single perspective, released from *sarx,* as it were. It becomes, in fact, daimonic. If this is the case, we might expect the physical body, now daimonized, to be able to contravene what we call physical laws.

It can, of course. We think immediately of fakirs who can bury themselves for days at a time in the earth, or of Zen Buddhist monks who are able, like Jesus, to walk on water. The spiritual training necessary for such feats has fallen into desuetude in our culture; but in monastic times they were common enough for men like St. John of the Cross to warn of the danger of confusing them with sanctity. A famous example of daimonic activity in a physical body (it was even suspected of being demonic, the work of the Devil) was the repeated levitations of St. Teresa of Avila. She experienced "raptures," not unlike the shaman's celestial journey, in which "...the Lord catches up the soul...and carries it right out of itself...and begins to show it the features of the Kingdom He has prepared for it." The raptures were sometimes so violent that she not only felt her soul being swept up by God, but was also lifted bodily off the ground so that her sisters had to hold her down.[9] (This is not all that exceptional — more than 100 Catholic saints were said to have levitated.)[10]

We might say that, unlike the abductees whose rational egos were floated up in their daimonic bodies, St. Teresa's daimonic ego remained in the physical body, which was sufficiently deliteralized as to simulate the celestial ascent of its daimonic counterpart. She was aware, however, that her levitations were not in good taste — she would shout, "Put me down, God!" — nor a sign of spiritual advancement (we remember that the well-known psychic, but otherwise ordinary man, D. D. Home, could float into the air at will). It is as if she knew that her celestial ascent should really — like the shaman's — be taking place less ostentatiously, in the daimonic body alone and without any accompanying physical flights. It was as if, in other words, she had an inkling of the literalizing influence of Christian dogma which, by polarizing man into either a spirit or a body, abolished the daimonic "both–and" perspective and so literalized spiritual ascent as physical "flight." (Analogously, Christian dogma literalizes spiritual rebirth as a "resurrection of the body.")

Christian or post-Christian cultures can only view the physical body in a literal way. For example, the UFO's light-beam paralyzes its victims before they are snatched into the Otherworld. Because the experience seems "real" to these abductees, they assume that it must be literal — and therefore that their physical bodies have been taken into "spacecraft." Non-Christian, traditional cultures also seem to view the physical body in a literal way. For instance, as Lady Wilde writes, describing fairy abductions among the Irish: "The evil influence of the fairy glance [like the UFO's light-beam] does not kill, but it throws the object into a death-like trance, in which the real body is carried off to some fairy mansion, while a log of wood, or some ugly deformed creature is left in its place, clothed with the shadow of the stolen form..."[11] But what on the surface seems like literalism on the part of fairy lore — the "real body" is taken — is actually the reverse: the physical body is imagined in the first instance as daimonic. The "real body" is the daimonic body which, once taken into the Otherworld, leaves behind (as Lady Gregory puts it) "a body in its likeness or the likeness of a body."[12] This expression attempts to describe the physical body when it is deprived of its daimonic ego-body — when it has "lost its soul." It becomes inanimate like a block of wood; an empty, ugly husk, barely recognizable as the "stolen" person. This, metaphorically, is how the physical body appears when, deprived of its daimonic counterpart, it becomes only physical — becomes literal.

The belief that the body left behind is actually a replacement (i.e. that an *exchange* has been made) expresses the reluctance on the part of traditional cultures to separate body and soul. They implicitly recognize that the physical and daimonic bodies are only two aspects of, two perspectives on, the same thing, as if the body were only the physical manifestation of soul, and soul the spiritual manifestation of body. They recognize, that is, that we humans are simultaneously quasi-physical, quasi-spiritual. *We, too, are daimonic.*

Soul and spirit

I have said that ego-consciousness has many perspectives, all of them more or less daimonic, except one — the rational and, above all, literalizing ego. In relation to daimonic reality itself — to *Anima Mundi* and its personification anima, *soul* — they are not daimonic. To put it another way, the daimonic ego is a soul in relation to the rational ego, but in relation to soul (world-soul, anima) it is *spirit*.

From time to time I have made a distinction between soul and spirit about which I ought now to be more explicit, since soul and spirit reflect a fundamental tension in human life.[13] For example, the drive towards integration, individuality, and unity is essentially a spiritual drive, as mono-theism in general (and Christianity in particular) is a spiritual religion. Soul, on the other hand, emphasizes disintegration, collectivity, and multiplicity. What we often call "major" religions are usually spiritual religions which barely recognize religions of the soul as religions at all — they are called animism or polytheism — because they have no single, "major," transcendent, divine principle, but rather stress the equality of many "minor" immanent daimonic images. As a kind of shorthand guide to spirit and soul, therefore, it may be helpful to draw up two lists of analogous concepts, attributes, and images which have been enduringly associated with them.

Thus, *Spirit:* God, monotheism, unity, the One, ego; heaven, transcendence, above, heights, ascent, "superior"; masculine, consciousness, rationality, light, fire, sun.

Soul: daimons, polytheism, multiplicity, the Many, anima; Earth, immanence, below, depths, descent, "inferior"; feminine, the unconscious, imagination, dark, water, moon.

Spirit and soul, it must be remembered, are not like two substances. They are symbols, like yang and yin, representing two slants on life, two perspectives. It is as though spirit were a white light diffracted into many colors by soul's prism, or as though soul's colors were concentrated into one white light by the prism of spirit. From the perspective of soul, spirit is many perspectives — all contained within soul itself and yet always trying to break free and impose one or another of its perspectives on soul as it were from the outside. From spirit's point of view, soul is one perspective — outside spirit and yet always somehow attached to it, entangling it, distracting spirit's rationalism with emotions, contradicting spirit's abstract concepts with concrete images, as it were from within.

Spirit and soul are reflections of each other. Thus my lists of their attributes are not meant to be seen as oppositional — opposition is only one way in which the tension between spirit and soul can be viewed.[14] Other ways are best expressed in the way the personifications of myth relate to each other: as sons to mothers, or husbands to wives; as antagonists or companions, enemies or lovers, and so on. For, as soon as spirit defines soul in one way, we find that this way of defining is already defined by soul according to whatever pairing spirit is in. Soul and spirit predetermine each other's perspective, defining each other simultaneously (except that "define" is spirit's word, not soul's). We cannot imagine outside these pairings, cannot stand outside these reciprocal perspectives — we can only view one from the other.[15] (Spirit's attempt to stand outside its pairings with soul, and its belief that it has done so, is precisely the rational ego, as I will shortly show.)

An example of the interaction between soul and spirit is the interpretation of myths. As products of Imagination, myths are the archetypal stories of soul. But modern mythographers (anthropologists and the like) come at them with scientific explanations and definitions. This is spirit at work. It wishes to find single underlying principles or unifying theories. But soul resists this process (there are always myths which escape the net of any one theory). It — I should perhaps say "she" — wants to be reflected, but not by any *one* concept or theory. She certainly does not want to be (and cannot be) *explained*. Soul recognizes the defining perspectives of spirit, but agrees to none, as if she were the sum total of all the theories that could be held about her. But there is no end to theorizing which — it dawns on us — is only mythologizing in another garb, another set of stories. Concepts, speculations, theories are continuous with the images, legends, myths they set out to explain. Even while they strike objective postures, as if they would stand outside myth, they are unwittingly determined by myth's own imaginative categories. Like Helen of Troy — always a cause of strife — soul looks on with amusement and despair as theories compete acrimoniously for the right to be the only theory, the "true" story.

And it is not only within "disciplines" — a real spirit word — that strife erupts. It also breaks out between disciplines, as long as each lays exclusive claim to the truth. Like the religious schisms of old, new schools of thought break away from the old and even form new disciplines, such as anthropology, psychology, sociology, and so on, which were almost unheard of 100 years ago. But the proliferation of disciplines is only the expression of further spirit perspectives, further attempts to imagine unimaginable Imagination.

This book, incidentally, is no exception. As a work of spirit, it has tried to elucidate soul, which I have been calling daimonic reality. But this is only one perspective on soul. It has also tried to draw attention to other perspectives — the collective unconscious, *Anima Mundi,* Imagination, and the Otherworld. Each of these seeks to approach soul from a slightly different angle (the term — or symbol — "soul" is itself only another metaphor). The common ground of these perspectives is that they are not imagined in an Apollonic, "scientific" spirit, which claims finally to define and explain soul; rather, they are imagined in a Hermetic spirit which allows soul in large measure to define itself. Thus, although they are unifying concepts, as spirit demands, they also take account of the many images which compose them.

By the modern criteria of "serious" scientific disciplines, this book can only appear inconsistent and unsystematic. It fails to classify and explain. But rigorous classification and explanation, admirable in themselves, will always tend to do violence to daimonic reality, either by forcing it into the straitjacket of a single perspective or, worse, by denying it altogether (scientism) or demonizing it (official Christendom). To force daimonic reality into a single perspective is to make soul an imitation of spirit. And this tells us more about ourselves and our own spirit-oriented culture than it does about daimonic reality. If "perspective" primarily means "seeing *through,*" then this book also aims to see through itself, aware that its perspective is also partial and incomplete. It would rather fail to describe reality, which is by nature daimonic, mysterious, and indescribable, than succeed in describing a false reality.

We are now in a better position to understand the sadness that sometimes hangs about the daimons, for instance in Irish myths and their elaboration in the early poems of W. B. Yeats.[16] It is as if the daimons sorrowed for the sorrow of men, which they cannot know. Ruled only by shadowy Necessity, they run the course of their lives in endless cycles, dying only to live and die again. There's a touch of *ennui* about the daimons. What they sorrow for, even hunger for, is that spirit whereby they may be discriminated, defined, made concrete; for, without spirit, soul can know "neither truth, nor law, nor cause."[17] By means of spirit soul knows itself.

At its best, a spiritual perspective regards the daimons, not as literal, but *as if* they were literal, just as traditional cultures recount their myths as if they were history. The daimons themselves insist on this as-if literalness, as we have seen from their traces, such as UFO landing marks and crop circles.

Reciprocally, spirit needs soul whose many daimons not only subvert, but also soften with their beauty, spirit's drive towards absolute unitary truth. As the hero searches for his princess, so spirit seeks to make connections with soul, perhaps through the diverse images of Art or Nature. Spirit needs soul to make the world personal, palliating its remote God with a personal Christ, human saints, and a human Virgin Mary. The dismembering of the shaman is the disintegrating of the ego, ruled by one of spirit's perspectives, into many perspectives; the forging of the "new body" is the construction of a new daimonic ego-body which can take on any of spirit's perspectives at will, moving freely through the Otherworld of soul.

We are daimonic — but we are not daimons. Like animals, daimons are sufficient unto themselves. We are both farther from divinity than they, and nearer, because the tension in us between spirit and soul engenders that self-reflection, that capacity for self-transformation, which they cannot know alone. Yet, through us, they can — and wish to — know; for our self-reflection is a reflection of them, their transformation our self-transformation.

The Heraclean ego

Every perspective of spirit which seeks to stand outside soul in the form of an ego can be represented by a god or goddess, but, above all — as we have seen — by a mythological hero. Each hero has a different style of approaching the Otherworld; each is paired — that is, both determining and determined by — a different aspect of soul, anima, like mutually reflecting mirrors. Aeneas has his Dido, for example; Odysseus his Circe, Calypso, and Penelope; Orpheus his Eurydice; Perseus his Andromeda; and so on. Thus we may ask: is there a hero analogous to that special, singular perspective of spirit I have called the rational ego? The answer is yes, and his name is Heracles (Hercules) who, above all, represents the pattern of heroic ego that predominates in modern Western culture.[18]

What is Heracles' attitude to soul, to daimonic reality, to the Underworld? It is eccentric, to say the least. He visits the Underworld of Hades in the course of his twelfth (and last) labor — which is to capture the guardian of Hades itself, Cerberus, the three-headed dog.[19] Where other heroes go to be initiated or instructed, Heracles goes solely to take. Club in hand, he bludgeons his way in, intimidating Charon to carry him across the river Styx. The shades of the dead flee from him in terror, just as the daimons run from our own hard-nosed rationalism. Throughout his visit, he treats the shades (the images, the daimons) as literal. Confronted by the shade of Meleager, he aims an arrow at him and has to be told that there is nothing to fear. Faced with the shade of Medusa the Gorgon, he draws his sword, before Hermes (who has of course accompanied him down) reassures him that she is only a phantom. Here, Heracles commits two crass errors: he not only mistakes the image of the Gorgon for the real Gorgon, but he also thinks that the real Gorgon can be vanquished head-on — in fact, brute force is useless against her because she turns all who look on her face to stone. (We shall be meeting the Gorgon again.) And so it goes on: Heracles muscles his way through the Underworld, wrestling Hades' herdsmen, slaughtering their cattle in order to feed the shades with blood — as if to literalize them back into life — and, finally, choking and chaining Cerberus before dragging him up into the daylight land of the living. In short, Heracles behaves just as the waking rational ego behaves in dreams, when it usurps the imaginative perspective of the daimonic ego. He seems, in fact, incapable of imagining. Rather than die metaphorically, as initiation demands, he kills literally, even attacking death itself (he wounds Hades in the shoulder). He embodies that myth within mythology itself which denies myth, just as our rational egos, grounded in soul, deny soul.

Because of the difficulty and danger of his last labor, the capture of Cerberus, Heracles asked if he might partake of the Eleusinian Mysteries before undertaking it. This, of course, would have initiated him into the secrets of death and rebirth, enabling his smooth passage into the Underworld. But he was either refused permission or, as other variants of the myth claim, permitted only to partake of the Lesser Mysteries (which were especially founded on his account). This lack of initiation implies exactly what I have been maintaining — that our rational egos remain uninitiated and thus ignorant of, and inimical to, the nature of daimonic reality.[20] The consequence of this is dire: Heracles, alone of all the heroes, goes mad (and kills his sons). "The initiation of the heroic ego…is not only a 'psychological problem'… It is cultural, and it is vast and crucial. The culture-hero Hercules, as well as all our mini-Herculean egos mimetic to that Man-God, is a killer among images. The image makes it mad, or rather evokes its madness, because heroic sanity insists on a reality it can grapple with…or bash with a club. Real equals corporeal. So it attacks the image, driving death from his throne, as if recognition of the image implies death for the ego."[21] (For "image," we can, of course, read "daimon.")

Too much of our recent history has been soul-slaughter, imagining the past as merely primitive and, muscle-bound with technology, bulldozing the sacred places, hunting the daimonic animals with high-velocity rifles, dispatching the jets to shoot down the UFOs, violating the moon-goddess with phallic rockets, and so on. Having severed all connection with the gods and daimons, we reckon we are getting away with it. But we aren't. The victory over the daimons is hollow; we simply make a hell of our world. And, as we drive out the daimons before us, they creep back in from behind, from within. We compel them to seize and possess and madden us. If we want to know our own fate, we would do well, perhaps, to look at the fate of Heracles. He neglected his wife, his soul, who, in order to rekindle his attention, sent him a shirt soaked in what she had been told was a love potion. But the potion was a poison that coursed over his body, corroding his too-solid flesh. The more he tore at the shirt, the more he tore himself to pieces. He was glad to find death on a burning pyre. (His wife killed herself out of remorse.)

This is a warning of what happens to spirit when it becomes divorced from its soul pairing, when it ceases to find its reflection in soul — and loses it. It becomes the solitary heroic rational ego which deludes itself into believing that there is no soul. It creates a correspondingly delusional world for itself which, deprived of its connection with a personal and personified counterpart, opens onto the soul's depths, as abysmal as deep space and as impersonal as the subatomic realm.

A note on technology

"Although there are many spirits, and many kinds of spirit, more and more the notion of 'spirit' has come to be carried by the Apollonic archetype, the sublimations of higher and abstract disciplines, the intellectual mind, refinements, and purifications."[22]

If, then, the Apollonic archetype represents the spirit of the age, and especially of science, the Heraclean archetype might be described as its instrument and will — its strong right arm — and hence the archetype of technology. Under the aegis of Apollo, we see the literalization of spirit's metaphors: upwards and onwards are science's watchwords; the "ascent of man"; Progress. In this respect, science is a secular version of the medieval mystic's ascent to "God who is on high" — which, in turn, is a spiritualized Christian version of the shaman's "celestial journey." (The latter, however, was preceded or at least balanced, we remember, by a corresponding descent to the subterranean, daimonic realm.) It is not therefore too far-fetched, I think, to see the invention of flight — often called an "age-old dream" — as a literalization of the shaman's journey, under the aegis of the Heraclean ego. We not only build aircraft, literalizing spiritual flight into physical, "muscular" flight, we also strive to fly higher and faster, finally initiating space programs whose first objective is to discredit the moon. She is no goddess, says Heracles; she has no power to madden or enchant — she's just dust.

Modern disquiet at the ascendancy of scientism has been signaled by a "return to Earth," notably in ecological movements which seek to combat scientism's detachment from (and hence oppression of) Nature. But these movements stand little chance of permanent success if they cast themselves in the same mold as scientism, advancing solutions from the same literal perspective as caused the problems. They must embrace a change in perspective, a change of heart, so that they re-imagine Earth as the embodiment of a world-soul, the violation of which is also a violation of their own souls.

However, I do not want to strike a facile anti-technological pose. I have named Heracles as the archetypal background to technology, but really I ought to say that his perspective entails the abuse of technology. The archetypal figure behind technology proper, and its correct use, is Daedalus, who invented the potter's wheel, the compass, and the saw.[23] He also built a machine resembling a cow in which Pasiphae could be hidden and so receive the sexual favors of Poseidon in the form of a bull. Thus technology, too, can mediate between humans and the gods! The offspring of this union was the Minotaur, half man and half bull(-god) — a daimonic creature, in other words. Daedalus built an intricate maze, the famous labyrinth, to house the Minotaur. The labyrinth is an image of soul. It is both an imaginative and technical structure, built like a shrine to accommodate a daimon. In addition, Pasiphae's husband, King Minos, was also said to have hidden there. Since Minos was appointed by Hades to judge the dead, we also see in the labyrinth a recognition of the soul's connection with death. Thus technology can embody soul and not necessarily oppose it.

We should not be surprised therefore if Daedalus expresses the right attitude to technology, as evidenced by his famous escape from Crete. He invented flight, fabricating the first pair of wings — and so becoming the first person to literalize the shaman's celestial journey. However, it was his son, Icarus, who abused the technology by flying too high on his wings towards the Apollonic sun. This is the hubris of technology which transcends its own limits — with the result we are all familiar with: the wax which held Icarus' wings together melted and he plunged to his death in the sea. Daedalus, on the other hand, using his new technology moderately, flew safely to Cumae, near Naples, where he dedicated his wings to Apollo and built him a temple, as if recognizing that the god was the scientific inspiration behind his technical innovation.

Siegfried's loss of soul

I ought here to touch on another myth whose hero, though very different from Heracles, has some telling characteristics in common. It is the Germanic myth of Siegfried, "the great hero of the German people."[24] I do not relish "translating" such myths into language and images other than their own; but I want to show that the Siegfried myth may well be as important as the Heraclean in understanding the modern rational ego. Specifically, the myth of Siegfried seems to provide much of the archetypal background for that singular perspective of spirit we might call the northern Protestant ego, from which the rational ego in large measure derives. (It is worth remembering here that it was the Mediterranean, Catholic form of Christianity which tended to Christianize the daimons — see Chapter 5 — while its Puritan, iconoclastic form, separated out at the Reformation as northern Protestantism, tended to demonize them.)

It may seem eccentric to cite a pagan myth as underlying a Christian development; but we will remember how thinly Christianity sometimes veils paganism, especially when we consider the dramatic resurgence of Germanic myth (notably Siegfried's) under Hitler's regime. At any rate, Siegfried and the northern Protestant ego share an important feature: they both suffer from loss of soul. (Another reason for recounting Siegfried's cautionary tale here is that it will appear again in the next chapter, in the course of our last otherworld journey.) The best-known version of the Siegfried myth is Wagner's operatic treatment of it in the *Ring* cycle. However, the version to which I will refer is the Norse one, where Siegfried is known as Sigurd, and Brunhilde as Brynhild.[25]

The parts of the plot which concern us are briefly as follows: Sigurd's first major heroic task is to kill the dragon Fafnir. He bathes in the dragon's blood and thereby becomes invulnerable, except for a small spot on his back. To be invulnerable is a dubious distinction; it implies that one is armored, intransigent, unwilling to let anything through. Here is the beginning of a spirit perspective rigidifying into a single-minded rational ego. Its soul counterpart in this case is personified by Brynhild. But she is not the usual princess; she is a Valkyr, one of Odin's warrior-maidens, cast out of the Otherworld for disobedience. There is no one like her in Greek mythology, except perhaps the Amazons, or else great Artemis, the cold huntress and moon-goddess. As a pair, Sigurd and Brynhild, ego and soul, both determine and reflect each other — and, splendid as they are, they are also hard and ruthless and martial.

Sigurd finds Brynhild on a mountain peak, in a tower surrounded by a wall of flame which only he can breach on his magical horse (reminiscent of the shaman's "spirit horse"). They fall in love. He then leaves her in order to perform more deeds of derring-do, so that he can be worthy of her hand in marriage. Actually he at once falls in with a king called Gunnar, to whom he becomes a blood brother. In other words, they become different aspects of the same person. Gunnar is like the rational ego which splits off from spirit and denies its connection with soul; or, vice versa, loss of connection with soul causes the rational ego to split off from spirit. At any rate, that the connection *is* lost is represented by the fact that Sigurd *forgets all about Brynhild.* It does not much matter that the cause of this untoward forgetfulness is attributed to an enchantment laid on Sigurd by Gunnar's mother, in order that Sigurd will fall in love with Gudrun, her daughter (and Gunnar's sister). The enchantment is like that waking daylight consciousness which banishes the dream images and returns us to this mundane world. Thus Sigurd forgets his true soul, Brynhild, in her otherworldly tower and marries Gudrun, the charming but shallow *hausfrau.*

Meanwhile, Gunnar has heard of Brynhild and determines to win her. Sigurd offers to help. But, arriving at the flame-encircled tower, Gunnar cannot traverse the fire, even when Sigurd lends him the magical horse. However, remembering one of his mother's spells, Gunnar decides to change shape with Sigurd. In other words, the rational ego imposes its perspective on the daimonic ego. Thus, in the guise of Gunnar — that is, identified entirely now with the rational ego — Sigurd breaches the wall of fire for the second time and wins Brynhild, who reckons herself (correctly) forgotten by Sigurd. She does not see Sigurd resuming his own appearance, nor does she know of his marriage to Gudrun until the latter informs her. Then her cold and mirthless attitude, so alien to the worldly household, grows more icy, remote, and incomprehensible to Gunnar and Gudrun.

As soon as he sees Brynhild at her wedding feast, Sigurd remembers everything — but can say nothing for the sake of Gunnar, his blood brother, and Gudrun, his wife. It is only when, after a year, Brynhild discovers from Gudrun that it was Sigurd, not Gunnar, who won her, that she confronts Sigurd, enabling him to explain what happened, that he was enchanted, etc. Brynhild begs him to leave with her at once so that they may live together as originally planned. But Sigurd will still not betray Gunnar and Gudrun.

Here, Sigurd gives up his second chance to become re-connected to the Otherworld of the Valkyr, as if he had become too contaminated with this world. What he had lost the first time through forgetfulness, he now willfully denies. It is precisely this willful denial of soul and of daimonic reality which is the hallmark of the rational ego and its close kin, the iconoclastic northern Protestant ego (which also, like Sigurd, emphasizes the priority of the ethical perspective over the erotic). And so the previous, temporary identification of Sigurd with Gunnar, of spirit with rational ego, is now made permanent. Sigurd can only merge with Gunnar or leave the stage. And so he does: the spurned Brynhild vengefully tells Gunnar that Sigurd really loves her and wishes him, Gunnar, dead (which is, from soul's point of view, no more than the truth). Whereupon Gunnar, to whom Sigurd has confided the place of his vulnerability, persuades his younger brother to kill Sigurd with a sword-thrust between the shoulder blades. Arrayed as if for a marriage feast, Brynhild takes her own life. Gunnar, as rational ego, is left in charge of a world devoid of both soul and of any other heroic perspective.

20

Approaching the Otherworld

The modern myth of gray aliens

It will by now be clear, I hope, that it matters very much how we approach the Otherworld. Accordingly, I will end this chapter, and this book, with two instructive examples of successful descents into the Underworld which, as I have said, is now more than ever the most appropriate spatial metaphor for daimonic reality.

However, conscious of having strayed rather far from actual apparitions, visions, and otherworld journeys, I would like to begin with a closer look at the aliens known as the grays, partly because they are related to (and can therefore throw light on) all daimons, and partly because they nevertheless constitute a special case, a modern manifestation which, reflecting our light, can teach us something about our present selves.

In one sense, the problem of the grays is not especially pressing. Only in the USA, it seems, have encounters with them risen to the surface and begun to be noticed by the instruments of official culture such as the press, the academic world, the Churches, and so on. This is testimony to the considerable groundswell of interest they have aroused in popular, unofficial culture. Books about them, unconsidered by "serious" or literary people, have sold not merely in thousands, but in millions. A 1991 survey of 6,000 American adults concluded that as many as 3.7 million abductions by grays may have taken place.[1] The survey, it is true, was conducted by members of the extraterrestrialist faction who therefore interpreted quite vague, quasi- or sub-daimonic experiences as evidence of abduction. But it revealed that daimonic experiences are — as anyone who bothers to ask around knows — extremely common. Moreover, whatever the case may be as regards the number or actuality of abductions, they constitute a grassroots belief, a modern constellation in the collective unconscious, a stirring of our universal Imagination, which may justly be called a contemporary myth.

If the myth is ignored or ridiculed by the orthodoxies, whether of science, religion, academia, literature, and so on, might it not be that it is these orthodoxies which are at fault rather than the myth itself? Might it be — horrors — precisely the worldview espoused by these orthodoxies that engenders a subculture, like a shadow, in which irrational, absurd, embarrassing events such as abductions are said to occur? The importance of "alien abductions" (to paraphrase C. S. Lewis) may well lie in their unimportance. It is the resistance of alien abductions to rational analysis which fascinates, almost as if their very duplicity were their chief message. The grays tell us little about themselves but may well be telling us a good deal about ourselves. They are like daimonic reality in the raw: powerful and immediate, yet frightening and ludicrous at the same time. Strangely crude, yet strangely complex, their abductions demonstrate a consistency comparable with, say, the consistency of reports describing the witches' Sabbat in medieval Europe.

I have no doubt that the grays will fade away as the imaginative configurations which contain them become exhausted. Perhaps they are already fading away — the claims of the extraterrestrialists seem to have reached a peak of extravagance which presages a collapse. But the grays will reappear in different shapes, while new variants of their myth will be woven out of the old threads. For daimons exist, and will continue to exist. Like the fairies, they retain the same shape as long as they are attached to a relatively unchanging landscape and to a relatively unchanging culture. But this does not make them any the less mysterious. So, too, it is not possible to explain the grays; but we are entitled to ask whether a changing landscape and culture has anything to do with the form in which they have chosen to appear — to ask, that is, "Why grays? Why now?" I have to say at once that I do not think this question can be answered. But that is no reason why we cannot reflect on them, mull them over, *mythologize*, in the hope of making some sense of them. For if we do not, the daimons may just grow more importunate, appearing out of Imagination in forms that will make the grays look like sweetness and light.

"Convenient rites"

By way of a preamble, we must remind ourselves that daimons like the grays may neither be all that new nor all that different from certain daimons of old. The Neoplatonist Porphyry (*c.* 232–*c.* 305), for instance, described something very like them. The domain of the air, he wrote, is governed by both good and bad daimons who have no solid body but neither do they have one shape, possessing rather a diversity of forms "which, impressed on their aerial part, are sometimes apparent, sometimes obscured." The bodies of malevolent daimons "are of a discordant temperament, on which account they inhabit that aerial space proximate to the earth…and for the most part govern things subject to their dominion with a turbulent malignity… For their manners are entirely violent and fraudulent, and destitute of the guardian preservation of better daemons; so that they machinate vehement and sudden snares with which they rush on the unwary; sometimes endeavoring to conceal their incursions, and sometimes acting with open violence against the subjects of their oppression."[2]

In a passage just before this one, Porphyry throws light on the reason for the daimons' malevolence. "A general persuasion obtains," he says, "that their influence is noxious and malignant if they are once angered because their accustomed worship is neglected; and that they are again beneficent if appeased by prayers and supplications, by sacrifices and convenient rites."[3]

The daimons are very close to us, in many ways closer to us than we are to ourselves. We are mistaken to neglect, in whatever form, such rites as are, or have been, universally practiced, from central Australia (where aboriginal tribes propitiate the "Alcheringa" or "Iruntarinia" daimons in order to acquire them as personal guardians or to secure their good will towards the community), to Ireland where, as we have seen, the fairies had to be propitiated nightly with token foodstuffs lest they ceased to ensure order and grew unruly. We tend to see in such rites only a literal meaning, as if they were primitive attempts to feed otherworldly beings. But they were never this. We confuse concrete actions with literal actions. The latter mean only what they seem to be on the surface. But concrete actions, combined with an idea, an imagining, are what constitute rites. They have an imaginative dimension, a depth, which lifts them out of literalness, turning them from action we merely *do* to actions we *perform*.

A rite, in other words, is a concrete form of imagining—everything depends on the "soul" we put into the action.[4] It is a recognition that without rites or, at least, without a sense of ritual in the way we approach our environment, we not only profane it (as is now the case) but we might also suffer unfortunate and concrete consequences (our homes really can be roughed up by neglected daimons).

Conversely, the ritual sense, even if conceived as without concrete action but as an imaginative approach, can transform the profane back into the sacred, re-animate the environment (profane word!) back into a habitable world. By giving soul back to the world, we allow the Soul of the World to show us its face again.

Thus it is less important that we perform actual rites than that we deepen and expand our imaginative lives to make room for the daimons. The social equivalent of this individual activity is the building of shrines, from household altars to city temples; for there is no area of personal, familial, or communal life which does not concern the daimons. Even beyond the city walls, in the wilderness that is the daimons' natural habitat, certain landmarks were traditionally designated shrines. Sometimes they were modified to make them more fit. Whatever the purpose of "fairy forts" in Ireland, for instance, it seems likely that this was not the least of it. Whether they were fairy places because they were sculpted out of the landscape to attract and house the fairies, or whether they were fairy places because fairies appeared there in the first instance, we cannot know. Since myth has it that they were built by Manannan, who was as near a deity as members of the Tuatha de Danann could be, both suppositions may be true: the people of Fairy built them to accommodate themselves. And this remains true regardless of whether or not human agency played a part.

To make room for the daimons is to set a distance between us and them. This enables us to reflect, and reflect on, them; or, perhaps more accurately, allows them to reflect themselves through us. Reflection is "an act of becoming conscious."[5] If we become conscious of the daimons, and remain mindful of them, we avoid becoming possessed by them. For we are always vulnerable to neurotic fixations and compulsions when unconscious daimons drive us to act out, against our will, their fixed mythic patterns. Of course there is no way we can break entirely free of the compelling power of the daimons, any more than we can sever ourselves with impunity from our own souls; but we can collaborate with them, through reflection and imagination, so that their compulsion begins to resemble what we think of as an artist's vocation. In this case, a dialogue is opened between us and our daimon, as if it were (as it often is) a Muse, so that there is struggle and passion, but also negotiation and inspirational exchange. We are no longer compelled to *act out* the daimonic pattern in a literal sense; rather, we are enabled to *body it forth* in imaginative acts — works of art, for example, or artifacts, or even ideas and hypotheses. All these, to a greater or lesser extent, contain and define the daimonic exuberance that might otherwise overwhelm us. Works of art are, in this respect, daimonic shrines, like the statues of the ancients which were wrought in order, magically, to draw down and contain a daimon or god.[6]

Why grays? Why now?

The ego, wrote Jung, is "that mirror in which the unconscious becomes aware of its own face."[7] And we might add that, reciprocally, the unconscious — soul — is a mirror in which the ego sees its own face. Since the rational ego does not recognize soul at all, the daimons are compelled to manifest as imitations of the ego's spirit perspective — we might say that spirit makes them in its own image. This is true, for example, of angels. They were originally daimons who became spiritualized by the Christian perspective into pure, pristine, sexless intelligences, without any of the darker, quasi-physical, more ambiguous attributes of the daimons. Analogously, the tall blond benevolent "Venusians" of the 1950s, who proffered bombastic BVM-style warnings about the danger of nuclear power, were daimons spiritualized (and literalized) by the secular usurper of religion, scientism.

From this point of view, the appearance of small and apparently malevolent gray aliens, which looks like a regression, is more like an improvement. They have recovered something of their original daimonic nature, not so much imitating the triumphal scientistic perspective as parodying it and so drawing attention to its darker side. They treat us much as we treat the natural world — sampling, analyzing, and operating on us with exemplary scientific detachment in their lab-like "spacecraft." They issue no warnings about the abuse of technology. They simply turn it against us, translating its potential for power, knowledge, and destruction into an image of a super-technology — which enthralls and initiates us, thereby destroying the technological perspective itself.

The grays are like the subterranean daimons who dismember the shaman. They need not be located in the Underworld because this is not a place but a metaphor for the soul's perspective. In our "space age," the metaphor "Underworld" has been replaced in part by "outer space": there is no room for the daimons on Earth and so they return from on high. (We remember, too, that this mythical inversion was already evident in Porphyry's time, among the Pythagoreans and Stoics, who transferred the site of Hades from the Underworld to the air.)[8] Traditional daimons such as fairies still exist in the natural habitats, ever dwindling, with which they have always been associated. But the grays come from outside Nature, like shadows or base reflections of the very rational ego which has been intent on clearing the Earth of them.

So the grays are an improvement on the earlier, scientistically correct aliens because they do not collaborate with the rational scientistic ego but contradict, and even attack, it. Their malevolence is perhaps only the tortuous movements of the soul as it struggles to free itself from the ego's straitjacket. Occasionally we glimpse within this twisting the daimons' native duplicity, their Hermetic mischief, signaling to us that, for all their technological posturing, it is a sham. For example, Whitley Strieber was woken one night by a jolt on the shoulder.[9] Three dwarfish grays stood by his bed. They wore blue overalls and had glittering deep-set eyes. Maintaining his rational stance, Strieber reacted "normally" — that is, literally and therefore inappropriately — by pressing the light switch by his bed. It took a supreme effort but, of course, it did not work. He then saw another alien with big black button eyes. As if satirizing Strieber's "normal" response, it was wearing a cardboard imitation of a blue double-breasted suit, complete with a triangle of handkerchief sticking out of the pocket. Strieber found their presence in the room "unimaginably powerful, and so strange";[10] yet there was "a sort of jollity about these beings...they seemed happy" — as if, maybe, there was a species of colorful Good People trying to peek out from behind the aliens' gray masks.

The physical appearance of the grays — skinny, hairless, all but earless, noseless, mouthless, etc. — is nondescript, except for their eyes. There is no surer sign, it seems, of a supernatural origin than something strange about the eyes. Many daimonic animals might be mistaken for a natural species were it not for their glowing red eyes — a feature we read about again and again. Equally penetrating, and potentially dangerous, are the lustrous silvery eyes of the Tuatha de Danann, the Good People, the Gentry. The eyes of the gray aliens — huge, almond-shaped, wholly black — seem to be a new phenomenon.

Eyes are traditionally the "windows of the soul." But the abductees scan them in vain for signs of recognition, sympathy, pity — any human expression at all. They are met with a blank implacable stare, which is commonly described as haunting, limitless, penetrating, electrifying. We see nothing in them; yet they are also fathomless. We can lose ourselves in them. Unlike our eyes, they do not reflect soul because they *are* soul. They shine darkly from the deep part of soul which is not personal, not expressive, not human, but unmoved and impersonal as the eyes of the old gods.[11] They are fathomless because, like soul, we can never get to the end of them. We see in them our own way of seeing. Thus some see age-old wisdom there; others see only the petrifying horror of the Gorgon's glare.

The error of humanism

The eyes of the grays gainsay another of our modern ideologies: humanism. They remind us that our very conception of the human is grounded in the inhuman, the daimonic, even the divine. For the aliens are like the daimons of our secular religion, loosely defined as a combination of materialism, scientism, and humanism. But daimons, by definition, have no place in these -isms; daimons are the opposite of them. And so they appear as if in a mirror distorted by our rationalistic view of things — appear as the most impoverished of daimons, the grays, whom we meet either with incredulity or else with humanistic explanations. The extraterrestrialists, it is true, recognize that the grays are like daimons in as much as they are (a) not human and (b) autonomous powers who can control us at will. In this lies the strength and popularity of their hypothesis or, as I prefer, myth. But they still retain the error of humanism by imagining the grays as analogous to humans, inhabiting their planets as we inhabit ours. In other words, they literalize the daimons, equating moreover their archetypal power with, of all things, a "super-technology."

Humanism would have us believe we are only human. But the heroes of old were half-human and half-gods. This is a metaphor for the pairing of the ego with a personification of the daimonic or divine. To abolish this half of the pairing is not to abolish the divine — gods are immortal — but rather to compel it to try and find expression through the human half, the ego. This results in the psychological condition known as inflation: the ego, having ceased to recognize and remain connected with the daimonic, becomes identified with it, as if the daimonic, having nowhere else to manifest itself, were compelled to invade the very realm from which it had been severed. The ego then becomes puffed up, beyond its natural limits, with the daimonic influx. It begins to imagine it has god-like powers (just as we imagine that we humans are the be all and end all); or, in extreme cases, imagines it is God (as in paranoid delusions). Indeed, our own humanistic view of ourselves contains, as I have intimated, elements of a delusional, paranoid condition.[12]

Most of the fashionable ways in which we seek to alleviate the sufferings of our souls — our psychopathology — rely either on humanistic models, such as psychotherapies, which interpret everything personally, or on spiritual models, by which we seek to transcend suffering by developing some sort of mystical "higher consciousness." Both methods are inimical to soul, which does not want to be humanized and personalized (it wants recognition of its inhuman and impersonal aspects); nor does it want to be transcended, raised up and made to conform with spirit's perspectives. In fact, from soul's point of view, such methods and disciplines do not, as they claim, free its daimons from repression, but inflict a further, more subtle form of repression.[13] To soul, they look like self-deception. Small wonder, then, if soul seeks to counter them with deceptions of its own — deceiving our self-deception into deeper truth.

Reports of abductions have come from many parts of the globe. But the majority — and, moreover, most of the grays' abductions — come from the USA. Some psychologists have asked why these sinister little creatures are especially interested in Americans. There is no answer to this question; but if I were to invent one, I might be tempted to say it has something to do with the American emphasis, in popular culture at least, on *feeling*. Nowhere else, perhaps, do people take so readily to psychotherapeutic models for dealing with mysteries and problems that used to be the preserve of religion. And these models are predominantly oriented towards "feeling." Not that feelings are a bad thing. We should by all means get in touch with them, feel our anger, grief, joy, and so on — feel good about ourselves.

But there is a sense in which this philosophy is simplistic, sentimental, and liable to lapse into mere hedonism.[14] The aliens tell us that feeling is not enough. They do not show feeling and they do not give a fig for ours. They ignore the cry of abductees that their human rights are being violated; they remind us instead that there are no rights without obligations — and our obligations towards the daimons have been sorely neglected. We are bewildered by the grays because they do not advance our belief in the primacy of feelings, warmth, personal growth, positiveness, light, "higher consciousness." They appear, on the contrary, to be unmoved, cold, paralyzing, negative, dark, and unconcerned with raising our consciousness. Budd Hopkins thinks that the grays need us to teach them emotion and how to give warmth to their children;[15] but, if this is so, he omits to mention what we need to learn from them in exchange. We must learn that beneath the warm shallows there are cold depths. The aliens reflect, compensate, and countermand our conscious attitudes, both showing us the face we show to them and showing us our other, unknown face. They initiate us into the Underworld, strip away our worldly perspective, and connect us downwards, backwards, to death. For what was the central initiatory ritual of Eleusis? It was the myth of Demeter, the Kore (Persephone), and Hades in which the soul (Kore) was forcibly removed from warm nurturing mothering life (Demeter), to marry alien Hades — the Rich One who is cold, immovable, and unnatural — where she becomes Persephone, "Bringer of Destruction."[16]

A guide to the Otherworld

Initiation can be thought of as a general term for any daimonic event which realigns our conscious viewpoint on the world, and introduces it to the Otherworld. If we identify ourselves with the rational ego, then the initiation will be — has to be — correspondingly fierce in order to introduce the whole notion of an otherworldly, daimonic reality. Alienated, we have to be — forcibly, if necessary, it seems — *alienized*. For, from the daimonic standpoint, we as rational egos are aliens while the aliens, the daimons, are part of ourselves. Alienizing means daimonizing: the rational ego is replaced by a daimonic ego which can slip into different shapes, different perspectives — all daimonic but all defining, and being defined by, soul in multifarious ways. Alienizing means being at ease with the aliens because one is an alien oneself.

Once we have been initiated into approaching the Otherworld on its own terms, from a daimonic point of view, each shift in perspective requires a lesser series of initiations, no more than imaginative jumps really, such as new and sudden insights provide. This is borne out by otherworld journeyers, such as abductees, who often report that as they grow accustomed to the aliens and offer less resistance to their petrifying world, their pain and fear diminish. At first, perhaps, they lose their paralyzing horror and are able to express anger towards the aliens; then the anger diminishes and they grow interested and watchful, even respectful. Many abductees notice that, even from the first, the terror was not in fact unalloyed — they sensed the shadowy presence of protective or guardian aliens.[17] Others report feelings akin to love for their abductors.[18]

Thus we can imagine approaching the Otherworld in a different spirit. Once initiated, we can begin to visit as pupils or explorers. Once acclimatized and equipped with guides, we might begin to travel there as tourists — or even spend prolonged periods there, like expatriates. It all depends on our attitude. For to cultivate the right attitude towards the daimons is, finally, to cultivate the right attitude towards life. As the hero of folktales reminds us, we must approach both in a flexible and mercurial spirit, with humor and humility, courage and courtesy, circumspection and a sense of wonder. In a lighter vein, the same rules apply to the otherworld journeyer as they do to any tourist. Here are a few tips from the Guide to the Otherworld:

Travel light. Don't believe everything you have been told, either for good or ill. Don't stay in hotels which replicate your own culture (you may as well have stayed at home). By all means drink the water, but sparingly at first, until you have built up immunity to its foreign properties. Don't expect the inhabitants to speak your language; rather, try and speak theirs (even stumbling attempts will be appreciated). Observe local customs; respect local gods. Talk less than you listen. Try to see as well as sightsee. Be polite but firm; take advice but do not be gullible. If in doubt, smile. Do not laugh at the natives, but don't be afraid to laugh. Avoid the black market — you are always liable to be taken for a ride, especially if you think you know better or best, or if you think you can get something for nothing. Barter but don't haggle. Do not be superior or aloof, but don't try to dress like a native (it's embarrassing). Don't join in the dancing unless you really have learned the steps. (Remember: you can never become one of them — you can only rejoice in their otherness. Against the odds, there can be fruitful exchange on the basis of mutual strangeness.)

Perseus and the Gorgon

If it is correct — and it is — to read psychological motifs in terms of mythology, it is also possible to read myths psychologically. (A daimonic consciousness, such as shamans possess, would not distinguish between mythology and psychology.) Thus, as an example of how the Otherworld can be approached in a way that is not Heraclean, for example, I would like to touch on a favorite myth, that of Perseus.[19] It would take far too long to give a full reading of his story which, although it is not lengthy, is very profound. Besides, it is not really possible, or desirable, to translate a myth into terms other than its own. However, there are parts of Perseus' story which can profit us when we are confronted with what is alien.

His job is to slay Medusa, one of the three Gorgons, and to bring back her head. Medusa inhabits a particular kind of Underworld, the western land of the Hyperboreans, where she lives among the weather-beaten images of men and beasts which she has turned to stone simply by looking at them. (It is her extreme ugliness — serpents for hair, huge teeth, protruding tongue, glaring eyes — which has petrified them.) Clearly, the direct, literalistic approach of Heracles is inappropriate here. His strength can only work against him, for he would be turned to stone before he could raise his club.

It is difficult to know what Medusa represents in the psychological sense. Everything seems to stop with her. We might guess that whenever we are deeply depressed, chronically "stuck," or, in extreme cases, catatonic, we are seeing the Medusa in us at work. She lies very deep down in the unconscious. She is a kind of bottom line, cold and unmoving, beyond which we cannot pass; and, as such, she is closely related to Hades, Thanatos, death.

It needs a lot of forethought and preparation to cope with Medusa. It needs the help of more than one perspective, of more than one god. Wisely, Perseus first of all consults Athene, who takes him to Deicterion in Samos, where images of the Gorgons were displayed so that he will be able to distinguish Medusa from her two sisters. Thus he learns, as it were, to assimilate what is already known about the unconscious and to differentiate contents which may appear alike. She also teaches him not to look at Medusa directly but only at her reflection, and for this she gives him a highly polished shield. This can be seen as the first of several attributes or virtues which Perseus, like a good shaman, has to acquire. We learn that reflection, the backward-looking absorption of past experience and images, is a key to broaching the Otherworld. From Hermes, Perseus acquires an adamantine sickle. This is a lethal weapon but, unlike the Heraclean club, it is sharp, incisive, and is connected less with warfare, say, than with harvesting.

The shield and the sickle will enable him to complete his task; but in order to return alive he needs three more things: a pair of winged sandals, like Hermes', for speed of flight; a wallet to contain the dangerous decapitated head; and the dark helmet of invisibility which belongs to Hades. In order to get these he has to make a preliminary journey into the Underworld, to the Stygian nymphs who have charge of these items. But in order to find *them*, he has first to visit the three Graeae who alone know where the Stygian nymphs can be found. The Graeae are the Gorgon's sisters whom, in Hermetic fashion, he outwits into giving him directions. In other words, a preliminary skirmish with the Gorgon-like, but less deadly contents of the unconscious enables him to orient himself to the underworld perspective.

Once he has located Medusa, Perseus approaches her by walking backwards and holding up his polished shield to catch her image so that he can avoid looking directly at her. Thus he is able to behead her over his shoulder with the Hermetic sickle. We notice that his approach is the opposite of Orpheus'. In looking back at his wife Eurydice as he was leading her out of the Underworld, Orpheus prematurely reflects ("looks back") — that is, he adopts an ego perspective which is inappropriate to the realm of soul, which separates itself from soul, driving it back and losing it (as Eurydice was lost). Perseus, on the other hand, demonstrates another, daimonic way of reflecting in the Underworld. Instead of assuming Orpheus' "normal" ego perspective, which engages the underworld (unconscious) image head-on, he hermetically reverses the procedure — *by advancing backwards and reflecting forwards*. Paradoxically, the ego perspective is guided forwards by the image of soul on which it is reflecting (looking back). To look at the procedure another way, we might say that the Gorgon is an image which is dangerous if met literally (directly, head-on), but which is neutralized when treated as the image of an image. Like a double negative, reflection renders her positive in the sense that it recognizes her as real but not literal. The image is dangerous if taken literally, but, taken seriously as an image, the Gorgon becomes vulnerable, able to be slain.

At once her corpse gives birth to the winged horse Pegasus and Chrysaor the warrior, both of whom had been begotten on Medusa by the sea-god Poseidon. Her slaying, then, is not mere destruction in the manner of Heracles, but a release of new forms of vital energy bred by the oceanic unconscious.

However, Perseus still has to escape the wrath of the Gorgon's two sisters, which he manages to do by slipping away under cover of his helmet of invisibility and by taking flight with the winged sandals. These pieces of shamanic equipment are really powers he has gained. The helmet, which belongs to Hades, signifies the perspective of death — the death of the conscious ego and the acquisition of the daimonic ego which, being at one with the daimonic realm, is invisible within it. The sandals signify the perspective of Hermes who, uniquely, was able to fly to and fro between the heights of Olympus, the surface of earth, and the depths of the Underworld whither he was charged with conducting the souls of the dead. It is Hermes, too, who helps Perseus carry the magical wallet which contains the Gorgon's head. This tells us that, in order to make dangerous unconscious contents conscious, we have to initiate a space within consciousness which has a Stygian affinity with death, and is therefore strong enough to contain those contents. But once contained — assimilated — the contents are no longer antagonistic; on the contrary, we can use their power as our own, as Perseus used the Gorgon's head to petrify his enemies. We notice that it is too heavy to be carried without Hermes' help.

There is more in the Perseus myth than I have space to discuss. But I might just mention one or two points about his further adventures, notably his winning of Andromeda. She had been chained, naked, to a cliff as a sacrifice to a female sea-monster who was ravaging her father's kingdom. To save her is the Orpheus-like part of Perseus' story. The sea monster is connected to Medusa, another version of Medusa, perhaps, through its connection with Poseidon. However, this time, it is not Perseus who looks at its reflection, but the monster who is distracted by Perseus' reflected image in the water, enabling him to fly down and decapitate it. We find that the way the unconscious copes with our images — imagines us — is as important as the way we imagine it.

The myth of Perseus reminds me of the Inuit (Eskimo) myth about the Mother of the Sea Creatures on whom all well-being depends.[20] In times of bad fishing, it is the task of the tribal shaman to visit this goddess and persuade her to release the needed creatures. The trouble is that, Medusa-like, she is a horrendously ugly hag, smelling of fish and with matted and tangled hair. Because she dwells at the bottom of the sea, the shaman's journey is particularly hazardous. He has to plunge downward in a state of trance or ecstasy for a prolonged period. There is always the risk, as with any venture into the daimonic realm of the unconscious, of "drowning." The method he uses to propitiate the Mother of the Sea Creatures is unexpected. There is no coercion, for instance, no question of drawing her up into consciousness since she is the ground of all being. Instead, he has simply to overcome his fear of her terrifying appearance and to comb her hair. Here, then, is another lesson on how to approach the Otherworld: with courage, respect, and tenderness.

The death of Siegfried: a modern shaman's journey

"The Greeks, a certain scholar has told me, considered that myths are the activities of the Daimons, and that the Daimons shape our characters and our lives. I have often had the fancy that there is some one myth for every man, which, if we but knew it, would make us understand all he did and thought."[21]

This remark of Yeats's is perhaps nowhere better exemplified than in my last tale of an otherworld journey, which graphically describes the interchangeability of depth psychology and mythology. It is of particular concern to us because it describes the initiation of a twentieth-century man into that more ancient and daimonic worldview which, as I have been insisting, is essential to the correct understanding of apparitions and visions. The man in question was a scientist and doctor — well-schooled, for example, in the latest psychology — but he was also, as it turned out, the modern

European equivalent of a shaman to whom paranormal events had occurred since early childhood. This had led him to pay attention, unusual in a scientist, to daimonic reality (or, as he thought of it, the unconscious psyche) in general and to dreams in particular.

In October 1913, this modern shaman, then aged about thirty-eight, was alone on a journey when he was suddenly seized by "an overpowering vision."[22] He saw a monstrous flood sweeping over the lowlands between the North Sea and the Alps, leaving behind "the floating rubble of civilization" and countless thousands of drowned bodies. Then the whole sea turned to blood. The vision lasted about an hour and left him bewildered, sickened, and ashamed of his own weakness. It occurred to him that the vision was prophetic, pointing to some kind of social upheaval; but since he could not envisage such a thing, he concluded that it must be to do with himself — that he was threatened by an imminent psychosis. The apocalyptic theme of his vision was continued in the spring of 1914, when he had three dreams in which an Arctic tidal wave froze the land to ice and killed all green living things. When, on the first of August, the World War I broke out, he was almost relieved. It seemed that his vision had, after all, been less to do with his own condition than with the state of Europe.

However, it also seemed that the fate of Europe was indeed inextricably bound up with his own psychic condition, as if he were a lightning conductor for the current storm. He began to be besieged by an incessant stream of what he called fantasies — by which he meant spontaneous, autonomous, and very powerful images, which surged up from the depths of the unconscious and presented themselves with visionary clarity. "I stood helpless before an alien world," he wrote. "Everything in it seemed different and incomprehensible. I was living in a constant state of tension… When I endured these assaults of the unconscious, I had an uncanny conviction that I was obeying a higher will…"[23] Because of this, he was determined to face up to the fantasies, to examine them and let "the inner voices speak afresh." But at times they grew so overpowering that his fear of being drowned by a psychosis revived. He took up yoga to hold the images in check — but only until he was calm enough to confront once again the salvo of images bursting out of his psyche. For he was simply aware of the danger of oriental disciplines, such as meditation and yoga, which seek to obliterate or to transcend the outpourings of Imagination, and so become a new kind of repression, denying the images life.

The task he had set himself required more than spiritual exercises. It also required Heraclean — he called it "demonic" — strength. Only by an almighty effort of the heroic ego could he hold at bay the bloody tide of madness. Apart from this brute strength of will, his other defense was scientific detachment. "From the beginning," he wrote, "I have conceived my voluntary confrontation with the unconscious as a scientific experiment, which I myself was conducting and in whose outcome I was vitally interested." He added: "Today I might equally say that it was an experiment that was being conducted on *me*." Like an abductee, he was finding that the person he thought of as himself, with its characteristically modern attributes of will, strength, integrity of ego, and detachment, had been seized and threatened with disintegration. Only with hindsight did he realize that there are daimonic powers to which the conscious ego is subordinate — powers, moreover, which are contradictory, confusing, and threatening (at least from the rational ego's point of view). "I was writing down fantasies that often struck me as nonsense, and towards which I had strong resistances. For as long as we do not understand their meaning, such fantasies are a diabolical mixture of the sublime and the ridiculous... Only by extreme effort was I finally able to escape from the labyrinth."

But to discover the meaning of his fantasies it was no longer sufficient to try and analyze them while simultaneously warding them off. Our shaman had no recourse but to give in to them. "In order to grasp the fantasies which were stirring in me 'underground,' I knew that I had to let myself plummet down into them, as it were. I felt not only violent resistance to this, but a distinct fear." Specifically he feared "losing command of [him]self," becoming a prey to the fantasy images and going insane. His projected journey, we notice, is downwards — the way of the shaman — not upwards like the mystic's striving. He chooses to go underground, where the dead live, where the daimons are, eschewing the transcending spiritual ascent towards the high gods.

Jung (for, of course, it is he) had no choice but to abandon the Heraclean ego, the Apollonic detachment, of modern Western man — and risk the descent.[24] If he did not, his unconscious images would take him over. Secondly, he realized that he could not expect his patients to make the necessary descents into the depths of their own souls if he had not dared to do likewise. For, as a good shaman, he was required to retrieve lost souls or to accompany them like a psychopomp — like Hermes — on their descents into the Underworld; and this he would be unqualified to do without having first made the journey on his own behalf. And so, on 12 December 1913, he took the decisive step. It was, he wrote, like dying. Perhaps it was worse, because a psychiatrist would fear madness more than death.

"I was sitting at my desk once more, thinking over my fears. Then I let myself drop. Suddenly it was as though the ground literally gave way beneath my feet, and I plunged down into the dark depths. I could not fend off a feeling of panic." He landed in a soft, sticky mass, in complete darkness. His eyes soon became accustomed to the gloom, which was more like a deep twilight. "Before me was the entrance to a dark cave, in which stood a dwarf with a leathery skin, as if he were mummified. I squeezed past him through the narrow entrance and waded knee deep through icy water to the other end of the cave, where, on a projecting rock, I saw a glowing red crystal." He lifted the crystal and saw running water in the hollow beneath. A corpse floated by, a youth with blond hair and a head wound. "He was followed by a gigantic black scarab and then by a red, newborn sun, rising up out of the depths of the water. Dazzled by the light, I wanted to replace the stone upon the opening, but then a fluid welled out. It was blood. A thick jet of it leaped up, and I felt nauseated." The blood spurted out for a long time before it ceased. Then the vision ended, leaving Jung stunned.[25]

He realized at once that he had witnessed "a hero and solar myth, a drama of death and renewal, the rebirth symbolized by the Egyptian scarab. At the end, the dawn of the new day should have followed" — but instead the blood poured out. Jung recalled his previous vision of blood sweeping over Europe and abandoned any attempt to understand the myth — the implication being that it would be explained by the later outbreak of war. He does not mention — not yet, at least — what seems fairly plain: having journeyed down into the cave of his own unconscious, he "lifts the lid" on the source of his chaotic images and of all his fears. But he found himself gazing, not at psychosis, but at a re-enactment of a heroic, solar myth — his own myth, in fact. However, it is not taking place at a personal level but at an impersonal, collective level. He has plumbed his own psyche to the point where his myth coincides with the myth behind modern Western man. He is no longer himself but the representative of an archetypal pattern; and the trail he blazed is one that we all, to some extent, have to follow. This is why I am dealing with Jung's experience in such detail. This reading is confirmed by a dream he had six days later and to which he attached extraordinary importance.

"I was with an unknown brown-skinned man, a savage, in a lonely rocky landscape. It was before dawn; the eastern sky was already bright, and the stars fading. Then I heard Siegfried's horn sounding over the mountains and I knew that we had to kill him. We were armed with rifles and lay in wait for him on a narrow path over the rocks." In one sense, this is the prelude to the earlier vision. Siegfried, the Teutonic solar hero and representative of the conscious, rational ego, will become the dead blond youth. In another sense, the dream is the sequel to the vision. Here is the beginning of the bright day that was missing, that was replaced by the gush of blood which will sweep so much away on both an individual and collective level. It symbolizes the death of Jung's entire worldview; it is the death of the old Europe, drowned in the blood of war. But it is also life — the uncontrollable surge of vital chthonic forces welling up from the Underworld. Swept away by the tide of blood, Siegfried will not rise again. The literal, single-minded perspective of light and consciousness and spiritual ascent has to die and give way to the metaphorical, paradoxical perspective of darkness, the unconscious, the descent into the daimonic realm of soul. The dream continued:

"Then Siegfried appeared high up on the crest of the mountain, in the first ray of the rising sun. On a chariot made of the bones of the dead, he drove at furious speed down the precipitous slope. When he turned a corner, we shot at him, and he plunged down, struck dead." Jung is filled, in the dream, with disgust, remorse, and unbearable guilt at having killed "something so great and beautiful." He wakes, turns the dream over in his mind, but is unable to understand it. He is about to fall asleep again when he hears a voice within him say: "You *must* understand the dream, and must do so at once... If you do not understand the dream, you must shoot yourself." There is a gun by the bed. Jung becomes frightened. He begins to reflect more deeply on the dream, and suddenly its meaning comes to him: it is "the problem that is being played out in the world. Siegfried, I thought, represents what the Germans want to achieve, heroically to impose their will, have their own way... *I had wanted to do the same* [my italics]. But now that was no longer possible. The dream showed that the attitude embodied by Siegfried, the hero, no longer suited me" — and, I might add, any of us. "Therefore it had to be killed."[26]

The warning voice of what was doubtless Jung's personal daimon told him that if he failed to understand the dream — the metaphor — he might have been forced to act it out literally, to undergo literal death (suicide) instead of initiatory death. In killing Siegfried he was killing that part of himself, that kind of ego which was no longer appropriate to his life, nor to our own twenty-first-century lives. It is a painful moment. Jung felt "an overpowering compassion, as though I myself had been shot: a sign of my secret identity with Siegfried, as well as of the grief a man feels when he is forced to sacrifice...his conscious attitudes." But "there are higher things than the ego's will, and to these one must bow."[27] Paradoxically, the beginning of an alliance with these higher things is an alliance with what we have hitherto regarded as lower — the primitive, shadow part of ourselves, the savage who initiates the killing.

These events marked a turning point in Jung's life. In a worldly sense, it was a downward turn. He broke away from Freud and from respectable psychology. He continued to think of himself as a scientist, but his science was not recognized by others. It addressed the irreducible facts of daimonic reality, in pursuit of which Jung allied himself with those other historically outcast scientists, the alchemists. He became a shaman, learning to control his voluntary descents into the daimonic realm, where he acquired such daimonic helpers as Philemon, who bestowed on him, to the gratitude of his patients, the gifts of healing and wisdom.

Epilogue: The Golden Chain

The tradition which forms the background to this book is hard to describe, because it has no name. We might tentatively call it, for convenience, the daimonic tradition. Although it appears in many disciplines, such as theology, philosophy, psychology, aesthetic theory, and so on, it is not itself a discipline. It is not a body of knowledge or system of thought. Rather it is a way of knowing and thinking, a way of seeing the world, which poets and visionaries have always possessed but which even they cannot stand outside of or formulate. Thus one cannot be taught the tradition, for example, as part of a university curriculum; one can only be initiated into it. Simply finding it out for oneself can be, like a quest, an act of self-initiation.

Like the eye which sees but which cannot see itself, the tradition only becomes a *tradition* when it has ceased to be congruent with the culture in which it is found and begins, as it were, to see itself. It ceases, in other words, to be an invisible perspective and becomes visible. In our culture it has become visible in writings which tend to be labeled "esoteric" or, worse, "occult." Such writings are only just visible, large shadowy shapes lurking beneath the surface of the prevailing orthodoxy. Occasionally they break the surface, usually and most successfully in the form of poetry, which is allowed for, perceived as unthreatening by the prevailing orthodoxy, because poetry can be dismissed as "only" poetry, only imaginary, and can even, if it begins to disturb, be ignored.

In the twentieth century, two examples of the tradition's breaking of the surface are the works of the poet W. B. Yeats and of the psychologist C. G. Jung. It is significant that both men were brought up in a rural environment where this traditional perspective was still active — where, in other words, daimonic reality was taken for granted. Both of them, for example, naturally accepted the reality of apparitions, visions, and the supernatural, as country people always have. Their early work reflects this acceptance, but also the desire to square the supernatural with the skeptical, educated world they had entered. Thus Yeats re-worked Irish myths into long poems and wrote about fairies, while Jung entitled his first thesis "On the Psychology and Pathology of So-called Occult Phenomena."[1]

Throughout their lives Yeats and Jung sought out precedents for, and affinities with, their visionary — their daimonic — standpoints. Between them they uncovered and studied just about every major proponent of our tradition. This is not surprising, because it is a feature of the tradition that it threads together all who discover it, to form a series of historical links. The alchemists called it the *Aurea Catena,* the Golden Chain;[2] and to grasp one link is to be connected to all the others. Having already joined the Golden Chain, so to speak, through his imaginative understanding of myth and folklore, Yeats found an immediate intellectual connection with it through the Romantic poets and especially William Blake, whose works he spent years editing. With Blake's help he was able to identify further links, such as the Swedish visionary Emmanuel Swedenborg and the German mystic Jacob Boehme — daimonic islands in the rational, post-Cartesian sea. He discovered the Neoplatonists and the Hermetic philosophers who had flourished in the first centuries after Christ — and who enjoyed a new lease of life at the Renaissance when Marsilio Ficino translated them into Latin. Through Ficino, new branches of the tradition grew up in such philosophers as Pico della Mirandola and Giordano Bruno — even a new religion, a mixture of Hermeticism, alchemy, and the Kabbalah (the Jewish esoteric tradition) which aspired to replace a Christianity riven by the conflict between Catholics and Protestants.[3]

At the same time, Yeats maintained an interest in contemporary, popular manifestations of the tradition, no matter how seemingly shady or frivolous. He kept in touch with Spiritualism, for instance, and studied ritual magic with the Order of the Golden Dawn. Above all, he saw that the life of a culture or nation was only as good as its imaginative life; and its imaginative life was embodied in its myths. Contemptuous of the profane ideologies which stood for myths in the modern world, he fought a losing battle to revitalize the soul of the Irish people through a revival of its authentic ancient myths in his poems and plays.

Jung similarly kept up a lifelong interest in his "occult phenomena," even to the point of recognizing the unrecognizable — the "flying saucers" whose meaning he alone was able to grasp early on, thanks to his immersion in our tradition. He was less conscious than Yeats of the tradition as it manifested in poetry and drama, except for the second part of Goethe's *Faust* which he proclaimed "a link in the *Aurea Catena* which has existed from the beginnings of philosophical alchemy and Gnosticism down to Nietzsche's *Zarathustra*. Unpopular, ambiguous, and dangerous, it is a voyage of discovery to the other pole of the world."[4] Instead, as the quotation suggests, Jung found it in the Gnostics and, supremely, in the alchemists, his own forebears, whose works were the historical counterpart of that myth-spinning imaginative life he had discovered empirically in the unconscious psyches of his patients.[5]

Like myths themselves, alchemy is always going on in our unconscious lives. But it seems to rise to the surface and become an activity only at certain times, perhaps when a particular culture has reached a particular evolutionary stage. Rooted in ancient Egypt, it was practiced in the Hellenistic culture which centered on Alexandria around the time of Christ. It was developed subsequently by the Arabs and, it seems, independently by the Chinese. It entered Europe in the twelfth century and reached its zenith towards the end of the sixteenth century. As a daimonic process, it was not a single classifiable activity, as the alchemists themselves recognized when they variously referred to it as Our Philosophy, Our Art, Our Science. In addition to these components, alchemy embraced Christian elements as images of its processes. It was like a last attempt to hold together under the banner of Imagination the disparate elements of spirit and matter, soul and body, inner and outer, before they flew apart. Thus the outward transformation of chemicals and metals mirrored the inward transformation of the alchemist himself, each acting on and reflecting the other. The Philosopher's Egg or Hermetic vessel in which his substances took on archetypal significance — Sun, Moon, King, Queen, Mercury, Sulphur, Fire, Water — was an image of soul itself in which fiery Imagination distils itself out of itself, forever separating, conjoining, mortifying, subliming, and multiplying.

I have elsewhere suggested[6] that the extraordinary and sudden efflorescence of imaginative activity at the turn of the seventeenth century, not only as poetry and drama, but also as the beginning of modern science, had been incubated in the secret vessels of the alchemists, which cracked open at that moment, as it were, to release their myth-laden gases into the mainstream of imaginative life. Just as alchemy had been conceived as an elemental drama, a "chemical theater," so, now, the finest dramas were rich in alchemical imagery (Shakespeare's *King Lear,* for example, and *The Tempest*).[7]

If alchemy had striven to hold together a unified, daimonic view of the world in which soul mediated, even while it distinguished, between spirit and matter, so too did Shakespearean drama. At least, this is the view held by Ted Hughes who, in *Shakespeare and the Goddess of Complete Being,*[8] identifies the myth (or, rather, the two myths) which provide the underlying dynamism of all Shakespeare's major plays. Central to these myths is the rejection of soul by the rational ego, and its dire consequences. The plays are like a series of variants on these myths, striving to express and thereby contain this crisis in the collective Imagination of Western culture. It was as if Shakespeare foresaw the dangers inherent in the triumph of the rational ego over soul, the disaster that would result in the denial of his own brand of mythopoeic Imagination. Hughes even argues, correctly, that the plays have a shamanic function:[9] they are like the otherworld journeys the shaman takes on behalf of the tribe in order to retrieve its lost soul and so heal the rift between soul and ego.

That Shakespeare's attempt at healing was unsuccessful — despite the radiant, reconciling imagery of *The Tempest* — the history of modern Western culture since that watershed moment has amply demonstrated. However, no matter how beleaguered the tradition becomes, it can never die out because daimonic reality needs no tradition to stay alive. It is always, and constantly, alive and able to re-imagine and renew itself in every generation, quite apart from any tradition, through spontaneous apparitions, visions, and otherworld journeys.

References

Introduction

1. Lewis, p. 122.
2. Randles, pp. 123-6.
3. Yeats (1959), p. 68.
4. Quoted in Raine, pp. 177-8.
5. Randles, pp. 153-6, pp. 162-4.
6. Bord (1985), p. 130.
7. Randles, p 218.
8. Jaffé, p. 21.
9. Kim Hansen, "UFO Casebook," in Evans with Spencer, pp. 66-7.
10. Quoted in Michael Cox, *Mysticism: the Direct Experience of God* (Wellingborough, 1983), pp. 126-7.
11. Randles and Whetnall, pp. 8-10.
12. Mary Purcell, "Our Lady of Silence," in Delaney, pp. 147f.
13. Quoted in Eliade (1977), p. 17.
14. Candida Lycett-Green, "In Pictogram Country..." , in *The Cereologist,* no. 2, Winter 1990, p. 11.
15. Letter to George and Thomas Keats, 21 December 1817.

1 Lights

1. Evans (1983), pp. 87-8.
2. ibid., pp. 100-101.
3. MacManus, pp. 111-12.
4. Randles, p. 115.
5. Needham (1978), pp. 27f.
6. Philip Mayer, "Witches," in Marwick, p. 57.

7. ibid.
8. Cynthia Hind, "UFOs and the African Tribal System," in Evans with Spencer, pp. 93f.
9. Jaffé, pp. 62-3.
10. Evans-Wentz, p. 83.
11. Mgr. John S. Kennedy, "The Lady in Tears," in Delaney, pp. 93-4.
12. Evans (1983), p. 105.
13. Mark Moravec, "UFOs as psychological and parapsychological phenomena," in Evans with Spencer, p. 306.

2 UFOs

1. Randles, pp. 75-6.
2. ibid.
3. Evans (1983), p. 99.
4. See Jung, *CW* 10, §589ff.
5. Kim Hansen, "UFO Casebook," in Evans with Spencer, pp. 48-9.
6. Jung, op. cit., §591, 614.
7. *Dialogue on Miracles*, 1:32, quoted in Zaleski, p. 51.
8. ibid.
9. Quoted by W. B. Yeats in Lady Gregory, p. 333.
10. Jaffé, pp. 76f.
11. Randles and Whetnall, p. 30.
12. Jung, op. cit., §783.
13. See Dodds, pp. 104-7.
14. Jung, op. cit., §627.
15. ibid.
16. ibid.
17. Randles, pp. 97-8.
18. ibid., pp. 119-20.
19. Quoted in Eliade (1977), p. 17.

3 Aliens and Fairies

1. Evans-Wentz, p. 133.
2. V. J. Olmos Ballester, *OVNIs. El Fenomeno Aterrizaje* (Barcelona, 1978), quoted in Evans (1983), p. 104.
3. Coral Lorenzen, "UFO occupants in United States Reports," in Bowen,

p. 160.

4. ibid., pp. 149-50.
5. Jacques Vallée, "The Pattern behind UFO landings," in Bowen, pp. 32f.
6. Quoted by Briggs (1967), p. 132.
7. Jaffé, p. 108.
8. Jung, *CW* 12, §203.
9. Keel (1973) p. 230.
10. Quoted in *The Circular*, vol. 2, no. 4 (January, 1992), pp. 18-19.
11. Quoted in Peter Hough "UFO Occupants," in Evans with Spencer, p. 127.
12. Quoted in Evans (1983), pp. 102-3.
13. Peter Hough, "The Development of UFO Occupants," in Spencer and Evans, p. 109.
14. Lorenzen, op. cit., in Bowen, pp. 144-5.
15. Charles Bowen, "Few and Far Between," in Bowen, p. 19.
16. Lorenzen, op. cit., in Bowen, p. 159.
17. Hough, op. cit., in Evans with Spencer, p. 128.
18. Keel (1973), p. 181
19. Briggs, p. 3.
20. ibid, pp. 3-4.
21. Evans-Wentz, p. 47.
22. Lady Gregory, pp. 60-61.
23. MacManus, pp. 44-5.
24. Evans-Wentz, pp. 242-3.
25. See Briggs (1967), Glossary, and Briggs (1976).
26. Evans-Wentz, p. 47.
27. In his *Apology for the Fables of Homer*, II.
28. Quoted in Raine and Harper, p. 376.
29. Sendivogius, *De Sulphure*, quoted in Jung, *CW* 12, §396.
30. Jung, *CW* 12, §399, 269.
31. Jung, *CW* 14, §410.
32. Jung, *MDR*, pp. 208-9.
33. Trans. E. R. Dodds, in *Pagan and Christian in an Age of Anxiety* (Cambridge, 1975), p. 37.
34. Dodds, p. 41.
35. *De Defectu Oraculorum*, 13.

4 Daimons

1. MacDonald, p. 39.
2. Dodds, pp. 41-3.
3. Jung, *MDR*, pp. 389-90.
4. e.g. in *Phaedrus.*
5. Dodds, p. 42.
6. Jaffé, p. 108.
7. Iamblichus, III, chapters III-IV.
8. Wallis, p. 71.
9. Dodds, p. 289.
10. Iamblichus, IX, chapter VI.
11. Yeats (1959), p. 336.
12. Jung, *MDR*, p. 390.
13. Quoted in Andreas Lommel, *Shamanism: The Beginning of Art* (New York, 1967), pp. 59-60.
14. ibid.
15. Briggs, p.131.
16. ibid., p. 132.
17. Gordon Creighton, "The Humanoids in Latin America," in Bowen, pp. 84f.
18. Bowen, pp. 19-20.
19. MacManus, pp. 135-6.
20. cf. Hillman (1972), p. 23.
21. cf. Hillman (1979), p. 23.
22. *Timaeus*, 30.
23. Jung, *CW* 13, §75.
24. Yeats (1959), p. 352.
25. Jung, *MDR*, p. 369.
26. ibid., p. 205.
27. Yeats (1959), p. 352.
28. Jung, *CW* 9, I, §291; cf. *CW* 10, §13.

5 A Little History of Daimons

1. I Cor. 10:20.
2. *De Divinatione daemonum*, cap iii, 7.
3. Quoted in Cohn, p. 71.

4. ibid.
5. Lines 8-18.
6. Lewis, p. 122.
7. ibid.
8. ibid, p. 137.
9. Quoted in M. W. Latham, *The Elizabethan Fairies* (Columbia, 1940), p. 16.
10. MacManus, p. 25.
11. Lewis, p. 138.
12. Yeats (1959), p. 64.
13. Quoted in Porter, p. 81.
14. Thomas, pp. 797-8.
15. ibid.
16. Evans-Wentz, p. 94.
17. Meurger, p. 59.
18. Personal communication from his brother; see also Kate Saunders, "The day a gnome got angry with me!" *Woman* magazine, 5 October 1992.
19. Sheldrake (1990), p. 97.
20. Wilson, pp. 109-19.
21. ibid., p. 118.
22. Camille Flammarion, *Mysterious Physic Forces* (Boston, 1907), pp. 441, 431.
23. Jung, *MDR*, p. 173.
24. e.g. Jung, *CW* 13, §54.

6 Beasts

1. Ms. Scholia to *Phaedo*, quoted in Iamblichus, pp. 339-40.
2. Iamblichus, I, chapter VIII.
3. See, for example, Michell (1983) and Michell and Rhone (1991).
4. Bord (1985), p. 87.
5. ibid., p. 92.
6. ibid., p. 88.
7. ibid., p. 85.
8. ibid., p. 87.
9. ibid., p. 94.
10. ibid.
11. MacManus, pp. 68-9.

12. ibid.
13. Briggs (1976), p. 301.
14. MacManus, p. 70.
15. Francis, p. 37.
16. Bord (1985), p. 57.
17. ibid., p. 75.
18. ibid., p. 76.
19. Francis, p. 37.
20. ibid., pp. 40-41.
21. ibid., p. 42.
22. ibid., p. 43.
23. ibid., pp. 44-45.
24. Bord (1985), pp. 50f.
25. ibid.
26. Francis, p, 50.
27. Bord (1985), pp. 138-9.
28. ibid., p. 142.
29. ibid., p. 141.
30. ibid., p. 139.
31. Bord (1982), p. 21.
32. ibid., p. 61.
33. ibid., p. 62.
34. ibid., p. 117.
35. ibid., pp. 132-3.
36. ibid., p. 71.
37. ibid., pp. 55-7.
38. ibid., p. 109.
39. ibid., pp. 118-20.

7 Seeing Things

1. "A Vision of the Last Judgment," in Blake, p. 617.
2. See Patrick Harpur, "Imaginary Reality," in *Magonia*, no. 32, March 1988.
3. The following is based on Bailey's account. See "Skull's Lantern: Psychological projection and the Magic Lantern," in *Spring*, 1986.
4. Jung, *MDR*, pp. 354-5.
5. ibid., p. 356.

6. W. B. Yeats, "The Statues," in Yeats (1967), p. 375.
7. Blake, p. 817, lines 29-30.
8. The following account of paranoia is drawn from James Hillman's definitive lecture *On Paranoia* (Eranos lectures 8, Spring Publications, Dallas, 1988).
9. Canetti, pp. 525f.
10. ibid.
11. Keel (1973), p. 279.

8 Ladies

1. Gilbert Cornu, "Pour une politique de la porte ouverte," in *Lumières dans la nuit* (Le Chambon, 1981-2), quoted in Evans (1986), p. 120.
2. McClure, p. 133.
3. Frances Parkinson Keyes, "Bernadette and the Beautiful Lady," in Delaney, pp. 115f.
4. Robert M. Maloy, "The Virgin of the Poor," in Delaney, pp. 241f.
5. Mgr. William C. McGrath, "The Lady of the Rosemary," in Delaney, pp. 175f.
6. Don Sharkey, "The Virgin with the Golden Heart," in Delaney, pp. 215f.
7. Ethel Cook Eliot, "Our Lady of Guadalupe in Mexico," in Delaney, pp. 39f.
8. Paris, 1977. Quoted in Evans (1986), p. 108.
9. Quoted in McClure, pp. 107-8.
10. McGrath, op. cit.
11. ibid.
12. For extensive testimony to the miracle at Fatima, see Haffert.
13. Jung (1979), p. 166.
14. ibid., p. 165.
15. ibid., p. 169.
16. M.-L. von Franz, "The Process of Individuation," in C. G. Jung (ed.), *Man and His Symbols* (London, 1978), p. 196.
17. Jaffé, p. 87.
18. ibid., p. 92.
19. Briggs (1967), p. 27.
20. Jaffé, pp. 93-4.
21. ibid., p. 95.
22. ibid., p. 96.

23. Lady Wilde, Vol. I, pp. 259-60.
24. Lady Gregory, p. 178.
25. Byrne, p. 63.
26. Brunvand, pp. 30-31.
27. Lady Gregory, p. 15.
28. Brunvand, p. 17.
29. ibid., p. 138.
30. Goss, p. 90.
31. ibid., p. 93.
32. Rojcewicz, p. 503.

9 Imagining Things

1. S. T. Coleridge, *Biographia Literaria* (1817; Everyman, London, 1965), p. 167.
2. "Making Knowing and Judging," in Auden, pp. 54-5.
3. ibid., p. 56.
4. ibid., p. 57.
5. Blake, p. 154.
6. Jung, *CW* 12, §394.
7. ibid., §396.
8. ibid., §394.
9. Mary Warnock, *Imagination* (Berkeley: Univ. of California, 1976), p. 202, quoted in Avens, p. 23.
10. Hillman (1975), pp. 125, 141.
11. ibid., p. x, cf. p. 69; cf. also Hillman (1983), p. 77.
12. cf. James Hillman, "Peaks and Vales," in James Hillman (ed.), *Puer Papers* (Dallas, 1979), pp. 57f.
13. G. S. Kirk, p. 17.
14. ibid., p. 19.
15. Needham (1978), p. 55.
16. ibid., pp. 65-6.
17. Conversation with John A. Keel, 23 August 1992.
18. Meurger, p. 36.
19. ibid.
20. ibid., p. 272.
21. Bord (1985), pp. 15-16.
22. ibid., p. 18.

23. Meurger, p. 163.
24. ibid., p. 162.
25. ibid., p. 124.
26. ibid., pp. 292-4.
27. ibid.
28. cf. Rojcewicz, p. 496.
29. Hillman (1975), p. 23.

10 Daimonic Traces

1. S. Campbell, "Close encounter at Livingstone," BUFORA, 1982, quoted in Evans (1983), pp. 20-21.
2. Bill Chalker, "Physical Traces," in Evans with Spencer, p. 187.
3. For photo and following details, see *Country Life* (Irish edition), 24 May 1973.
4. ibid.
5. Keel (1973), pp. 174-5.
6. ibid., pp. 71-2.
7. Hartland, p. 136.
8. Keel (1973), pp. 176-7.
9. McClure, p. 112.
10. Ethel Cook Eliot, op. cit., in Delaney pp. 39f.
11. Evans (1983), p. 66.
12. Roger Patterson shot 30 ft. of 16 mm film of "a female Bigfoot" at Bluff Creek, N. California, on 20 October 1967.
13. Evans (1983), p. 63.
14. Bord (1985), p. 21.
15. See Bill Chalker, op. cit.
16. *History of the Goths*, III, p. 10, quoted in Lewis Spence, *British Fairy Origins* (Wellingborough, 1981), p. 180.

11 Circles

1. Candida Lycett-Green, "In pictogram country: notes from a Wiltshire village," in *The Cereologist*, no. 2, Winter 1990, p. 11.
2. Delgado and Andrews (1989), pp. 49-50.
3. ibid., pp. 127f.
4. See, for example, Delgado and Andrews (1990), p. 13; for photos of

anomalous lights, see Jürgen Krönig (ed.), *Spuren im korn* (Frankfurt, 1992), pp. 168-9.

5. Patrick Harpur, "Running rings around the corn," in *The Guardian,* 16 May 1991.
6. G. T. Meaden, "Crop circles and the plasma vortex," in Noyes, p. 77.
7. *The Cereologist* no. 2, Winter 1990, p. 5.
8. See *The Cereologist* nos. 3, 4, 5, and 6.
9. Delgado and Andrews (1990), pp. 15-16.
10. *The Cereologist*, no. 4, Summer 1991, p. 7.
11. ibid., no. 5, Winter 1991/2, pp. 3-6.
12. Lectures by George Wingfield and John Macnish at *The Cereologist* 1st Annual "Cornference," Glastonbury, Somerset, on 7/8 September 1991.
13. See Jung, *CW* 8, §816f.
14. Jaffé, p. 192.
15. See, for example, the account of Plotinus' doctrine in Wallis, p. 61.
16. Quoted in Raine and Harper, pp. 192-3.
17. Sheldrake (1981).
18. Bob Rickard, "Clutching at Straws: Whirls, winds, witches and fairies," in *Fortean Times*, no. 53, Winter 1989/90, pp. 62-4.

12 Structures

1. Lévi-Strauss (1970), p. 12. But the translation is taken from *Yale French Studies* (1966; New York, 1970).
2. G. S. Kirk, p. 83.
3. Keel (1988), pp. 63f.
4. Plotinus, II, 2, 2.
5. Hillman (1975), p. 14; cf. Plotinus, IV, 3, 11.
6. See Hillman (1975), p. 149; also Hillman (1983), p. 73.
7. See Hillman (1975), p. 119.
8. *American Magazine*, October 1909.
9. See *The Cereologist*, no. 7, Harvest 1992.
10. Raine and Harper, pp. 460-61.
11. Quoted by Thomas Taylor in Iamblichus, p. 260.
12. Iamblichus, I, chapter XX, pp. 78-9.
13. Raine and Harper, pp. 484-5.
14. Hillman (1975), p. 130.
15. Hillman (1979), pp. 36-8.

16. Hillman (1975), p. 132.
17. López-Pedraza, pp. 53f.
18. See Campbell (1988), p. 294n.
19. cf. James Hillman (ed.), *Puer Papers* (Dallas, 1979), pp. 67-9.
20. See Radin, *passim.*
21. See Alice Karlsdottir, "Loki, Father of Strife," in *Gnosis*, no. 19. Spring 1991, p. 33.
22. Campbell (1988), p. 327.
23. *Bhagavad Gita*, 10, 20.
24. cf. "The Joker in the Pack," in Auden, pp. 255-6.
25. ibid.

13 The Otherworld

1. Hillman (1975), p. xi.
2. Dodds, p. 111.
3. cf. Alderson Smith.
4. See Capra.
5. ibid.
6. For example, Jones.
7. See Needham (1983).

14 Missing Time

1. A good account of the Avis story is to be found in Rimmer, pp. 18f; further details can be found in Andrew Collins, "The Aveley Abduction," in *Flying Saucer Review*, vol. 23, no. 6, April 1978, and vol. 24, no. 1, June 1978.
2. See, for example, Moody; Ring.
3. Hopkins (1988a), p. 5.
4. Hartland, chapters, VII-IX.
5. cf. Rimmer, pp. 57-8.
6. ibid., pp. 113-14.
7. Jung, *MDR*, p. 141.
8. Rimmer, pp. 21-5.

15 Supernatural Branding

1.   Hopkins (1988a), p. 14.
2.   ibid., p. 193.
3.   ibid., pp. 32f.
4.   ibid., pp. 48-9.
5.   ibid., p. 86.
6.   Hopkins (1988b), p. 216.
7.   ibid., pp. 119-44.
8.   ibid., p. 122.
9.   ibid., pp. 178-9.
10. ibid., p. 179.
11. ibid., p. 189.
12. ibid., pp. 195-7.
13. ibid., p. 137.
14. ibid., pp. 198-9.
15. Hopkins (1988b), p. 6.
16. Evans-Wentz, p. 73.
17. Personal communication to the author, 6/2/92.
18. Robert Kirk, pp. 58-9.
19. ibid., p. 59.
20. See Briggs (1967), chapter I.
21. Bede, chapter 12, pp. 284f.
22. ibid., p. 287.
23. Zaleski, p. 79.
24. ibid.
25. MacDonald, pp. 40-41.
26. Evans (1983), p. 50; Rojcewicz, pp. 489-90.
27. De la Bedoyere, pp. 241-3.
28. St Teresa of Avila, *The Flaming Heart* (1624), p. 419, quoted in Michael Cox, *Mysticism* (Wellingborough, 1983), p. 197.

16 Changelings

1.   Rimmer, pp. 25-6.
2.   ibid., p. 27.
3.   ibid., p. 28.
4.   ibid., pp. 28-9.

5. For this story, I follow Méheust, pp. 352-3.
6. ibid., p. 354.
7. ibid., p. 357, n. 8.
8. ibid.
9. Bord (1982), p. 24.
10. ibid., p. 43.
11. ibid., pp. 44-6.
12. For this story, I follow Kim Hansen, "UFO Casebook," in Evans with Spencer, pp. 56-9; also Rimmer, pp. 36-8.
13. Hopkins (1988a), pp. 165f.
14. ibid., p. 171
15. ibid., pp. 172-4.
16. ibid., pp. 136f.
17. ibid., pp. 157-9.
18. Lady Gregory, p. 364.
19. Hartland, p. 101.
20. Hopkins (1988a), pp. 212-14.
21. ibid., p. 193.
22. ibid., pp. 193-8.
23. ibid., pp. 224-6.
24. ibid., pp. 201-2.
25. John Rhys, *Y Cymmrodor*, vol. V, p. 70, quoted in Hartland, pp. 37-8.
26. Quoted in Hartland, pp. 38-9.
27. Randles and Whetnall, p. 104.
28. Bord (1985), p. 147.
29. Randles and Whetnall, p. 107.
30. Hartland, p. 43.
31. See G. S. Kirk, and J. E. Raven, *The Presocratic Philosophers* (Cambridge, 1957), p. 210.

17 Human Demons

1. Mike Dash, "Satan and the Social Workers: Recent British Ritual Abuse Scares," in *Fortean Times*, no. 57. Spring 1991, p. 46.
2. ibid., p. 47.
3. Bob Rickard, "Satanic Child Abuse Mania," in *Fortean Times*, no. 57. Spring, 1991, p. 57.
4. See Cohn, chapter I: "Prelude in Antiquity."

5. See Needham (1978), Part 2: "Synthetic Images."

6. Cohn, p. 101.

7. ibid.

8. Since writing this, I have found scholarly support for this connection between witches, fairylore, and shamanism in Ginzburg.

9. e.g. in *The Witch-Cult in Western Europe* (London, 1921).

10. e.g. Alan Macfarlane, *Witchcraft in Tudor and Stuart England*, (London, 1970).

11. Rickard, op. cit. pp. 54-6.

12. John Michell, "Satanic Curses: Bogus Social Workers and Demonic Abductors," in *Folklore Frontiers*, no. 12, p. 6.

13. Mike Dash, "The Case of the Phantom Social Workers," in *Fortean Times*, no. 57, Spring 1991, p. 43.

14. ibid., p. 44.

15. ibid.

16. Mitchell, op. cit., p. 5.

17. Dash, op. cit., pp. 44-5.

18. ibid., p. 44.

19. Evans (1986), p. 141.

20. ibid., pp. 142-3.

18 Daimonic Humans

1. Eliade (1989), pp. 34-6.

2. Méheust, p. 354.

3. ibid., p. 353.

4. Eliade (1989), p. 36.

5. Hopkins (1988a), p. 218.

6. Eliade (1989), pp. 46-7.

7. ibid., pp. 137-8.

8. ibid., pp. 300f.

9. Eliade (1977), p. 302.

10. Commentary on *First Alcibiades*, quoted in Raine and Harper, pp. 460-61.

11. Hopkins (1988a), p. 43.

12. Eliade (1989), p. 86.

13. See John Fuller, *The Interrupted Journey* (New York, 1966).

14. The seminal work on dreaming as initiation is Hillman (1979), e.g. p.

112.
15. Randles (1983), pp. 216-7.
16. Hopkins (1988a), p. 22.
17. The following account is taken from Keel (1973), pp. 273-5; for a fuller account still, see John A. Keel, *The Mothman Prophecies* (New York, 1975; re-issued IllumiNet Press, Avondale Estates, GA., 1991).
18. cf. Hillman (1979), pp. 85,112.

19 Soul and Body

1. II Cor. 12: 2-4.
2. Jung, *CW* 10, §714.
3. cf. Jung *CW* 8, §217, 577, 587, 392-6.
4. Hillman (1979), p. 104.
5. ibid., p. 105.
6. See W. H. Myers, et al. (1886); also Wilson (1987), pp. 115-6.
7. I Cor. 15: 44.
8. For a full discussion of *soma* and *sarx*, see Macquarrie, pp. 39-46.
9. Teresa of Avila, pp. 136-7.
10. Strieber (1989), p. 86.
11. Lady Wilde, vol. I, p. 52.
12. Lady Gregory, introduction.
13. See Hillman (1975), pp. 67-70.
14. cf. Hillman (1979), pp. 74-85.
15. cf. Hillman (1985), chapter 10, "Anima in the Syzygy," pp. 167-83.
16. cf. Lady A. Gregory*, Gods and Fighting Men* (1904; Gerrards Cross, 1976); Yeats (1967).
17. Hillman (1975), p. 69.
18. Hillman (1979), pp. 110-17.
19. Graves, vol. 2, pp. 153f.
20. cf. Hillman (1979), p. 112.
21. ibid., p. 115.
22. Hillman (1975), p. 69.
23. Graves, vol. I, pp. 312f.
24. Picard, p. viii.
25. ibid., pp. 214f.

20 Approaching the Otherworld

1. Reported in Dennis Stacy, "Alien abortions, avenging angels," in *Magonia,* no. 44, October 1992, p. 15.
2. *De Abstinentia*, Book II, quoted in Raine and Harper, pp. 189-90.
3. ibid.
4. cf. Hillman (1975), p. 137.
5. Jung, *CW* 11, §235, n. 9.
6. See Yates (1964), p. 37, 41.
7. Jung, *CW* 14, §129.
8. Dodds, p. 111.
9. Strieber (1988), p. 171.
10. ibid., p. 173.
11. cf. ibid., pp. 105-6.
12. cf. Hillman (1975), pp. 187-8.
13. ibid., p. 70.
14. ibid., p. 66.
15. Hopkins (1988a), p. 190.
16. cf. Hillman (1979), p. 49, 208.
17. Strieber (1988), p. 262.
18. ibid., p. 105.
19. My account comes from Graves, vol. I, pp. 237-42.
20. Recounted in Larsen, p. 87.
21. "At Stratford-on-Avon," in W. B. Yeats, *Essays and Introductions* (London, 1969), p. 107.
22. Jung, *MDR*, p. 199.
23. ibid., p. 201.
24. ibid., p. 202.
25. ibid., p. 203.
26. ibid., pp. 204-5.
27. ibid., p. 205.

Epilogue; The Golden Chain

1. In C. G. Jung, *Psychiatric Studies* (1902), *CW* I (London, 1970).
2. cf. Jung, *MDR*, p. 213 and n.
3. See, for example, Yates (1964), (1983).
4. Jung, *MDR*, p. 213.

5. ibid., p. 231.
6. Harpur (1990).
7. See, for example, Charles Nicholl, *The Chemical Theatre* (London, 1980).
8. London, 1992.
9. Hughes, pp. 372, 430, 435-6.

Select Bibliography

Anon., Early Irish Myths and Sagas, trans. Jeffrey Gantz (London, 1981).

— *Sir Orfeo*, ed. A. J. Bliss (Oxford, 1966).

Alderson Smith, Peter, *W. B. Yeats and the Tribes of Danu* (Gerrards Cross, 1987).

Auden, W. H., *The Dyer's Hand* (London, 1963).

Austen, A. W. (ed.), *Teachings of Silver Birch* (London, 1938).

Avens, Roberts, *Imagination is Reality* (Dallas, 1980).

Barrett, William, *Death of the Soul* (Oxford, 1987).

Bede, *A History of the English Church and People*, trans. Leo Sherley-Price (London, 1955).

Blake, William, *Complete Writings*, ed. Geoffrey Keynes (London, OUP, 1966).

Boehme, Jacob, *The Signature of All Things and Other Writings* (Cambridge and London, 1969).

Bord, Janet and Colin, *The Bigfoot Casebook* (London, 1982).

— *Alien Animals* (London, 1985).

Bowen, Charles (ed.), *The Humanoids* (London, 1974).

Briggs, K. M., *The Fairies in Tradition and Literature* (London, 1967).

— *Dictionary of Fairies* (London, 1976).

Brunvand, Jan Harold, *The Vanishing Hitchhiker: American Urban Legends and Their Meanings* (London, 1983).

Byrne, Patrick F., *Tales of the Banshee* (Cork, 1987).

Campbell, Joseph, *Creative Mythology* (London, 1976).

— *The Hero with a Thousand Faces* (London, 1988).

Canetti, Elias, *Crowds and Power* (London, 1984).

Capra, Fritjof, *The Tao of Physics* (London, 1975).

Cereologist, The (also called *Cerealogist*), ed. John Michell (11 Powis Gdns, London, W11 1JG).

Cohn, Norman, *Europe's Inner Demons* (Sussex Univ. Press, 1975).

de la Bedoyere, Michael, *Francis*: *A Biography of the Saint of Assisi* (London, 1976).

Delaney, John J. (ed.), *A Woman Clothed with the Sun* (New York, 1961).

Delgado, Pat, and Andrews, Colin, *Circular Evidence* (London, 1989).

— *Crop Circles: The Latest Evidence* (London, 1990).

Dionysius the Areopagite, *The Divine Names* and *The Mystical Theology*, trans. C. E. Rolt (London, 1940).

Dodds, E. R., *The Greeks and the Irrational* (Univ. of California, Berkeley, 1951).

Eliade, Mircea, *From Primitives to Zen* (London, 1977).

— *Shamanism: Archaic Techniques of Ecstasy* (London, 1989).

Evans, Hilary, *The Evidence for UFOs* (Wellingborough, 1983).

— *Visions Apparitions Alien Visitors* (Wellingborough, 1986).

Evans, Hilary, with Spencer, John (eds.), *UFOs 1947-1987* (London, 1987).

Evans-Wentz, W. Y., *The Fairy-Faith in Celtic Countries* (Oxford, 1911; Gerrards Cross, 1977).

Fort, Charles, *The Complete Books of Charles Fort* (New York, 1974).

Fortean Times, eds. Robert Rickard and Paul Sieveking (current editor: Mark Pilkington, 9, Dallington St., London, EC1V OBQ).

Francis, Di, *Cat Country* (Newton Abbot, Devon, 1983).

Ginzburg, Carlo, *Ecstasies: Deciphering the Witches' Sabbath*, trans. R. Rosenthal (London, 1990).

Goss, Michael, *The Evidence for Phantom Hitch-hikers* (Wellingborough, 1984).

Graves, Robert, *The Greek Myths* (London, 1955).

Gregory, Lady, *Visions and Beliefs in the West of Ireland* (1920; Gerrards Cross, 1976).

Haffert, John M., *Meet the Witnesses* (AMI Press, Washington, NJ, 1961).

Harpur, Patrick (ed.), *Mercurius; or, the Marriage of Heaven and Earth* (London, 1990)

Harpur, Patrick, *The Philosophers' Secret Fire: A History of the Imagination* (London, 2002; Chicago, 2003)

Hartland, Edwin Sidney, *The Science of Fairy Tales* (London, 1891)

Hillman, James, "An essay on Pan" (Berne, 1972), in Roscher, W. H., and Hillman, James, *Pan and the Nightmare* (Dallas 1972).

— *Re-Visioning Psychology* (New York, 1975).

— *The Dream and the Underworld* (New York, 1979).

— *Healing Fiction* (New York, 1983).

— *Anima: An Anatomy of a Personified Notion* (Dallas, 1985).

Hopkins, Budd, *Intruders: The Incredible Visitations at Copley Woods* (London, 1988a).

— *Missing Time* (Ballantine, New York, 1988b).

Hughes, Ted, *Shakespeare and the Goddess of Complete Being* (London, 1992).

Iamblichus, *On the Mysteries of the Egyptians, Chaldeans and Assyrians*, trans. T. Taylor (London, 1821).

Jaffé, Aniela, *Apparitions* (Univ. of Dallas, 1979).

Jones, Roger, *Physics as Metaphor* (London, 1983).

Jung, C. G., *Memories, Dreams, Reflections* (*MDR*) (London, 1967).

— *The Archetypes and the Collective Unconscious*, *CW* (*Collected Works*) 9, Part I (London, 1968).

— *The Structure and Dynamics of the Psyche*, *CW* 8 (London, 1969).

— *Civilization in Transition*, *CW* 10 (London, 1964).

— *Psychology and Alchemy*, *CW* 12 (London, 1968).

— *Alchemical Studies*, *CW* 13 (London, 1968).

— *Psychology and Religion: West and East*, *CW* 11 (London, 1969).

— *Mysterium Coniunctionis*, *CW* 14 (London, 1970).

— *Answer to Job* (London, 1979).

Keel, John A., *Operation Trojan Horse* (London, 1973).

— *Disneyland of the Gods* (New York, 1988).

Kirk, G. S., *The Nature of Greek Myths* (London, 1974).

Kirk, Rev Robert, *The Secret Commonwealth* (1691), ed. Stewart Sanderson (Cambridge, 1976).

Larsen, Stephen, *The Shaman's Doorway* (Barrytown, NY, 1988).

Lévi-Strauss, Claude, *The Raw and the Cooked* (London, 1970).

— *The Savage Mind* (London, 1972).

— *Structural Anthropology I*, trans. Claire Jacobson and Brooke Grundfest Schoepf (London, 1977).

Lewis, C. S., *The Discarded Image* (Cambridge, 1964).

López-Pedraza, Rafael, *Hermes and his Children* (Einsiedeln, Switzerland, 1989).

MacDonald, Hope, *When Angels Appear* (Grand Rapids, Michigan, 1982).

MacManus, Dermot, *The Middle Kingdom* (Gerrards Cross, 1959).

Macquarrie, John, *An Existentialist Theology: A Comparison of Heidegger and Bultmann* (London, 1973).

Magonia, ed. John Rimmer (John Dee Cottage, 5 James Terrace, Mortlake Churchyard, London SW14 8HB).

Marwick, Max (ed.), *Witchcraft and Sorcery* (London, 1970).

McClure, Kevin, *The Evidence for Visions of the Virgin Mary* (Wellingborough, 1983).

Méheust, Bertrand, "UFO Abductions as Religious Folklore" in Evans with Spencer, pp. 352-8.

Meurger, Michel, with Gagnon, Claude, *Lake Monster Traditions: a Cross Cultural Analysis* (London, 1988).

Michell, John, *The New View over Atlantis* (London, 1983).

Michell, John, and Rhone, Christine, *Twelve-Tribe Nations and the Science of Enchanting the Landscape* (London, 1991).

Midgley, Mary, *Evolution as a Religion* (London, 1985).

Moody, Raymond A., Jr., *Life After Life* (Atlanta, 1975; New York and Harrisburg, Pa., 1976).

Myers, Frederic W. H., with Gurney, Edmund, and Podmore, Frank, *Phantasms of the Living,* vols. I and II (London, 1886).

Myers, F. W. H., *Human Personality and Its Survival of Bodily Death* (New York, 1961).

Needham, Rodney, *Primordial Characters* (Univ. of Virginia, 1978).

— *Against the Tranquility of Axioms* (Univ. of California Press, 1983).

Noyes, Ralph (ed.), *The Crop Circle Enigma* (Bath, 1990).

Paracelsus, *Selected Writings*, ed. Jolande Jacobi (Princeton, 1958).

Picard, Barbara Leonie, *Tales of the Norse Gods and Heroes* (Oxford, 1953).

Plato, *The Republic*, trans. H. D. P. Lee (London, 1955).

— *Timaeus*, trans. H. D. P. Lee (London, 1971).

— *Phaedrus and Letters VII and VIII*, trans. Walter Hamilton (London, 1973).

Plotinus, *The Enneads*, trans. Stephen Mackenna (London, 1956).

Porter, Roy, *Mind-forg'd Manacles* (London, 1990).

Radin, Paul, *The Trickster: A Study in American Indian Mythology* (London, 1956).

Raine, Kathleen, *William Blake* (London, 1970).

Raine, Kathleen, and Harper, George Mills (eds.), *Thomas Taylor the Platonist: Selected Writings* (London, 1969).

Randles, Jenny, *The Pennine UFO Mystery* (St. Albans, 1983).

Randles, Jenny, and Whetnall, Paul, *Alien Contact* (London, 1981).

Rimmer, John, *The Evidence for Alien Abductions* (Wellingborough, 1984).

Ring, Kenneth, *Life at Death: A Scientific Investigation of the Near-Death Experience* (New York, 1980).

Rojcewicz, Peter M., "Fairies, UFOs, and Problems of Knowledge" in Narváez, Peter (ed.), *The Good People: New Fairylore Essays* (New York, 1991).

Sheldrake, Rupert, *A New Science of Life: The Hypothesis of Formative Causation* (London, 1981).

— *The Rebirth of Nature* (London, 1990).

Spencer, John, and Evans, Hilary (eds.), *Phenomenon* (London, 1988).

Spring: A Journal of Archetype and Culture (P.O. Box 222069, Dallas, Texas 75222).

Strieber, Whitley, *Communion* (London, 1988).

— *Transformation* (London, 1989).

Teresa of Avila, *The Life of Saint Teresa of Avila*, trans. J. M. Cohen (London, 1957).

Thomas, Keith, *Religion and the Decline of Magic* (London, 1978).

Wallis, R. T., *Neoplatonism* (London, 1972).

Wilde, Lady F. S., *Ancient Legends, Mystic Charms and Superstitions of Ireland*, 2 vols. (London, 1887).

Wilson, Colin, *Afterlife* (London, 1987).

Yates, Frances A., *Giordano Bruno and the Hermetic Tradition* (London, 1964).

— *The Art of Memory* (London, 1984).

— *The Occult Philosophy in the Elizabethan Age* (London, 1983).

Yeats, W. B., *Mythologies* (London, 1959).

— *A Vision* (London, 1962).

— *Collected Poems* (London, 1967).

Zaleski, Carol, *Otherworld Journeys* (Oxford, 1988).

Index